11.00

$11\frac{00}{N}mc$

Essay Index

J

2-8-72

D0713056

PERIODICAL ESSAYS
OF THE
EIGHTEENTH CENTURY

Periodical Essays of the Eighteenth Century

Edited by
George Carver

Essay Index

BOOKS FOR LIBRARIES PRESS
FREEPORT, NEW YORK

STANDARD BOOK NUMBER:

8369-1555-0

LIBRARY OF CONGRESS CATALOG CARD NUMBER:

70-99621

PRINTED IN THE UNITED STATES OF AMERICA

TO

E. D. C.

UNA MATER VALET CENTUM
SCOLASTICOS

PREFACE

The growing interest in the literature of the eighteenth century, as witnessed by the increase in the number of college courses devoted to its study and by the multiplication of books making more accessible its contribution, must be offered as justification for the present volume.

In particular, however, *Periodical Essays of the Eighteenth Century* endeavors, by presenting the work of some twenty men in some sixty representative selections, to show the essay as reaching the climax of its development as a type of literary expression and to indicate its decline before the advent of the reviews of the nineteenth century. Moreover, in choosing the pieces to be included, the editor has been guided by the desire not only to reveal the progress of the essay as a type but to offer some evidence of social progress as well. Towards these ends, then, he has selected essays of representative excellence having to do with many phases of life and idea; but more than this, he has ever been mindful of the fact that the eighteenth and twentieth centuries have much in common—hence, the book will be found to contain much that, except for exigencies of style, might have been written yesterday.

It is his hope, then, that the volume may be found useful both to students of the literature of the eighteenth century and to those of the history of the essay as well.

G. C.

Pittsburgh
December, 1929

CONTENTS

INTRODUCTION

I

WITH the appearance of the first issue of the *Tatler* on April 12, 1709, the essay as a literary type may be said to have come of age. There had been excellent examples published previously, to be sure; nothing could be better than the work of Bacon, of the "character" writers, Overbury, Hall, and Earle, and of Owen Felltham and James Howell, during the early part of the seventeenth century; of Browne, Fuller, Milton, and Jeremy Taylor during the years of Puritan control; or of Cowley, Butler, Temple, Dryden, and John Locke during the Restoration. Nevertheless, until the age of Anne the essay was unimportant as an influence. It had taken form, and its canons, for the most part, had been established prior to the advent of Steele and Addison; but the social demands made upon it had not been such that it had yet attained its fullest development.

After the turn of the century, however, the face of social England changed, and, as always, with social change came literary change as well. The seventeenth century had been turmoil, but turmoil that had been broached from within and had been almost wholly confined to English soil. With the flight of James, however, in 1688, began the exploitation on the part of foreign monarchs and the heroic struggle on the part of the people to work some sort of order out of the resulting chaos. Not only this, but activity in France, in the Netherlands, in America, and in Asia, beginning early and extending throughout the century to such degree that Sir John Seeley in his *Expansion of England* could say "the expansion of England abroad, in the New World, and in Asia is the formula which sums up for England the history of the eighteenth century" so wrought upon the English consciousness that there arose a pressing demand for order, for standards of conduct, for effective means of governing the affairs of life. That such demands were as old as civilization made no more difference than did the failure of previous epochs to supply them. The demands arose anew and scores of literary reputations may be traced in their beginnings to the apparent success with which the clamor was answered.

The success of Alexander Pope, for instance, might almost be said to rest upon his ability to interpret the needs of a generation in search of social and intellectual health. Much the same statement might be made concerning Richardson, Smollett, Fielding, and Sterne. What was thus true of poets and novelists who achieved fame during the second decade of the century and thereafter was likewise true of the essayists contemporary and immediately preceding; but particularly true of the contributors to the *Tatler*, the *Spectator*, and the *Guardian*, during the years 1709–1714, that is, when the essay may be said to have reached the climax of its development, a condition quite natural at that time inasmuch as the essay more than any other literary form was adaptable to the requirements of the age for a cleansing influence.

For, whatever else may be said of it, the essay is primarily a vehicle of creative criticism. That it is not unique in this respect goes, naturally, without saying; nevertheless, when one considers the circumstances under which it came to be, and the course of its progress through the seventeenth century, one becomes aware that to think of it in terms of anything less than creative criticism is to do it something less than justice.

One remembers that when it first emerged as a distinct literary form the forces of the Renaissance were at work reshaping the minds of men. Men had always thought—a few of them, that is. But by 1580, the date of Montaigne's first printing, more were thinking and thinking differently. Europe was becoming saturated with the learning of the ancients, and the results were far-reaching. Nationalism was beginning. New types of leaders were molding autocracies at the expense of the old communal ways. Individualism was awakening, aroused by increased opportunity. With the separation of England, France, and Spain into national units, a contingency hastened, perhaps, by the rapid advance of the Protestant Reformation, the old mass thinking and mass control were dying. Men began to consider themselves more nearly as free agents, and as far as their natural enemies, hunger and cold, could be placated, to act upon the thought. The result was a new heaven and a new earth in politics, in art, in literature, in religion, in life in general. And so it was that the essay came to be. The new ideas, new habits of thought, required a new vehicle for their expression. The drama, the chronicle, the romance were inadequate. What better, then, could be found than the old prose forms, the discourses and dialogues, of the classical and oriental writers —of Cicero and Seneca, of Plato and Aristotle, of Confucius and Mencius, of the authors of Ecclesiastes, Ecclesiasticus, and the Book of Proverbs—but these forms refurbished and brought up to date to suit the spirit of the age? The time was ripe, and the agent was at hand in the person of Michel de Montaigne. Hence the essay appeared, a short prose composition exactly fitted to its purpose, that of communicating the ideas of men of rich intelligence to a generation seeking adjustment to an environment spiritually and intellectually new.

II

At the opening of the seventeenth century, therefore, men found the essay ready for use, and they were not slow in putting it to work. Mention has already been made of the "aphoristic" writers, like Bacon and his immediate followers; of the "character" writers, like Hall, Overbury, and Earle; of Feltham and Howell; of the Puritans; and of the Restorationists. These men all contributed not only to the progress of English thought through their incomparable writings but, by reason of such contribution, to the progress of the essay as well, through their adaptation of its possibilities to the exigencies of their demands. Without their work in the form, the essay would much more slowly have reached the state of its perfection. But these men were not periodical essayists. We are more nearly concerned with those who were.

According to Professor Walter Graham of the University of Illinois, whose book, *The Beginnings of English Literary Periodicals*, published by the Oxford University Press in 1926, is unique in its distinction as a study of early periodical literature, "the earliest remote ancestors of modern literary journals were the book notices of the seventeenth century, appearing as the first advertisements in newsbooks." Following these, the earliest periodical publications were serialized book abstracts, one of the most important of which, started as an imitation of the French *Journal des Savans* and aided, no doubt, by the *Philosophical Transactions of the Royal Society*, begun in 1665, became the *Mercurias Librarius*, or, as it is better known, the Term Catalogue, which was issued from 1668 to 1709.

But something more than book extracts was demanded by the ever-increasing desire for knowledge that gathered force toward the end of the third quarter of the seventeenth century; hence a so-called "question and answer" paper was established by a bookseller named John Dunton, the idea being to answer questions propounded by subscribers—an undertaking not unlike certain departments of our present-day newspapers. In the columns of Dunton's *Athenian Mercury*, therefore, were "resolved the nice and curious questions proposed by the ingenious," and it was the editor's wish that his journal become of interest wherever people gathered to discuss matters "close to their business and bosoms." Journals of book abstracts, then, and "question and answer" papers, of which there were many examples prior to the end of the century, one may consider as being the logical ancestors of the periodical as a publication; and although to us nowadays they may seem the very epitome of dullness, they are none the less illuminating in that they indicate a growing intellectual sensitivity on the part of the general public, a trait which, becoming more and more widespread with the passage of time, aided in making possible the effectiveness of Addison and Steele.

But if there was an intellectual curiosity which helped to call into being the journals of information, there was likewise a craving for amusement that called forth the journals of entertainment.

These last had their beginning in satirical political pamphlets, but with the undoubted success of the journals of information to encourage them, the publishers of pamphlets turned their attention toward the serial. So decided was their success, moreover, that by 1680 there was a reading public for allegories dealing with social and political matters, such as *Advice from Parnassus*, 1680, and *Heraclitus Ridens*, 1681. These, together with burlesque papers like *Democritus Ridens*, *Mercurias Infernus*, *News from the Land of Chivalry*, and *Mercurias Bifrons*, all serve to shadow forth something of the facetiousness that during the eighteenth century was to come into its own. A more pretentious group of journals, however, appeared about 1690: *Poor Robin's Occurrences and Remarks*, *Rambles Around the World*, and *Momus Ridens*, the last a paper somewhat in the manner of the, later, *Tatler*, as it contained "comical remarks on publick reports" dated "From Westminster," "From Whitehall," etc. But probably the most widely read of the group was Edward Ward's *London Spy*. It flourished from 1698 to 1700 as a monthly, making use of the essay form and being written in the first person (again in anticipation of the *Tatler* and its followers). One of the *Spy's* most interesting characteristics (also from the point of view of its being anticipatory) is the use it made of a countryman's being shown about London by a city acquaintance, a suggestion, although by no means the only one, of Sir Roger de Coverley of *Spectator* fame.[1] Other periodicals

---

[1]For information concerning the *London Spy* and, in fact, most of the periodicals of the seventeenth century, the writer is indebted to Professor Walter Graham, whose work has been mentioned in the body of this introduction.

not entirely dissimilar were John Harris's *The English Lucian*, 1698; Ward's *Weekly Comedy*, 1699; "Sylvester Partridge's" *The Infallible Astrologer*, 1700; and the *Merry Mercury*, 1700.

One of the chief characteristics of this whole group so far mentioned was salaciousness, a quality not often found in their successors of the eighteenth century; nevertheless, because of the various technical devices used by one or the other of them, like dating certain numbers from one place and others from another, or like announcing and maintaining *dramatis personae;* and because of the fact that many of them while amusing in intent were nevertheless also reformatory, they bear no slight relationship to the periodicals that were later to appear.

In addition to this quite ephemeral type there was another —one perhaps more stable, and surely much more respectable. The chief periodical included here is, no doubt, the *Gentleman's Journal*, 1692. It was edited by Peter Anthony Motteux, who modeled it upon *Le Mercure Galant*, a Parisian journal of gossip and court news. The *Journal* was a miscellany of every kind of matter that had thus far served to attract readers: news, questions and answers, translations, poems, essays, fables, even a "Lovers' Gazette," the legitimate forbear of our present-day "Advice to the Love-Lorn" columns. One of the most important contributions made by the *Journal* to literary progress was the effect it had toward removing the rather widespread prejudice against fiction and poetry then existing; the first two numbers contained, in addition to the usual features, a considerable amount of verse and not a little criticism; but starting with the third each number contained a so-called novel and the amount of criticism was so far increased as to have become a feature.

The *Gentleman's Journal*, successful as it was from the beginning, was, naturally, not without imitators. The most important follower, however, did not appear until 1731, when the *Gentleman's Magazine* was issued, and it is curious to

note that, although this magazine is usually considered to be
the first of the modern type, it contained, from its inception,
only one departure from the standard established by the
Journal. Among the other, and more immediate followers
are to be found *Miscellanies over Claret*, or *Friends to the
Tavern the Best Friends to Poetry*, 1697; *Mercurias Theologi-
cus*, or *Monthly Instructor*, a journal of religious influence;
and the *Weekly Entertainer*, a direct forerunner of the *Spectator* in that it was printed upon a single sheet and contained
a single essay. These, then, and the various journalistic
undertakings of Defoe, most especially his *Weekly Review*
which contained a section called the *Mercure Scandale*,
"Advice from the Scandalous Club, being a weekly history of
nonsense, impertinence, vice and debauchery";[1] together
with the *Monthly Miscellany*, 1707, one of the earliest
literary journals, and the *Muses Mercury*, 1707, constitute a
sort of roll-call of seventeenth century periodicals. And
these last in connection with the essays collected and published in book form furnish the background against which
the essay was to make its appearance as the dominant
literary type during the age of Queen Anne.

III

Thus more than a century of experimentation passed during which many minds, each contributing a modicum toward
the perfection of the essay, so wrought upon it that Richard
Steele, when the time came for him to choose a medium by
which he might interpret his generation to itself, found
ready at hand the ideal instrument. For in 1709 and immediately thereafter the function of authorship was to
mediate between the governing and the governed, for one
thing; and to point the way toward self-realization through
adjustment to an ever-shifting condition of environment, for

---

[1]Defoe's *Weekly Review* was a newspaper more nearly than a literary
periodical, and, as such, points only indirectly toward the theme of this
sketch.

another. One did not become a writer during the age of
Anne because he felt within him the glow of inspiration to
work out his destiny in terms of the beautiful, accepting
reward as a possible result, but because he wished to make
his way in the world. Writing was a means toward that
end, and if one possessed sufficient talent to draw the attention of powerful individuals to himself, he was enlisted in the
service of whatever party happened for the moment to be
in power. If he were of easy conscience politically, like
Defoe, for instance, who managed to serve either Whig or
Tory with equal facility, in fact at one time to serve both, his
way was not too difficult; but if he were more sensitive, as
were both Addison and Steele, who severed the friendship of a
lifetime because of political difference, then the way was not
so smooth. At all events during the first decade of the
eighteenth century there happened to converge the three
elements most essential for success in no matter what undertaking: personality, opportunity, and medium—and all were
of first quality.

The medium we understand; a century had gone into developing a short prose composition, both the limits and the
essence of which were ideally suited not only to interest but
also to affect the class most vitally concerned. Not only this,
but the class itself, because of the intensity of English
activity both at home and abroad, had never been so sensitive
to the necessity of knowing itself the better in order the better
to survive.

Sometimes a most trivial practical detail may influence
enormously toward moral or spiritual change. One remembers the old epigram about the horseshoe nail and the loss
of a kingdom. It happened late during the preceding
century that a Turkish merchant had returned to England
bringing along a native servant, an adept at making coffee.
It also happened that the servant made the coffee in a public
house and served his master where everyone could see what
was toward. In no long time a demand arose for coffee served
after the fashion adopted by this man, a demand so insistent

that he left the service of his master and established a coffee-house, the forerunner of the institution with which the history of the essay is so closely bound up that it seems almost as if it were as important an influence as was Richard Steele himself. For by 1709 there were scores of coffee-houses in London. But by this time they had taken on the characteristics of clubs in which men congregated to discuss whatever was uppermost at the moment. It was here that the bulk of what were middle-class readers was to be found, for the most part, deep in the discussion not of a chimerical idealism, nor of commonplace details of personal business, but of the social, intellectual, and moral movements of the time. What better, then, than to design a periodical which would engage the interest of coffee-house patrons? There can be small doubt that something like this idea entered the mind of Steele.

Here, almost ready made, was an opportunity; it only needed a personality properly endowed to bring it to life. And such a one was Steele. He was, at the time when he conceived the idea of the *Tatler*, governmental gazetteer, and as such had immediate access to channels of news. Besides, he was already an author of some power, having published one book, *The Christian Hero*, and produced some three or four plays. So, impelled by these circumstances, and aided, no doubt, by something of a hint from Defoe's *Review*, he launched his project, the purpose of which is best described in his own words, appearing in the first volume of the collected *Tatler* papers as part of the dedication: "The general purpose of this paper is to expose the false arts of life, to pull off the disguises of cunning, vanity, and affectation, and to recommend a general simplicity in our dress, our discourse, and our behavior." This description may be augmented by the design as set forth in the first number, where he says that he will date papers having to do with learning from the coffee-house known as the Grecian; those having to do with poetry from Will's; with foreign and domestic news from St. James'; with gallantry, pleasure, and entertainment from White's;

and papers having to do with any other matters from "My own Apartment."

How successful he was in his undertaking is clear from a comment made upon him by John Gay: "It is incredible to conceive the effect his writings have made upon the Town; how many thousand follies they have either quite banished or given a very great check! how much countenance they have added to Virtue and Religion! how many people they have rendered happy, by showing them it was entirely their own fault if they were not so! and, lastly, how entirely they have convinced our young fops and gay fellows of the values and advantages of learning!" Gay wrote this passage in 1711, after the *Tatler* had run its course. For it ended with 271st paper on January 2, 1711.

Many conjectures have been made concerning the abrupt close to which the *Tatler* was brought. No doubt one reason for its discontinuance was that late in 1710 Steele lost his position as gazetteer, and so was cut off from the sources of news. But perhaps the most important reason was that both he and Addison, who had joined the enterprise with the publication of the eighteenth paper, seemed to find themselves circumscribed by the rules laid down in the first paper. At all events, toward the end both editors seemed to grow lackadaisical; as if, having undertaken to provide their readers with certain kinds of information and amusement and yet having realized that even their best, under the self-imposed conditions, was none too good, their interest in the project became perfunctory. That this last is not illogical would appear from the fact that hardly had the *Tatler* come to an end than the *Spectator* began, for on March 1, 1711, appeared the first number—with all the freshness of a newly conceived undertaking. Only this time there was no definite announcement of topics to be treated, Addison remaining content to remark (in the tenth paper) merely: "Since I have raised to myself so great an audience, I shall spare no pains to make their instruction agreeable, and their diversion useful. For these reasons I shall endeavor to enliven morality with wit, and to temper wit with morality, that my readers may, if possible, both ways find their account in the speculation of the day. And to the end that their virtue and discretion may not be short transient starts of thought, I have resolved to refresh their memories from day to day, till I have resolved them out of that desperate state of vice and folly into which the age is fallen." This is Addison's view of what a periodical should be, a view which, according to Dr. Hugh Walker's *The English Essay and Essayists*, may in something account for the discontinuance of the *Tatler* and the establishment of the *Spectator* in its place. For in the first-named, Steele was the dominant figure, Addison occupying only the position of contributor; but in the second, Addison emerged as the coadjutor, equally responsible with Steele.

And it is unquestionable that in this combination both Addison and Steele were at their best. Steele's brilliant initiative and his quick imagination were tempered by the classical restraint of Addison. Steele provided a freshness of perception and a vivid style; Addison, scholarship, artistic sense, and a stability of purpose that went a long way toward sustaining the *Spectator* through its 635 incomparable numbers.

One may well say *incomparable* here, for it is in the papers of the *Spectator* that one finds the essay to have attained its perfection. In the *Tatler* were contained the best examples of periodical writing thus far produced, but these were no more than a trying out, so to speak, of the medium. It was left for the later journal to appeal so strongly to the general public that Addison could write, "My publisher tells me that there are already [Monday, March 12, 1711] three thousand [copies] distributed every day: so that if I allow twenty readers [the *Spectator*, like all periodicals of the time, was distributed to coffee-houses as well as to individual subscribers] to every paper, which I look upon as a modest computation, I may reckon about three score thousand disciples in London and Westminster." It is natural to suppose that so wide a circle of influence could have been attained only because of the accuracy with which the public's state of mind was gauged, and more than this, because of the urbanity with which "morality was enlivened with wit, and wit tempered with morality."

For, whatever else it may have been, the age of Anne was urbane; it was sure that it knew what it wanted and it was fastidious as to the manner in which its wants were supplied. It could be appealed to only in terms of its interests, and then in terms of an expression subtly forceful and delicately adequate. The result was that in finding its audience, the essay found also its manner, "that peculiar intimacy with the public," according to Leigh Hunt, which, established by Montaigne, augmented by Addison and Steele, and revived by Charles Lamb and William Hazlitt in the nineteenth century, has now become fixed as the chief mark of its identity.

By means of the accuracy with which they observed their generation, then, together with the appropriateness of their manner, Addison and Steele brought about a definite advance in popularizing knowledge, in elevating taste, in inspiring enthusiasm for reform, and, generally, in "making reason and the will of God prevail," if we may borrow the phrase of Matthew Arnold. But more than this—by some obscure manifestation of genius they were enabled to penetrate the sophistication of the age until they touched its soul, awakening it to new perceptions of human life and the possibilities of its further development.

IV

As has been said before, authorship during the age of Anne was far more dependent upon politics than it ever has been since. Steele, we remember, was enabled to establish the *Tatler* at least partly because of his government position, and we know that his discontinuance of the periodical and the loss of his position very nearly coincided. Addison, naturally, was a politician also; he had begun his career as the

result of his poem, *The Campaign*, composed at the request of
Lord Godolphin, the lord treasurer, in celebration of the Duke
of Marlborough's victory at the Battle of Blenheim. The
immediate success of the poem won for him the favor of the
ruling party, and such were his political talents that he rose
rapidly in the service, having by 1710 become so powerful that
upon his reëlection to Parliament Swift could remark of him,
"If he had a mind to be chosen king, he would hardly be
denied." Hence, although his contemporaries were more or
less under the thumb of either the Whigs or the Tories,
Addison, as an author, could remain aloof from either influence. And it is clear that he did so, at least when writing
for the *Spectator*, for the *Spectator* papers are singularly free
from political coloration. Not so Steele. Not only was he
more or less dependent upon political favor, but in spite of
his success as a journalist, he continued in touch with state
affairs. As a matter of fact, not long before the *Spectator*
was temporarily discontinued, in December, 1712, Steele un-
dertook to establish a new journal, the *Guardian*, the first
number of which appeared on March 12, 1713. The *Guardian*
was issued daily for more than six months, until October 2,
1713. Both Addison and Steele were the chief contributors,
although at first Addison wrote nothing. The latter half of
the *Guardian* papers, however, show Addison as writing far
more than Steele, who was becoming more and more deeply
involved in politics—he was elected to Parliament and
eventually knighted—so that he could ill afford the time demanded by his various journalistic projects. Nevertheless,
immediately upon the discontinuance of the *Guardian*, which
showed something of a political tinge, Steele founded the
Englishman, a periodical devoted almost wholly to politics,
which he conducted without the assistance of Addison.
Moreover, Addison in 1715 established the *Freeholder* in-
dependently of Steele. Altogether, Addison and Steele,
either in combination or separately, established almost a
dozen journals. Not one of these, however, was of the
quality of the *Spectator*. They appeared, were issued for a

few months, perhaps a year, and were then discontinued to make room for new ones.

It is safe to say that during the six years between 1709 and 1715 the periodical essay was the dominant literary form. One must not suppose that Addison and Steele were alone as proprietors of periodicals. In fact, Dr. George S. Marr, in his *The Periodical Essayists of the Eighteenth Century*, lists twenty-three journals that flourished during the first fifteen years of the century. That such enterprises were profitable is easily understood especially when one considers the amount of advertising that very early began to be included; and they continued to be profitable in spite of the Stamp Duty imposed in 1712, which required the payment of a tax of a halfpenny upon every half sheet published.

However, although many imitators sprang up in the wake of the *Spectator*, nothing comparable to it in either literary quality or social influence ever appeared. Among the 148 periodicals which Dr. Marr considers, for instance, not more than seven in addition to those already mentioned are worthy of remark: the *Rambler*, which appeared in 208 numbers between March 20, 1750, and March 14, 1752, was written almost entirely by Dr. Samuel Johnson; the *Adventurer*, in 140 numbers between November 7, 1752, and March 8, 1754, was composed chiefly by Johnson and John Hawkesworth; the *World*, in 209 numbers between January 4, 1753, and December 30, 1756, was edited by Edward Moore under the patronage of Horace Walpole and the Earl of Chesterfield; the *Connoisseur*, in 140 numbers between January 31, 1753, and September 30, 1756, was written by George Colman and Bonnell Thornton, with the exception of a handful of papers by William Cowper and one or two by Chesterfield; the *Idler*, in 103 numbers between April 15, 1758, and April 5, 1760, in the columns of the *Universal Chronicle* was, again, written almost wholly by Samuel Johnson; the *Citizen of the World* papers, which appeared in the *Public Ledger* during 1760 and 1761, were composed by Oliver Goldsmith; and the *Lounger*, which was issued in Edinburgh between 1785 and 1787, was written chiefly by Henry Mackenzie, whose reputation, however, rests almost entirely upon his novel, *The Man of Feeling*.[1]

Immediately the question looms: why did nothing appear during the remainder of the century which will bear comparison with what appeared during the years 1709 to 1714?

The answer lies buried beneath an obscurity of conjecture, any attempt to define which would extend to several times the space available for this sketch. In order to approximate an answer, however, one should recall that the essay came into being as the result of that precious heritage of the Renaissance, scepticism. The credulity of the ages preceding having been somewhat dispelled, new attitudes, new ways of thinking demanded a new instrument. As the seventeenth century advanced, and the necessities of scepticism multiplied under pressure of the popularity of the essay's appeal, this instrument became ever more and more effective until during the years immediately following the Revolution of 1688, when the results of scepticism could in some fashion be measured, the essay stood upon the brink of maturity. And it is no more than natural that the expository form should grow in demand at a time when, for instance, the royal prerogative began to be limited, religious tolerance to be recognized, an improvement in the administration of justice to be sought, the possibilities of increase in economic power to be remarked, and the clamor of the people for education to be heeded. Of all this the *Tatler*, the *Spectator*, and the *Guardian*, and their contemporaries were aware. And upon such awareness they proceeded to success.

It may be that they were so successful that the efforts of those who followed them could attain to nothing more than mediocrity, or it may be that they served the cause of en-

---

[1]Another journal which has been drawn upon in the selection of the essays comprising this book is the *Examiner*. It was established by the Tories in 1710 in opposition to the *Tatler*, and was continued for four years under various editors, one of whom was Jonathan Swift. The *Examiner* was wholly political; it is remembered only because of Swift's connection with it.

lightenment to such effect that the added demands made upon it were too heavy for so slight an instrument. At all events it is plain that between the discontinuance of the *Guardian* and the establishment of the *Rambler*, a period of some forty years, there is neither essayist nor periodical worthy of particular note. And yet there is no dearth of literary production.

On the contrary, for during these years Alexander Pope attained his position in literature because of his philosophically humane poetry, Jonathan Swift established himself as the great English satirist, and Defoe, Richardson, and Fielding pointed out the way which has been followed by modern fiction. The interesting point here is that, although achieving his reputation in another form, each of these writers occasionally made use of the essay as a medium. Pope contributed a number of papers to the *Guardian* and would have written more if he had not feared the consequences of political entanglement. Swift wrote a number of periodical essays for the *Tatler* and for his own *Examiner;* but one of the papers by which he is best known as an essayist, the one on *Style* reprinted in the present collection, is remarkable for the mistaken idea regarding language that it reveals. Defoe, although his periodical contributions amounted literally to hundreds, is forever enshrined in literature as the author of *Robinson Crusoe.* Fielding's essays between the chapters of *Tom Jones* reveal him as an essayist of power and discrimination, while his papers in the *Champion* and the *True Patriot* are only a trifle less distinctive. And Richardson's *Familiar Letters on Important Occasions*, although not to be thought of as work in the field of the periodical essay, is nevertheless a collection of didactic essays of considerable interest—yet Richardson the potential essayist is lost completely in Richardson the actual novelist. Hence, it may be, as has frequently been suggested, that after the *Guardian* the demands made by a people growing ever more and more enlightened by reason of an ever-increasing intellectual curiosity imposed too heavy a burden upon the essay and, as a result, the essay form was absorbed into other forms or was eclipsed in popularity by them.

That it was absorbed into the novel, its special prerogative, social criticism, being thus usurped by the longer, more flexible form, is plain to anyone who reads the early novelists. That it was taken over by the newspaper, and so became the "news article," is likewise plain when one measures the degree to which the newspaper was gaining over the periodical in circulation and influence. For instance, in the first number of the *Gentleman's Magazine* (1731) a writer remarked, "Newspapers are of late so multiplied as to render it impossible, unless a man makes it his business to consult them all." But that the demand for the single essay periodical had evolved into a demand for a periodical of wider scope and more universal appeal, as evidenced by the establishment of the monthly magazines, is likewise to be remembered in any consideration of the decline of the essay in influence and popularity. These, of course, carried essays, and it would be perhaps impossible to over-emphasize the effect such essays had in diffusing knowledge and in adding to the reading public. Ambrose Philips, the editor of the *Free Thinker*, a liberal Whig journal of considerable weight, stated in 1718: "Of all the methods which have been practiced to inform mankind and to convey wisdom and knowledge to the multitude, that of throwing out short lectures from the press upon stated days is far more effectual and more convincing than any other." Nevertheless, during the third decade of the century these "short lectures" no longer sufficed; a more pretentious medium was required.

The requirement was satisfied by the appearance of two magazines, for instance, among a host of others—the *Gentleman's Magazine*, in 1731, and the *London Magazine, or the Gentleman's Monthly Intelligencer*, in 1732, both of which had long and honorable careers, the last surviving until 1779. These, together with their less well known contemporaries, harked back somewhat to the periodicals of the seventeenth century—especially to the *Gentleman's Journal* (1692)—for precedent. The *Gentleman's Magazine*, in particular, carried letters to the editor, memoirs, antiquities, sometimes accompanied by illustrative plates, verse, and book notices, besides the usual essays. In addition, however, it published notices of births, marriages, and deaths, and stock prices current. In its own words it contained "more in quantity and greater variety than any book of its kind and price. All the pieces of wit, humor, or intelligence daily offered to the public in the newspapers, and therewith some other matters of use and amusement that will be communicated to us." The *London Magazine*, likewise, printed book notices, items of news, verse, and original essays, but different from the other journals of the time, it carried also essays taken over from its competitors. The first number, for instance, takes over eight items from eight different journals, some of which are authentic reprints, but in some instances the original has been paraphrased, or even parodied. Perhaps the magazine can best be characterized by a quotation from the preface to the first number: "As the miscellaneous kind of writing is in its own nature peculiarly engaging, variety of subjects having a certain quality of unbending and entertaining the mind; so this work may boast of a greater variety in less compass than any other kind of performance, and truly answers our motto, *multum* (we might say *plurima*) *in parvo*." Hence, while the essay was still a principal item in periodical publication, it was no longer relied upon to carry the burden alone; interests had gradually become so diversified as a result of the ever-widening reading public that no one type of writing could long remain in the ascendant. As a matter of fact, by 1750 all the literary forms with which we are familiar, except the short story as developed by Edgar Allan Poe, were under full exploitation. The essay never again was to wield anything like its former influence— except for a short time early in the nineteenth century— as the main feature of the critical reviews.

However, during the decade 1750–1760, because of the prestige of Dr. Samuel Johnson, the brilliance of Oliver

Goldsmith, and the influence of the politically powerful group of writers who were affiliated with the Earl of Chesterfield in the publication of the *World*, there was something of a revival of interest in the essay as written by Addison and Steele. These later compositions were for the most part cast in a more substantial mold than had formerly been the case. Except at infrequent intervals the matter treated was serious and the manner dignified if not ponderous. The reading public of the day was intent upon being informed—an effect, perhaps, of the increasingly apparent intellectual democracy which was making possible more and more freedom of inquiry into political and religious affairs—and it looked upon the periodical press as the source of its information. The result was that between the years 1753 and 1792 the publication of newspapers and magazines was doubled. However, although Johnson, when he established the *Rambler* (while in the midst of compiling his dictionary), was beginning to be looked upon as the great literary figure he eventually became, he lacked that last atom of inspiration which was necessary to bring his essays to life. We read them because in their way they mark another milestone in the history of literature, and because, occasionally, they are authentic contributions to the *genre;* nevertheless, nothing that Johnson wrote either for the *Rambler* or the *Idler* is comparable to the use he made of the essay in his *Lives of the Poets.* The *Rambler* was not signally successful, and while in the *Idler* he produced some of his best periodical work, so far had the essay periodical declined in favor that the *Idler* papers were published in the columns of a newspaper, the *Universal Chronicle.*

It is true also of Goldsmith's *Citizen of the World* papers that they were published as part of a newspaper, this time the *Public Ledger.* They were afterward collected and reprinted in book form, to be sure, and became very popular. Not even the essays of Goldsmith were considered sufficiently powerful to carry the entire weight of a periodical. And yet for us Goldsmith figures among the very greatest of

English essayists, requiring, as he does, to be considered in the canon distinguishing Bacon, Addison and Steele, Charles Lamb, and William Hazlitt.

And so the essay tapers off in quality and hence in influence during the remainder of the century, being absorbed into the more imposing novel, being added as a feature to the newspaper and to the magazines, and yet continuing to reappear from time to time with some show of its former brilliance. But not often; the spirit of the age had shifted. The eager expectancy with which the century had opened had dimmed, whether because of England's added wisdom, or because of the apparent futility of its hopes—who shall say? At all events, the essay having served its purpose remained quiescent, almost as if gathering strength before the storm of the French Revolution, a storm which was to arouse it to renewed activity in its special field—creative criticism—during the century to come.

PERIODICAL ESSAYS
OF THE
EIGHTEENTH CENTURY

JONATHAN SWIFT

1667 Was born in Dublin of a comparatively wealthy English family.

1673 Entered Kilkenny Grammar School

1682 Entered Trinity College, Dublin.

1686 Was granted a degree by special favor.

1689–1694 Lived in the household of Sir William Temple, a relative, spending his time in study, and making the acquaintance of distinguished men.
Met Esther Johnson (the "Stella" of the *Journals*).

1695 Took orders, and became Prebend of Kilroot.

1696–1699 Lived again with Sir William Temple.

1699 Occurred the death of Temple, without financial benefit to Swift. Went to Ireland as chaplain and secretary to the Earl of Berkeley.

1701 Received the living at Laracor, Ireland.

1701–1709 Went often to London in the service of the church and to further his own ends, particularly in the cultivation of Whig acquaintances.

1704 Published *The Tale of a Tub*, and *The Battle of the Books*.

1708 Published *Argument Against Abolishing Christianity*.

1709–1710 Contributed to the *Tatler*.

1710–1711 Edited the *Examiner*, a political journal.

1711 Published *The Conduct of the Allies*.

1711–1713 Wrote the *Journal to Stella*. (Not published until 1766.)

1713 Was appointed Dean of St. Patrick's in Dublin.
Published *Cadenus and Vanessa*.
Became a member of the Scriblerus Club.

1714 Retired permanently to Dublin, upon the death of Queen Anne and the fall of the Tories.

1720 Published *Proposal for the Universal Use of Irish Manufactures*, launching his defense of Ireland.

1724 Published *Drapier Letters*, becoming a hero of Ireland.

1726 Published *Gulliver's Travels*.

1729 Published *A Modest Proposal*.

1738 Became afflicted with mental disorder.

1745 Died, and was buried in St. Patrick's Cathedral, Dublin.

1

PULPIT ELOQUENCE[1]

THE subject of the discourse this evening was eloquence and graceful action. Lysander, who is something particular in his way of thinking and speaking, told us, "a man could not be eloquent without action; for the deportment of the body, the turn of the eye, and an apt sound to every word that is uttered, must all conspire to make an accomplished speaker. Action in one that speaks in public is the same thing as a good mien in ordinary life. Thus, as a certain insensibility in the countenance recommends a sentence of humour and jest, so it must be a very lively consciousness that gives grace to great sentiments. The jest is to be a thing unexpected; therefore your undesigning manner is a beauty in expressions of mirth; but when you are to talk on a set subject, the more you are moved yourself, the more you will move others.

"There is," said he, "a remarkable example of that kind. Æschines, a famous orator of antiquity, had pleaded at Athens in a great cause against Demosthenes; but having lost it, retired to Rhodes. Eloquence was then the quality most admired among men, and the magistrates of that place, having heard he had a copy of the speech of Demosthenes, desired him to repeat both their pleadings. After his own he recited also the oration of his antagonist. The people expressed their admiration of both, but more of that of Demosthenes. 'If you are,' said he, 'thus touched with hearing only what that great orator said, how much would you have been affected had you seen him speak? for he who hears Demosthenes only, loses much the better part of the oration.' Certain it is that they who speak gracefully are very lamely represented in having their speeches read or repeated by unskilful people; for there is something native to each man, so inherent to his thoughts and sentiments, which it is hardly possible for another to give a true

[1]*Tatler*, No. 66. Saturday, September 10, 1709.

idea of. You may observe in common talk, when a sentence of any man's is repeated, an acquaintance of his shall immediately observe, 'That is so like him, methinks I see how he looked when he said it.'

"But of all the people on the earth, there are none who puzzle me so much as the clergy of Great Britain, who are, I believe, the most learned body of men now in the world: and yet this art of speaking, with the proper ornaments of voice and gesture, is wholly neglected among them; and I will engage, were a deaf man to behold the greater part of them preach, he would rather think they were reading the contents only of some discourse they intended to make, than actually in the body of an oration, even when they were upon matters of such a nature as one would believe it were impossible to think of without emotion.

"I own there are exceptions to this general observation, and that the dean we heard the other day together is an orator. He has so much regard to his congregation, that he commits to his memory what he is to say to them; and has so soft and graceful a behaviour, that it must attract your attention. His person, it is to be confessed, is no small recommendation; but he is to be highly commended for not losing that advantage; and adding to the propriety of speech, which might pass the criticism of Longinus, an action which would have been approved by Demosthenes. He has a peculiar force in his way, and has charmed many of his audience, who could not be intelligent hearers of his discourse were there not explanation as well as grace in his action. This art of his is useful with the most exact and honest skill: he never attempts your passions until he has convinced your reason. All the objections which he can form are laid open and dispersed before he uses the least vehemence in his sermon; but when he thinks he has your head, he very soon wins your heart; and never pretends to show the beauty of holiness until he has convinced you of the truth of it.

"Would every one of our clergymen be thus careful to

recommend truth and virtue in their proper figures, and show so much concern for them as to give them all the additional force they were able, it is not possible that nonsense should have so many hearers as you find it has in dissenting congregations, for no reason in the world but because it is spoken extempore; for ordinary minds are wholly governed by their eyes and ears; and there is no way to come at their hearts but by power over their imaginations.

"There is my friend and merry companion Daniel; he knows a great deal better than he speaks, and can form a proper discourse as well as any orthodox neighbour.   But he knows very well that to bawl out, 'My beloved!' and the words 'grace! regeneration! sanctification! a new light! the day! the day! ay, my beloved, the day! or rather the night! the night is coming!' and 'judgment will come when we least think of it!' and so forth.   He knows, to be vehement is the only way to come at his audience. Daniel, when he sees my friend Greenhat come in, can give a good hint, and cry out, 'This is only for the saints! the regenerated!'   By this force of action, though mixed with all the incoherence and ribaldry imaginable, Daniel can laugh at his diocesan, and grow fat by voluntary subscription, while the parson of the parish goes to law for half his dues. Daniel will tell you, it is not the shepherd, but the sheep with the bell, which the flock follows.

"Another thing, very wonderful this learned body should omit, is learning to read; which is a most necessary part of eloquence in one who is to serve at the altar; for there is no man but must be sensible that the lazy tone and inarticulate sound of our common readers depreciates the most proper form of words that were ever extant in any nation or language, to speak their own wants, or his power from whom we ask relief.

"There cannot be a greater instance of the power of action than in little parson Dapper, who is the common relief to all the lazy pulpits in town.   This smart youth has a very good memory, a quick eye, and a clean handkerchief.   Thus equipped, he opens his text, shuts his book fairly, shows he has no notes in his Bible, opens both palms, and shows all is fair there too. Thus, with a decisive air, my young man goes on without hesitation; and though from the beginning to the end of his pretty discourse, he has not used one proper gesture, yet, at the conclusion, the churchwarden pulls his gloves from off his hands; 'Pray, who is this extraordinary young man?' Thus the force of action is such, that it is more prevalent, even when improper, than all the reason and argument in the world without it." This gentleman concluded his discourse by saying, "I do not doubt but if our preachers would learn to speak, and our readers to read, within six months' time we should not have a dissenter within a mile of a church in Great Britain."

ON STYLE[1]

From my own Apartment, September 27.

THE following letter has laid before me many great and manifest evils in the world of letters which I had overlooked; but they open to me a very busy scene, and it will require no small care and application to amend errors which are become so universal. The affectation of politeness is exposed in this epistle with a great deal of wit and discernment; so that whatever discourses I may fall into hereafter upon the subjects the writer treats of, I shall at present lay the matter before the World without the least alteration from the words of my correspondent.

"To ISAAC BICKERSTAFF, ESQ.,

"SIR,

"There are some abuses among us of great consequence, the reformation of which is properly your province, though as far as I have been conversant in your papers, you have not yet considered them. These are, the deplorable ignor-

---

[1] *Tatler*, No. 230. Tuesday, September 27, 1710.

ance that for some years hath reigned among our English writers, the great depravity of our taste, and the continual corruption of our style. I say nothing here of those who handle particular sciences, divinity, law, physic, and the like; I mean, the traders in history and politics, and the *belles lettres;* together with those by whom books are not translated, but (as the common expressions are) 'done out of French, Latin,' or other language, and 'made English.' I cannot but observe to you, that till of late years a Grub-Street book was always bound in sheepskin, with suitable print and paper, the price never above a shilling, and taken off wholly by common tradesmen, or country pedlars, but now they appear in all sizes and shapes, and in all places. They are handed about from lapfuls in every coffeehouse to persons of quality, are shown in Westminster-Hall and the Court of Requests. You may see them gilt, and in royal paper, of five or six hundred pages, and rated accordingly. I would engage to furnish you with a catalogue of English books published within the compass of seven years past, which at the first hand would cost you a hundred pounds, wherein you shall not be able to find ten lines together of common grammar or common sense.

"These two evils, ignorance and want of taste, have produced a third; I mean, the continual corruption of our English tongue, which, without some timely remedy, will suffer more by the false refinements of twenty years past, than it hath been improved in the foregoing hundred: And this is what I design chiefly to enlarge upon, leaving the former evils to your animadversion.

"But instead of giving you a list of the late refinements crept into our language, I here send you the copy of a letter I received some time ago from a most accomplished person in this way of writing, upon which I shall make some remarks. It is in these terms.

"'SIR,

"'I *cou'dn't* get the things you sent for all *about Town.*— I *thôt* to *ha'* come down myself, and then *I'd ha' brôut'um;*

but I *han't don't*, and I believe I *can't do't*, that's *pozz.*—*Tom* begins to *g'imself* airs because *he's* going with the *plenipo's.* —'Tis said, the *French* King will *bamboozl' us agen*, which *causes many speculations.* The *Jacks*, and others of that *kidney*, are very *uppish*, and *alert upon't*, as you may see by their *phizz's.*—*Will Hazzard* has got the *hipps*, having lost *to the tune of* five hundr'd pound, *thô* he understands play very well, *nobody better.* He has promis't me upon *rep*, to leave off play; but you know 'tis a weakness *he's* too apt to *give into, thô* he has as much wit as any man, *nobody more.* He has lain *incog* ever since.—The *mobb's* very quiet with us now.—I believe you *thôt* I *banter'd* you in my last like a *country put.*—I *sha'n't* leave Town this month, *&c.'*

"This letter is in every point an admirable pattern of the present polite way of writing; nor is it of less authority for being an epistle. You may gather every flower in it, with a thousand more of equal sweetness, from the books, pamphlets, and single papers, offered us every day in the coffee-houses: and these are the beauties introduced to supply the want of wit, sense, humour, and learning, which formerly were looked upon as qualifications for a writer. If a man of wit, who died forty years ago, were to rise from the grave on purpose, how would he be able to read this letter? And after he had gone through that difficulty, how would he be able to understand it? The first thing that strikes your eye is the *breaks* at the end of almost every sentence; of which I know not the use, only that it is a refinement, and very frequently practised. Then you will observe the abbreviations and elisions, by which consonants of most obdurate sound are joined together, without one softening vowel to intervene; and all this only to make one syllable of two, directly contrary to the example of the Greeks and Romans; altogether of the Gothic strain, and a natural tendency towards relapsing into barbarity, which delights in monosyllables, and uniting of mute consonants; as it is observable in all the Northern languages. And this is still more visible in the next refinement, which consists in pronouncing the first syllable in a word that has many, and dismissing the rest; such as *phizz*, *hipps*, *mobb*, *pozz.*, *rep.* and many more; when we are already overloaded with monosyllables, which are the disgrace of our language. Thus we cram one syllable, and cut off the rest; as the owl fattened her mice, after she had bit off their legs to prevent their running away; and if ours be the same reason for maiming words, it will certainly answer the end; for I am sure no other nation will desire to borrow them. Some words are hitherto but fairly split, and therefore only in their way to perfection, as *incog* and *plenipo:* but in a short time it is to be hoped they will be further docked to *inc* and *plen*. This reflection has made me of late years very impatient for a peace, which I believe would save the lives of many brave words, as well as men. The war has introduced abundance of polysyllables, which will never be able to live many more campaigns; *Speculations, operations, preliminaries, ambassadors, palisadoes, communication, circumvallation, battalions*, as numerous as they are, if they attack us too frequently in our coffeehouses, we shall certainly put them to flight, and cut off the rear.

"The third refinement observable in the letter I send you, consists in the choice of certain words invented by some *pretty fellows;* such as *banter, bamboozle, country put*, and *kidney*, as it is there applied; some of which are now struggling for the vogue, and others are in possession of it. I have done my utmost for some years to stop the progress of *mobb* and *banter*, but have been plainly borne down by numbers, and betrayed by those who promised to assist me.

"In the last place, you are to take notice of certain choice phrases scattered through the letter; some of them tolerable enough, till they were worn to rags by servile imitators. You might easily find them, though they were not in a different print, and therefore I need not disturb them.

"These are the false refinements in our style which you ought to correct: First, by argument and fair means; but if those fail, I think you are to make use of your authority as censor, and by an annual *index expurgatorius* expunge all words and phrases that are offensive to good sense, and condemn those barbarous mutilations of vowels and syllables. In this last point the usual pretence is, that they spell as they speak; a noble standard for language! to depend upon the caprice of every coxcomb, who, because words are the clothing of our thoughts, cuts them out, and shapes them as he pleases, and changes them oftener than his dress. I believe, all reasonable people would be content that such refiners were more sparing of their words, and liberal in their syllables: and upon this head I should be glad you would bestow some advice upon several young readers in our churches, who coming up from the university, full fraught with admiration of our town politeness, will needs correct the style of their prayer-books. In reading the absolution, they are very careful to say *'Pardons and absolves;'* and in the Prayer for the Royal Family, it must be, *endue'um, enrich'um, prosper-'um,* and *bring'um.* Then in their sermons they use all the modern terms of art, *sham, banter, mob, bubble, bully, cutting, shuffling,* and *palming,* all which, and many more of the like stamp, as I have heard them often in the pulpit from such young sophisters, so I have read them in some of those sermons that have made most noise of late. The design, it seems, is to avoid the dreadful imputation of pedantry, to shew us, that they know the town, understand men and manners, and have not been poring upon old unfashionable books in the university.

"I should be glad to see you the instrument of introducing into our style that simplicity which is the best and truest ornament of most things in life, which the politer ages always aimed at in their building and dress, (*simplex munditiis*[1]) as well as their productions of wit. It is manifest, that all new, affected modes of speech, whether borrowed from the court, the town, or the theatre, are the first perishing parts in any language, and, as I could prove by many hundred instances, have been so in ours. The writings of Hooker, who was a country clergyman, and of Parsons the Jesuit,

---

[1] Of simple elegance.

both in the reign of Queen Elizabeth, are in a style that, with very few allowances, would not offend any present reader; much more clear and intelligible than those of Sir H. Wotton, Sir Robert Naunton, Osborn Daniel the historian, and several others who writ later; but being men of the court, and affecting the phrases then in fashion, they are often either not to be understood, or appear perfectly ridiculous.

"What remedies are to be applied to these evils I have not room to consider, having, I fear, already taken up most of your paper. Besides, I think it is our office only to represent abuses, and yours to redress them.

"I am, with great respect,

"Sir,

"Your, &c."

THE ART OF POLITICAL LYING[1]

WE ARE told the devil is the father of lies, and was a liar from the beginning; so that, beyond contradiction, the invention is old: and, which is more, his first essay of it was purely political, employed in undermining the authority of his prince, and seducing a third part of the subjects from their obedience: for which he was driven down from heaven, where (as Milton expresses it) he had been viceroy of a great western province; and forced to exercise his talent in inferior regions among other fallen spirits, poor or deluded men, whom he still daily tempts to his own sin, and will ever do so, till he be chained in the bottomless pit.

But although the devil be the father of lies, he seems, like other great inventors, to have lost much of his reputation by the continual improvements that have been made upon him.

Who first reduced lying into an art, and adapted it to politics, is not so clear from history, although I have made some diligent inquiries. I shall therefore consider it only according to the modern system, as it has been cultivated

---

[1]*Examiner*, No. 15. Thursday, November 2, 1710.

these twenty years past in the southern part of our own island.

The poets tell us that, after the giants were overthrown by the gods, the earth in revenge produced her last off-spring, which was Fame. And the fable is thus interpreted: that when tumults and seditions are quieted, rumours and false reports are plentifully spread through a nation. So that, by this account, lying is the last relief of a routed, earth-born, rebellious party in a state. But here the moderns have made great additions, applying this art to the gaining of power and preserving it, as well as revenging themselves after they have lost it; as the same instruments are made use of by animals to feed themselves when they are hungry, and to bite those that tread upon them.

But the same genealogy cannot always be admitted for political lying; I shall therefore desire to refine upon it, by adding some circumstances of its birth and parents. A political lie is sometimes born out of a discarded statesman's head, and thence delivered to be nursed and dandled by the rabble. Sometimes it is produced a monster, and licked into shape: at other times it comes into the world completely formed, and is spoiled in the licking. It is often born an infant in the regular way, and requires time to mature it; and often it sees the light in its full growth, but dwindles away by degrees. Sometimes it is of noble birth, and some-times the spawn of a stock-jobber. Here it screams aloud at the opening of the womb, and there it is delivered with a whisper. I know a lie that now disturbs half the kingdom with its noise, [of] which, although too proud and great at present to own its parents, I can remember its whisperhood. To conclude the nativity of this monster, when it comes into the world without a sting it is still-born; and whenever it loses its sting it dies.

No wonder if an infant so miraculous in its birth should be destined for great adventures; and accordingly we see it has been the guardian spirit of a prevailing party for almost twenty years. It can conquer kingdoms without

fighting, and sometimes with the loss of a battle. It gives
and resumes employments; can sink a mountain to a mole-
hill, and raise a mole-hill to a mountain; has presided for
many years at committees of elections; can wash a blacka-
moor white; make a saint of an atheist, and a patriot of a
profligate; can furnish foreign ministers with intelligence,
and raise or let fall the credit of the nation. This goddess
flies with a huge looking-glass in her hands, to dazzle the
crowd, and make them see, according as she turns it, their
ruin in their interest, and their interest in their ruin. In
this glass you will behold your best friends, clad in coats
powdered with *fleurs de lis* and triple crowns; their girdles
hung round with chains, and beads, and wooden shoes;
and your worst enemies adorned with the ensigns of liberty,
property, indulgence, moderation, and a cornucopia in their
hands. Her large wings, like those of a flying-fish, are of no
use but while they are moist; she therefore dips them in mud,
and, soaring aloft, scatters it in the eyes of the multitude,
flying with great swiftness; but at every turn is forced to
stoop in dirty ways for new supplies.

I have been sometimes thinking, if a man had the art
of the second sight for seeing lies, as they have in Scotland
for seeing spirits, how admirably he might entertain himself in this town, by observing the different shapes, sizes,
and colours of those swarms of lies which buzz about the
heads of some people, like flies about a horse's ears in
summer; or those legions hovering every afternoon in Exchange alley, enough to darken the air; or over a club of
discontented grandees, and thence sent down in cargoes to be
scattered at elections.

There is one essential point wherein a political liar differs
from others of the faculty, that he ought to have but a
short memory, which is necessary according to the various
occasions he meets with every hour of differing from himself
and swearing to both sides of a contradiction, as he finds the
persons disposed with whom he has to deal. In describing
the virtues and vices of mankind, it is convenient, upon

every article, to have some eminent person in our eye, from whom we copy our description. I have strictly observed this rule, and my imagination this minute represents before me a certain great man famous for this talent, to the constant practice of which he owest his twenty years' reputation of the most skilful head in England for the management of nice affairs. The superiority of his genius consists in nothing else but an inexhaustible fund of political lies, which he plentifully distributes every minute he speaks, and by an unparalleled generosity forgets, and consequently contradicts, the next half-hour. He never yet considered whether any proposition were true or false, but whether it were convenient for the present minute or company to affirm or deny it; so that, if you think fit to refine upon him by interpreting everything he says, as we do dreams, by the contrary, you are still to seek, and will find yourself equally deceived whether you believe or not: the only remedy is to suppose that you have heard some inarticulate sounds, without any meaning at all; and besides, that will take off the horror you might be apt to conceive at the oaths wherewith he perpetually tags both ends of every proposition; although, at the same time, I think he cannot with any justice be taxed with perjury when he invokes God and Christ, because he has often fairly given public notice to the world that he believes in neither.

Some people may think that such an accomplishment as this can be of no great use to the owner, or his party, after it has been often practised and is become notorious; but they are widely mistaken. Few lies carry the inventor's mark, and the most prostitute enemy to truth may spread a thousand without being known for the author: besides, as the vilest writer has his readers, so the greatest liar has his believers; and it often happens that, if a lie be believed only for an hour, it has done its work, and there is no farther occasion for it. Falsehood flies, and truth comes limping after it, so that when men come to be undeceived it is too late; the jest is over, and the tale has had its effect: like a man who

has thought of a good repartee when the discourse is changed
or the company parted; or like a physician who has found out
an infallible medicine after the patient is dead.

Considering that natural disposition in many men to lie,
and in multitudes to believe, I have been perplexed what to
do with that maxim so frequent in everybody's mouth,
that truth will at last prevail. Here has this island of ours,
for the greatest part of twenty years, lain under the influence
of such counsels and persons, whose principle and interest
it was to corrupt our manners, blind our understanding,
drain our wealth, and in time destroy our constitution both
in church and state, and we at last were brought to the
very brink of ruin; yet, by the means of perpetual misrepre-
sentations, have never been able to distinguish between our
enemies and friends. We have seen a great part of the
nation's money got into the hands of those who, by their
birth, education, and merit, could pretend no higher than to
wear our liveries; while others, who, by their credit, quality,
and fortune, were only able to give reputation and success
to the Revolution, were not only laid aside as dangerous and
useless, but loaded with the scandal of Jacobites, men of
arbitrary principles, and pensioners to France; while truth,
who is said to lie in a well, seemed now to be buried there
under a heap of stones. But I remember it was a usual
complaint among the Whigs, that the bulk of the landed
men was not in their interests, which some of the wisest
looked on as an ill omen; and we saw it was with the utmost
difficulty that they could preserve a majority, while the
court and ministry were on their side, till they had learned
those admirable expedients for deciding elections and influencing distant boroughs by powerful motives from the city.
But all this was mere force and constraint, however upheld
by most dexterous artifice and management, until the people
began to apprehend their properties, their religion, and
the monarchy itself in danger; when we saw them greedily
laying hold on the first occasion to interpose. But of this
mighty change in the dispositions of the people I shall dis-

course more at large in some following paper: wherein I shall endeavour to undeceive or discover those deluded or deluding persons who hope or pretend it is only a short madness in the vulgar, from which they may soon recover; whereas, I believe it will appear to be very different in its causes, its symptoms, and its consequences; and prove a great example to illustrate the maxim I lately mentioned, that truth (however sometimes late) will at last prevail.

JOSEPH ADDISON

1672 Was born in Wiltshire, the son of a clergyman.
1686 Entered Charterhouse School, where he formed a friendship with Richard Steele.
1687 Entered Queen's College, Oxford.
1693 Proceeded M. A.
1694 Published *An Account of the Greatest English Poets*.
1697–1711 Held a fellowship at Magdalen College, Oxford.
1699 Obtained a pension of £300 through the influence of Charles Montague, who afterward became the Earl of Halifax, on account of his potential political usefulness.
Went abroad to finish his education.
1701 Published *A Letter from Italy*.
1703 Returned from the continent because his pension was discontinued after the death of King William during the resultant political turmoil.
1704 Published *The Campaign*, a poem extolling Marlborough's victory at the battle of Blenheim, at the instigation of Lord Godolphin, and became well known and widely popular.
1706 Became Under Secretary of State.
Produced *Rosamond*, an opera.
1709–1711 Became secretary to the Lord Lieutenant of Ireland.
Contributed to the *Tatler*.
1711 Lost his office upon the rise of the Tories to power.
Founded, with Richard Steele, the *Spectator*.
1713 Produced *Cato*, a classical tragedy.
1714 Returned to office upon the return of the Whigs to power.
1715 Founded the *Freeholder*, a political journal.
Produced *The Drummer*, a comedy.
1716 Married the Countess of Warwick.
1717–1718 Served with the Earl of Sunderland as Secretary of State.
1719 Became involved in a political controversy with Richard Steele.
Died and was buried in Westminster Abbey.

TOM FOLIO[1]

Faciunt næ intelligendo, ut nihil intelligant.[2]
(Ter. *Andria*, Prol. 17.)

TOM FOLIO is a broker in learning, employed to get together good editions, and stock the libraries of great men. There is not a sale of books begins till Tom Folio is seen at the door. There is not an auction where his name is not heard, and that too in the very nick of time, in the critical moment, before the last decisive stroke of the hammer. There is not a subscription goes forward, in which Tom is not privy to the first rough draught of the proposals; nor a catalogue printed, that does not come to him wet from the press. He is an universal scholar, so far as the title-page of all authors, knows the manuscripts in which they were discovered, the editions through which they have passed, with the praises or censures which they have received from the several members of the learned world. He has a greater esteem for Aldus and Elzevir than for Virgil and Horace. If you talk of Herodotus, he breaks out into a panegyric upon Harry Stephens. He thinks he gives you an account of an author when he tells you the subject he treats of, the name of the editor, and the year in which it was printed. Or if you draw him into further particulars, he cries up the goodness of the paper, extols the diligence of the corrector, and is transported with the beauty of the letter. This he looks upon to be sound learning and substantial criticism. As for those who talk of the fineness of style, and the justness of thought, or describe the brightness of any particular passages, nay, though they themselves write in the genius and spirit of the author they admire, Tom looks upon them as men of superficial learning and flashy parts.

---

[1]*Tatler*, No. 158. April 13, 1710.

[2]While they endeavour to show their learning, they make it appear that they understand nothing.

I had yesterday morning a visit from this learned idiot
(for that is the light in which I consider every pedant), when
I discovered in him some little touches of the coxcomb which
I had not before observed. Being very full of the figure
which he makes in the republic of letters, and wonderfully
satisfied with his great stock of knowledge, he gave me broad
intimations that he did not "believe" in all points as his forefathers had done. He then communicated to me a thought
of a certain author upon a passage of Virgil's account of the
dead, which I made the subject of a late paper. This thought
has taken very much among men of Tom's pitch and understanding, though universally exploded by all that know how
to construe Virgil, or have any relish of antiquity. Not to
trouble my reader with it, I found upon the whole that Tom
did not believe in a future state of rewards and punishments
because Æneas, at his leaving the empire of the dead, passed
through the gate of ivory, and not through that of horn.
Knowing that Tom had not sense enough to give up an
opinion which he had once received, that I might avoid
wrangling, I told him that Virgil possibly had his oversights
as well as another author. "Ah! Mr. Bickerstaff," says
he, "you would have another opinion of him if you would
read him in Daniel Heinsius' edition. I have perused him
myself several times in that edition," continued he; "and
after the strictest and most malicious examination, could find
but two faults in him: one of them is in the Æneid, where
there are two commas instead of a parenthesis; and another
in the third Georgic, where you may find a semicolon turned
upside down." "Perhaps," said I, "these were not Virgil's
faults, but those of the transcriber." "I do not design it,"
says Tom, "as a reflection on Virgil: on the contrary, I know
that all the manuscripts declaim against such a punctuation.
Oh! Mr. Bickerstaff," says he, "what would a man give to
see one simile of Virgil writ in his own hand?" I asked him
which was the simile he meant, but was answered, "Any
simile in Virgil." He then told me all the secret history in
the commonwealth of learning: of modern pieces that had

the names of ancient authors annexed to them; of all the books
that were now writing or printing in the several parts of
Europe; of many amendments which are made, and not yet
published; and a thousand other particulars, which I would
not have my memory burdened with for a Vatican.

At length, being fully persuaded that I thoroughly admired him and looked upon him as a prodigy of learning, he
took his leave. I know several of Tom's class who are professed admirers of Tasso without understanding a word of
Italian, and one in particular that carries a Pastor Fido in his
pocket, in which I am sure he is acquainted with no other
beauty but the clearness of the character.

There is another kind of pedant who, with all Tom Folio's
impertinences, hath greater superstructures and embellishments of Greek and Latin, and is still more insupportable
than the other, in the same degree as he is more learned. Of
this kind very often are editors, commentators, interpreters,
scholiasts, and critics, and in short, all men of deep learning
without common sense. These persons set a greater value
on themselves for having found out the meaning of a passage
in Greek, than upon the author for having written it; nay,
will allow the passage itself not to have any beauty in it, at
the same time that they would be considered as the greatest
men of the age for having interpreted it. They will look
with contempt upon the most beautiful poems that have
been composed by any of their contemporaries; but will
lock themselves up in their studies for a twelvemonth together
to correct, publish, and expound such trifles of antiquity as
a modern author would be contemned for. Men of the
strictest morals, severest lives, and the gravest professions
will write volumes upon an idle sonnet that is originally in
Greek or Latin, give editions of the most immoral authors, and
spin out whole pages upon the various readings of a lewd expression. All that can be said in excuse for them is that their
works sufficiently show that they have no taste of their authors, and that what they do in this kind is out of their great
learning and not out of any levity or lasciviousness of temper.

A pedant of this nature is wonderfully well described in six lines of Boileau, with which I shall conclude his character:

> *Un Pédant enviré de sa vaine science,*
> *Tout hérissé de Grec, tout bouffi d'arrogance,*
> *Et qui, de mille auteurs retenus mot pour mot,*
> *Dans sa tête entassés n'a souvent fait qu'un sot,*
> *Croit qu'un livre fait tout, & que, sans Aristote,*
> *La raison ne voit goutte, & le bon sens radote.*[1]

ADVENTURES OF A SHILLING[2]

Per varios casus, per tot discrimina rerum,
Tendimus.——[3]   Virg. *Aen.* I. 208.

I WAS last night visited by a friend of mine, who has an inexhaustible fund of discourse, and never fails to entertain his company with a variety of thoughts and hints that are altogether new and uncommon. Whether it were in complaisance to my way of living, or his real opinion, he advanced the following paradox: that it required much greater talents to fill up and become a retired life than a life of business. Upon this occasion he rallied very agreeably the busy men of the age, who only value themselves for being in motion and passing through a series of trifling and insignificant actions. In the heat of his discourse, seeing a piece of money lying on my table, "I defy," says he, "any of these active persons to produce half the adventures that this twelve-penny piece has been engaged in, were it possible for him to give us an account of his life."

---

[1]Brimfull of learning see that pedant stride,
Bristling with horrid Greek, and puff'd with pride!
A thousand authors he in vain has read,
And with their maxims stuff'd his empty head;
And thinks that without Aristotle's rule,
Reason is blind, and common sense a fool.

[2]*Tatler*, No. 249. Saturday, November 11, 1710.

[3]Through various fortunes and events, we move.

My friend's talk made so odd an impression upon my mind, that soon after I was a-bed I fell insensibly into an unaccountable reverie, that had neither moral nor design in it, and cannot be so properly called a dream as a delirium.

Methought the shilling that lay upon the table reared itself upon its edge, and, turning the face towards me, opened its mouth, and in a soft silver sound, gave me the following account of his life and adventures:

"I was born," says he, "on the side of a mountain, near a little village of Peru, and made a voyage to England in an ingot under the convoy of Sir Francis Drake. I was, soon after my arrival, taken out of my Indian habit, refined, naturalized, and put into the British mode, with the face of queen Elizabeth on one side, and the arms of the country on the other. Being thus equipped, I found in me a wonderful inclination to ramble, and visit all the parts of the new world into which I was brought. The people very much favored my natural disposition, and shifted me so fast from hand to hand, that, before I was five years old, I had travelled into almost every corner of the nation. But in the beginning of my sixth year, to my unspeakable grief, I fell into the hands of a miserable old fellow, who clapped me into an iron chest, where I found five hundred more of my own quality who lay under the same confinement. The only relief we had, was to be taken out and counted over in the fresh air every morning and evening. After an imprisonment of several years, we heard somebody knocking at our chest, and breaking it open with an hammer. This we found was the old man's heir, who, as his father lay dying, was so good as to come to our release. He separated us that very day. What was the fate of my companions I know not: as for myself, I was sent to the apothecary's shop for a pint of sack. The apothecary gave me to an herb-woman, the herb-woman to a butcher, the butcher to a brewer, and the brewer to his wife, who made a present of me to a nonconformist preacher. After this manner I made my way merrily through the world; for, as I told

you before, we shillings love nothing so much as travelling.
I sometimes fetched in a shoulder of mutton, sometimes
a play-book, and often had the satisfaction to treat a templer
at a twelve-penny ordinary, or carry him with three friends to
Westminster-hall.

"In the midst of this pleasant progress which I made
from place to place, I was arrested by a superstitious old
woman, who shut me up in a greasy purse, in pursuance of
a foolish saying, 'that while she kept a queen Elizabeth's
shilling about her, she would never be without money.'
I continued here a close prisoner for many months, until at
last I was exchanged for eight-and-forty farthings.

"I thus rambled from pocket to pocket until the beginning of the civil wars, when, to my shame be it spoken, I
was employed in raising soldiers against the king: for, being
of a very tempting breadth, a sergeant made use of me to
inveigle country fellows, and lift them into the service of the
Parliament.

"As soon as he had made one man sure, his way was,
to oblige him to take a shilling of a more homely figure,
and then practice the same trick upon another. Thus I
continued doing great mischief to the crown, until my
officer chancing one morning to walk abroad earlier than
ordinary, sacrificed me to his pleasures, and made use of
me to seduce a milk-maid. This wench bent me, and gave
me to her sweetheart, applying more properly than she
intended the usual form of, 'to my love and from my love.'
This ungenerous gallant marrying her within a few days
after, pawned me for a dram of brandy; and drinking me out
next day, I was beaten flat with an hammer, and again set
a-running.

"After many adventures, which it would be tedious to
relate, I was sent to a young spendthrift, in company with
the will of his deceased father. The young fellow, who I
found was very extravagant, gave great demonstrations of
joy at receiving the will; but opening it, he found himself
disinherited, and cut off from the possession of a fair estate

by virtue of my being made a present to him. This put him into such a passion, that, after having taken me in his hand, and cursed me, he squirred me away from him as far as he could fling me. I chanced to light in an unfrequented place under a dead wall, where I lay undiscovered and useless during the usurpation of Oliver Cromwell.

"About a year after the King's return, a poor cavalier, that was walking there about dinner-time, fortunately cast his eye upon me, and, to the great joy of us both, carried me to a cook's shop, where he dined upon me, and drank the King's health. When I came again into the world, I found that I had been happier in my retirement than I thought, having probably by that means escaped wearing a monstrous pair of breeches.

"Being now of great credit and antiquity, I was rather looked upon as a medal than an ordinary coin; for which reason a gamester laid hold of me, and converted me to a counter, having got together some dozens of us for that use. We led a melancholy life in his possession, being busy at those hours wherein current coin is at rest, and partaking the fate of our master; being in a few moments valued at a crown, a pound, or sixpence, according to the situation in which the fortune of the cards placed us. I had at length the good luck to see my master break, by which means I was again sent abroad under my primitive denomination of a shilling.

"I shall pass over many other accidents of less moment, and hasten to that fatal catastrophe when I fell into the hands of an artist, who conveyed me under ground, and, with an unmerciful pair of sheers, cut off my titles, clipped my brims, retrenched my shape, rubbed me to my inmost ring; and, in short, so spoiled and pillaged me, that he did not leave me worth a groat. You may think what confusion I was in to see myself thus curtailed and disfigured. I should have been ashamed to have shown my head, had not all my old acquaintance been reduced to the same shameful figure, excepting some few that were punched through the belly. In the midst of this general calamity, when everybody thought our misfortune irretrievable, and our case desperate, we were thrown into the furnace together, and, as it often happens with cities rising out of a fire, appeared with greater beauty and lustre than we could ever boast of before. What has happened to me since this change of sex which you now see, I shall take some other opportunity to relate. In the meantime, I shall only repeat two adventures, as being very extraordinary, and neither of them having ever happened to me above once in my life. The first was, my being in a poet's pocket, who was so taken with the brightness and novelty of my appearance, that it gave occasion to the finest burlesque poem in the British language, entitled, from me, 'The Splendid Shilling.' The second adventure, which I must not omit, happened to me in the year 1703, when I was given away in charity to a blind man; but indeed this was by mistake, the person who gave me having thrown me heedlessly into the hat among a pennyworth of farthings."

PURPOSE OF THE *SPECTATOR*[1]

Non aliter quam qui adverso vix flumine lembum
Remigiis subigit: si brachia forte remisit,
Atque illum in præceps prono rapit alveus amni.[2]
Virg. *Georg.* I, 201.

It is with much satisfaction that I hear this great city inquiring day by day after these my papers, and receiving my morning lectures with a becoming seriousness and attention. My publisher tells me that there are already three thousand of them distributed every day. So that if I allow twenty readers to every paper, which I look upon as a modest

---

[1] *Spectator*, No. 10. Monday, March 12, 1711.

[2] So the boat's brawny crew the current stem,
And, slowly advancing, struggle with the stream:
But if they slack their hands, or cease to strive,
Then down the flood with headlong haste they drive. **Dryden.**

computation, I may reckon about three-score thousand disciples in London and Westminster, who I hope will take care to distinguish themselves from the thoughtless herd of their ignorant and unattentive brethren. Since I have raised to myself so great an audience, I shall spare no pains to make their instruction agreeable, and their diversion useful. For which reasons I shall endeavour to enliven morality with wit, and to temper wit with morality, that my readers may, if possible, both ways find their account in the speculation of the day. And to the end that their virtue and discretion may not be short, transient, intermitting starts of thought, I have resolved to refresh their memories from day to day, till I have recovered them out of that desperate state of vice and folly into which the age is fallen. The mind that lies fallow but a single day, sprouts up in follies that are only to be killed by a constant and assiduous culture. It was said of Socrates, that he brought philosophy down from heaven, to inhabit among men; and I shall be ambitious to have it said of me, that I have brought philosophy out of closets and libraries, schools and colleges, to dwell in clubs and assemblies, at tea-tables and in coffee-houses.

I would therefore in a very particular manner recommend these my speculations to all well-regulated families, that set apart an hour in every morning for tea and bread and butter; and would earnestly advise them for their good to order this paper to be punctually served up, and to be looked upon as a part of the tea-equipage.

Sir Francis Bacon observes, that a well-written book, compared with its rivals and antagonists, is like Moses's serpent, that immediately swallowed up and devoured those of the Egyptians. I shall not be so vain as to think, that where the *Spectator* appears, the other public prints will vanish; but shall leave it to my reader's consideration, whether, is it not much better to be let into the knowledge of one's self, than to hear what passes in Muscovy or Poland; and to amuse ourselves with such writings as tend to the wearing out of ignorance, passion, and prejudice, than such as naturally conduce to inflame hatreds, and make enmities irreconcilable?

In the next place, I would recommend this paper to the daily perusal of those gentlemen whom I cannot but consider as my good brothers and allies, I mean the fraternity of spectators, who live in the world without having anything to do in it; and either by the affluence of their fortunes, or laziness of their dispositions, have no other business with the rest of mankind, but to look upon them. Under this class of men are comprehended all contemplative tradesmen, titular physicians, fellows of the Royal Society, Templars that are not given to be contentious, and statesmen that are out of business; in short, every one that considers the world as a theatre, and desires to form a right judgment of those who are the actors on it.

There is another set of men that I must likewise lay a claim to, whom I have lately called the blanks of society, as being altogether unfurnished with ideas, till the business and conversation of the day has supplied them. I have often considered these poor souls with an eye of great commiseration, when I have heard them asking the first man they have met with, whether there was any news stirring? and by that means gathering together materials for thinking. These needy persons do not know what to talk of, till about twelve o'clock in the morning; for by that time they are pretty good judges of the weather, know which way the wind sits, and whether the Dutch mail be come in. As they lie at the mercy of the first man they meet, and are grave or impertinent all the day long, according to the notions which they have imbibed in the morning, I would earnestly intreat them not to stir out of their chambers till they have read this paper, and do promise them that I will daily instil into them such sound and wholesome sentiments, as shall have a good effect on their conversation for the ensuing twelve hours.

But there are none to whom this paper will be more useful, than to the female world. I have often thought there has not been sufficient pains taken in finding out proper employments and diversions for the fair ones. Their amusements seem contrived for them, rather as they are women, than as they are reasonable creatures; and are more adapted to the sex than to the species. The toilet is their great scene of business, and the right adjusting of their hair the principal employment of their lives. The sorting of a suit of ribbons is reckoned a very good morning's work; and if they make an excursion to a mercer's or a toy-shop, so great a fatigue makes them unfit for anything else all the day after. Their more serious occupations are sewing and embroidery, and their greatest drudgery the preparation of jellies and sweetmeats. This, I say, is the state of ordinary women; though I know there are multitudes of those of a more elevated life and conversation, that move in an exalted sphere of knowledge and virtue, that join all the beauties of the mind to the ornaments of dress, and inspire a kind of awe and respect, as well as love, into their male beholder. I hope to increase the number of these by publishing this daily paper, which I shall always endeavour to make an innocent if not an improving entertainment, and by that means at least divert the minds of my female readers from greater trifles. At the same time, as I would fain give some finishing touches to those which are already the most beautiful pieces in human nature, I shall endeavour to point out all those imperfections that are the blemishes, as well as those virtues which are the embellishments of the sex. In the meanwhile I hope these my gentle readers, who have so much time on their hands, will not grudge throwing away a quarter of an hour in a day on this paper, since they may do it without any hindrance to business.

I know several of my friends and well-wishers are in great pain for me, lest I should not be able to keep up the spirit of a paper which I oblige myself to furnish every day: but to make them easy in this particular, I will promise them faithfully to give it over as soon as I grow dull. This I know will be matter of great raillery to the small wits; who will frequently put me in mind of my promise, desire me to keep my word, assure me that it is high time to give over, with many other little pleasantries of the like nature, which men of a little smart genius cannot forbear throwing out against their best friends, when they have such a handle given them of being witty. But let them remember that I do hereby enter my caveat against this piece of raillery.

WESTMINSTER ABBEY[1]

Pallida mors æquo pulsat pede pauperum tabernas
Regumqueturres, O beate Sexti.
Vitæ summa brevis spem nos vetat inchoare longam,
Jam te premet nox fabulæque manes,
Et domus exilis Plutonia.——[2]

Hor. *Od.* I, iv. 13.

WHEN I am in a serious humour, I very often walk by myself in Westminster Abbey; where the gloominess of the place, and the use to which it is applied, with the solemnity of the building, and the condition of the people who lie in it, are apt to fill the mind with a kind of melancholy, or rather thoughtfulness, that is not disagreeable. I yesterday passed a whole afternoon in the churchyard, the cloisters, and the church, amusing myself with the tombstones and inscriptions that I met with in those several regions of the dead. Most of them recorded nothing else of the buried person, but that he was born upon one day, and died upon another: the whole history of his life being comprehended in those two circumstances that are common to all mankind. I could not but look upon these registers of existence, whether of brass or marble, as a kind of satire upon the departed per-

---

[1]*Spectator*, No. 26. Friday, March 30, 1711.
[2]With equal foot, rich friend, impartial fate
Knocks at the cottage, and the palace gate:
Life's span forbids thee to extend thy cares,
And stretch thy hopes beyond thy years:
Night soon will seize, and you must quickly go
To story'd ghosts, and Pluto's house below.   Creech.

sons; who left no other memorial of them, but that they were
born, and that they died.   They put me in mind of several
persons mentioned in the battles of heroic poems, who
have sounding names given them, for no other reason but
that they may be killed, and are celebrated for nothing but
being knocked on the head.

$$\Gamma\lambda a\hat{v}\kappa\acute{o}\nu \ \tau\epsilon \ M\epsilon\delta\acute{o}\nu\tau a \ \tau\epsilon \ \Theta\epsilon\rho\sigma\iota\lambda o\chi\acute{o}\nu \ \tau\epsilon^1$$
                          Hom.

The life of these men is finely described in holy writ by
"the path of an arrow," which is immediately closed up and
lost.

Upon my going into the church, I entertained myself
with the digging of a grave; and saw in every shovelful of
it that was thrown up, the fragment of a bone or skull intermixed with a kind of fresh mouldering earth, that some
time or other had a place in the composition of an human
body.   Upon this I began to consider with myself, what
innumerable multitudes of people lay confused together under
the pavement of that ancient cathedral; how men and
women, friends and enemies, priests and soldiers, monks
and prebendaries, were crumbled amongst one another, and
blended together in the same common mass; how beauty,
strength, and youth, with old age, weakness, and deformity,
lay undistinguished in the same promiscuous heap of matter.

After having thus surveyed this great magazine of mortality, as it were in the lump, I examined it more particularly
by the accounts which I found on several of the monuments
which are raised in every quarter of that ancient fabric.
Some of them were covered with such extravagant epitaphs,
that if it were possible for the dead person to be acquainted
with them, he would blush at the praises which his friends
have bestowed on him. There are others so excessively modest, that they deliver the character of the person departed in
Greek or Hebrew, and by that means are not understood

---

[1]Glaucus, and Medon, and Thersilochus.

once in a twelve-month. In the poetical quarter, I found there
were poets who had no monuments, and monuments which
had no poets. I observed, indeed, that the present war had
filled the church with many of these uninhabited monuments,
which had been erected to the memory of persons whose
bodies were, perhaps, buried in the plains of Blenheim, or in
the bosom of the ocean.

I could not but be very much delighted with several
modern epitaphs, which are written with great elegance
of expression and justness of thought, and therefore do
honour to the living as well as to the dead. As a foreigner
is very apt to conceive an idea of the ignorance or politeness
of a nation from the turn of their public monuments and
inscriptions, they should be submitted to the perusal of men
of learning and genius before they are put in execution. Sir
Cloudesley Shovel's monument has very often given me great
offense. Instead of the brave, rough, English admiral, which
was the distinguishing character of that plain, gallant man,
he is represented on his tomb by the figure of a beau, dressed
in a long periwig, and reposing himself upon velvet cushions
under a canopy of state. The inscription is answerable to
the monument; for, instead of celebrating the many remarkable actions he had performed in the service of his country,
it acquaints us only with the manner of his death, in which
it was impossible for him to reap any honour. The Dutch,
whom we are apt to despise for want of genius, show an infinitely greater taste of antiquity and politeness in their
buildings and works of this nature, than what we meet with
in those of our own country. The monuments of their ad-
mirals, which have been erected at the public expense, represent them like themselves, and are adorned with rostral
crowns and naval ornaments, with beautiful festoons of sea-
weed, shells, and coral.

But to return to our subject. I have left the repository
of our English kings for the contemplation of another day,
when I shall find my mind disposed for so serious an amusement. I know that entertainments of this nature are apt to

raise dark and dismal thoughts in timorous minds and gloomy imaginations; but for my own part, though I am always serious, I do not know what it is to be melancholy; and can therefore take a view of nature in her deep and solemn scenes, with the same pleasure as in her most gay and delightful ones. By this means I can improve myself with those objects, which others consider with terror. When I look upon the tombs of the great, every emotion of envy dies in me; when I read the epitaphs of the beautiful, every inordinate desire goes out; when I meet with the grief of parents upon a tombstone, my heart melts with compassion; when I see the tomb of the parents themselves, I consider the vanity of grieving for those whom we must quickly follow. When I see kings lying by those who deposed them, when I consider rival wits placed side by side, or the holy men that divided the world with their contests and disputes, I reflect with sorrow and astonishment on the little competitions, factions, and debates of mankind. When I read the several dates of the tombs, of some that died yesterday, and some six hundred years ago, I consider that great day when we shall all of us be contemporaries, and make our appearance together.

THE ROYAL EXCHANGE[1]

Hic segetes, illic veniunt felicius uvae:
Arborei foetus alibi atque injussa virescunt
Gramina. Nonne vides, croceos ut Tmolus odores.
India mittit ebur, molles sua thura Sabaei?
At Chalybes nudi ferrum, virosaque Pontus
Castorea, Eliadum palmas Epirus equarum?
Continuo has leges aeternaque foedera certis
Imposuit Natura locis——[2]

Virg. *Georg.* I, 54.

THERE is no place in the town which I so much love to frequent as the Royal Exchange. It gives me a secret satisfaction, and, in some measure, gratifies my vanity, as I am an Englishman, to see so rich an assembly of countrymen and foreigners consulting together upon the private business of mankind, and making this metropolis a kind of emporium for the whole earth. I must confess I look upon high-change to be a great council, in which all considerable nations have their representatives. Factors in the trading world are what ambassadors are in the politic world; they negotiate affairs, conclude treaties, and maintain a good correspondence between those wealthy societies of men that are divided from one another by seas and oceans, or live on the different extremities of a continent. I have often been pleased to hear disputes adjusted between an inhabitant of

---

[1] *Spectator*, No. 69. Saturday, May 19, 1711.

[2] This ground with Bacchus, that with Ceres suits;
That other loads the trees with happy fruits;
A fourth with grass, unbidden, decks the ground:
Thus Tmolus is with yellow saffron crown'd;
India black ebon and white iv'ry bears;
And soft Idume weeps her odrous tears:
Thus Pontus sends her beaver stones from far:
And naked Spaniards temper steel for war:
Epirus for th' Elean chariot breeds
(In hopes of palms) a race of running steeds.
This is th' original contract; these the laws
Impos'd by nature and by nature's cause.

Dryden

Japan and an alderman of London, or to see a subject of the Great Mogul entering into a league with one of the Czar of Muscovy. I am infinitely delighted in mixing with these several ministers of commerce, as they are distinguished by their different walks and different languages: sometimes I am justled among a body of Armenians: sometimes I am lost in a crowd of Jews; and sometimes make one in a group of Dutch-men. I am a Dane, Swede, or Frenchman at different times, or rather fancy myself like the old philosopher, who upon being asked what country-man he was, replied, that he was a citizen of the world.

Though I very frequently visit this busy multitude of people, I am known to nobody there but my friend Sir Andrew, who often smiles upon me as he sees me bustling in the crowd, but at the same time connives at my presence without taking any further notice of me. There is indeed a merchant of Egypt, who just knows me by sight, having formerly remitted me some money to Grand Cairo; but as I am not versed in the modern Coptic, our conferences go no further than a bow and a grimace.

This grand scene of business gives me an infinite variety of solid and substantial entertainments. As I am a great lover of mankind, my heart naturally overflows with pleasure at the sight of a prosperous and happy multitude, insomuch that at many public solemnities I cannot forbear expressing my joy with tears that have stolen down my cheeks. For this reason I am wonderfully delighted to see such a body of men thriving in their own private fortunes, and at the same time promoting the public stock; or in other words, raising estates for their own families, by bringing into their country whatever is wanting, and carrying out of it whatever is superfluous.

Nature seems to have taken a particular care to disseminate her blessings among the different regions of the world, with an eye to this mutual intercourse and traffic among mankind, that the natives of the several parts of the globe might have a kind of dependence upon one another, and be united together by their common interest. Almost every degree produces something peculiar to it. The food often grows in one country, and the sauce in another. The fruits of Portugal are corrected by the products of Barbadoes: the infusion of a China plant sweetened with the pith of an Indian cane. The Philippick Islands give a flavour to our European bowls. The single dress of a woman of quality is often the product of an hundred climates. The muff and the fan come together from the different ends of the earth. The scarf is sent from the torrid zone, and the tippet from beneath the Pole. The brocade petticoat rises out of the mines of Peru, and the diamond necklace out of the bowels of Indostan.

If we consider our own country in its natural prospect, without any of the benefits and advantages of commerce, what a barren uncomfortable spot of earth falls to our share! Natural historians tell us, that no fruit grows originally among us, besides hips and haws, acorns and pig-nuts, with other delicacies of the like nature; that our climate of itself, and without the assistances of art, can make no further advances towards a plum than to a sloe, and carries an apple to no greater a perfection than a crab: that our melons, our peaches, our figs, our apricots, and cherries, are strangers among us, imported in different ages, and naturalized in our English gardens; and that they would all degenerate and fall away into the trash of our own country, if they were wholly neglected by the planter, and left to the mercy of our sun and soil. Nor has traffic more enriched our vegetable world, than it has improved the whole face of nature among us. Our ships are laden with the harvest of every climate: our tables are stored with spices, and oils, and wines: our rooms are filled with pyramids of China, and adorned with the workmanship of Japan: our morning's-draught comes to us from the remotest corners of the earth: we repair our bodies by the drugs of America, and repose ourselves under Indian canopies. My friend Sir Andrew calls the vineyards of France our gardens; the spice-islands our hot-beds; the Persians our silk-weavers, and the Chinese our potters. Nature indeed furnishes us with the bare necessaries of life, but traffic gives us a great variety of what is useful, and at the same time supplies us with every thing that is convenient and ornamental. Nor is it the least part of this our happiness, that whilst we enjoy the remotest products of the north and south, we are free from those extremities of weather which give them birth; that our eyes are refreshed with the green fields of Britain, at the same time that our palates are feasted with fruits that rise between the tropics.

For these reasons there are not more useful members in a commonwealth than merchants. They knit mankind together in a mutual intercourse of good offices, distribute the gifts of nature, find work for the poor, add wealth to the rich, and magnificence to the great. Our English merchant converts the tin of his own country into gold, and exchanges his wool for rubies. The Mahometans are clothed in our British manufacture, and the inhabitants of the frozen zone warmed with the fleeces of our sheep.

When I have been upon the 'Change, I have often fancied one of our old kings standing in person, where he is represented in effigy, and looking down upon the wealthy concourse of people with which that place is every day filled. In this case, how would he be surprized to hear all the languages of Europe spoken in this little spot of his former dominions, and to see so many private men, who in his time would have been the vassals of some powerful baron, negotiating like princes for greater sums of money than were formerly to be met with in the royal treasury! Trade, without enlarging the British territories, has given us a kind of additional empire: it has multiplied the number of the rich, made our landed estates infinitely more valuable than they were formerly, and added to them an accession of other estates as valuable as the lands themselves.

SIR ROGER'S CHAPLAIN[1]

——*Hinc tibi copia*
Manabit ad plenum, benigno
Ruris honorum opulenta cornu.[2]
Hor. *Epist.* I, xvii, 14.

HAVING often received an invitation from my friend Sir Roger de Coverley, to pass away a month with him in the country, I last week accompanied him thither, and am settled with him for some time at his country-house, where I intend to form several of my ensuing speculations. Sir Roger, who is very well acquainted with my humour, lets me rise and go to bed when I please, dine at his own table or in my chamber, as I think fit, sit still and say nothing without bidding me be merry. When the gentlemen of the country come to see him, he only shows me at a distance. As I have been walking in his fields I have observed them stealing a sight of me over an hedge, and have heard the knight desiring them not to let me see them, for that I hated to be stared at.

I am the more at ease in Sir Roger's family because it consists of sober and staid persons; for, as the knight is the best master in the world, he seldom changes his servants; and as he is beloved by all about him, his servants never care for leaving him; by this means his domestics are all in years, and grown old with their master. You would take his *valet de chambre* for his brother, his butler is gray-headed, his groom is one of the gravest men that I have ever seen, and his coachman has the looks of a privy counsellor. You see the goodness of the master even in the old house-dog, and in a gray pad that is kept in the stable with great care and tenderness, out of regard to his past services, though he has been useless for several years.

----

[1]*Spectator*, No. 106. Monday, July 2, 1711.
[2]Here plenty's liberal horn shall pour
Of fruits for thee a copious show'r
Rich honors of the quiet plain.

I could not but observe with a great deal of pleasure the joy that appeared in the countenances of these ancient domestics upon my friend's arrival at his country-seat. Some of them could not refrain from tears at the sight of their old master; every one of them pressed forward to do something for him, and seemed discouraged if they were not employed. At the same time the good old knight, with a mixture of the father and the master of the family, tempered the inquiries after his own affairs with several kind questions relating to themselves. This humanity and good-nature engages everybody to him, so that when he is pleasant upon any of them, all his family are in good humour, and none so much as the person whom he diverts himself with; on the contrary, if he coughs, or betrays any infirmity of old age, it is easy for a stander-by to observe a secret concern in the looks of all his servants.

My worthy friend has put me under the particular care of his butler, who is a very prudent man, and, as well as the rest of his fellow-servants, wonderfully desirous of pleasing me, because they often heard their master talk of me as of his particular friend.

My chief companion, when Sir Roger is diverting himself in the woods or the fields, is a very venerable man who is ever with Sir Roger, and has lived at his house in the nature of a chaplain above thirty years. This gentleman is a person of good sense and some learning, of a very regular life and obliging conversation; he heartily loves Sir Roger, and knows that he is very much in the old knight's esteem, so that he lives in the family rather as a relation than a dependent.

I have observed in several of my papers that my friend Sir Roger, amidst all his good qualities, is something of an humorist, and that his virtues as well as imperfections are, as it were, tinged by a certain extravagance, which makes them particularly *his*, and distinguishes them from those of other men. This cast of mind, as it is generally very innocent in itself, so it renders his conversation highly agreeable, and more delightful than the same degree of sense and virtue would appear in their common and ordinary colours. As I was walking with him last night, he asked me how I liked the good man whom I have just now mentioned, and without staying for my answer, told me that he was afraid of being insulted with Latin and Greek at his own table, for which reason he desired a particular friend of his, at the University, to find him out a clergyman rather of plain sense than much learning, of a good aspect, a clear voice, a sociable temper, and, if possible, a man that understood a little of backgammon. "My friend," says Sir Roger, "found me out this gentleman, who, besides the endowments required of him, is, they tell me, a good scholar, though he does not show it; I have given him the parsonage of the parish, and, because I know his value, have settled upon him a good annuity for life. If he outlives me, he shall find that he was higher in my esteem than perhaps he thinks he is. He has now been with me thirty years, and though he does not know I have taken notice of it, has never in all that time asked anything of me for himself, though he is every day soliciting me for something in behalf of one or other of my tenants, his parishioners. There has not been a lawsuit in the parish since he has lived among them; if any dispute arises they apply themselves to him for the decision; if they do. not acquiesce in his judgment, which I think never happened above once, or twice at most, they appeal to me. At his first settling with me I made him a present of all the good sermons which have been printed in English, and only begged of him that every Sunday he would pronounce one of them in the pulpit. Accordingly he has digested them into such a series that they follow one another naturally and make a continued system of practical divinity."

As Sir Roger was going on in his story, the gentleman we were talking of came up to us; and upon the knight's asking him who preached to-morrow (for it was Saturday night), told us the Bishop of St. Asaph in the morning and Dr. South in the afternoon. He then showed us his list of preachers for the whole year, where I saw with a great deal of pleasure

Archbishop Tillotson, Bishop Saunderson, Dr. Barrow, Dr. Calamy, with several living authors who have published discourses of practical divinity. I no sooner saw this venerable man in the pulpit but I very much approved of my friend's insisting upon the qualifications of a good aspect and a clear voice; for I was so charmed with the gracefulness of his figure and delivery as well as with the discourses he pronounced, that I think I never passed any time more to my satisfaction. A sermon repeated after this manner is like the composition of a poet in the mouth of a graceful actor.

I could heartily wish that more of our country clergy would follow this example; and, instead of wasting their spirits in laborious compositions of their own, would endeavour after a handsome elocution and all those other talents that are proper to enforce what has been penned by greater masters. This would not only be more easy to themselves, but more edifying to the people.

WILL WIMBLE[1]

Gratis anhelans, multa agendo nihil agens.[2]
Phædrus, *Fab.* II, v, 3.

As I was yesterday morning walking with Sir Roger before his house, a country fellow brought him a huge fish, which, he told him, Mr. William Wimble had caught that very morning; and that he presented it, with his service to him, and intended to come and dine with him. At the same time he delivered him a letter, which my friend read to me as soon as the messenger left him:—

"SIR ROGER,—

"I desire you to accept of a jack, which is the best I have caught this season. I intend to come and stay with you a week, and see how the perch bite in the Black River.

---

[1] *Spectator*, No. 108. Wednesday, July 4, 1711.
[2] Out of breath to no purpose, and very busy about nothing.

I observed with some concern, the last time I saw you upon the bowling-green, that your whip wanted a lash to it; I will bring half a dozen with me that I twisted last week, which I hope will serve you all the time you are in the country. I have not been out of the saddle for six days last past, having been at Eton with Sir John's eldest son. He takes to his learning hugely.

"I am, sir, your humble servant,
"WILL WIMBLE"

This extraordinary letter and message that accompanied it made me very curious to know the character and quality of the gentleman who sent them, which I found to be as follows: Will Wimble is younger brother to a baronet, and descended of the ancient family of the Wimbles. He is now between forty and fifty, but, being bred to no business and born to no estate, he generally lives with his elder brother as superintendent of his game. He hunts a pack of dogs better than any man in the country, and is very famous for finding out a hare. He is extremely well versed in all the little handicrafts of an idle man; he makes a may-fly to a miracle, and furnishes the whole country with angle-rods. As he is a good-natured, officious fellow, and very much esteemed upon account of his family, he is a welcome guest at every house, and keeps up a good correspondence among all the gentlemen about him. He carries a tulip-root in his pocket from one to another, or exchanges a puppy between a couple of friends that live perhaps in the opposite sides of the county. Will is a particular favourite of all the young heirs, whom he frequently obliges with a net that he has weaved or a setting-dog that he has made himself. He now and then presents a pair of garters of his own knitting to their mothers or sisters, and raises a great deal of mirth among them by inquiring as often as he meets them, *how they wear.* These gentleman-like manufactures and obliging little humours make Will the darling of the country.

Sir Roger was proceeding in the character of him, when

he saw him make up to us with two or three hazel-twigs in his hand that he had cut in Sir Roger's wood, as he came through them, in his way to the house. I was very much pleased to observe on one side the hearty and sincere welcome with which Sir Roger received him, and on the other, the secret joy which his guest discovered at sight of the good old knight. After the first salutes were over, Will desired Sir Roger to lend him one of his servants to carry a set of shuttle-cocks he had with him in a little box to a lady that lived about a mile off, to whom it seems he had promised such a present for above this half year. Sir Roger's back was no sooner turned but honest Will began to tell me of a large cock-pheasant that he had sprung in one of the neighbouring woods, with two or three other adventures of the same nature. Odd and uncommon characters are the game that I look for and most delight in; for which reason I was as much pleased with the novelty of the person that talked to me as he could be for his life with the springing of a pheasant, and therefore listened to him with more than ordinary attention.

In the midst of his discourse the bell rung to dinner, where the gentleman I have been speaking of had the pleasure of seeing the huge jack he had caught served up for the first dish in a most sumptuous manner. Upon our sitting down to it he gave us a long account how he had hooked it, played with it, foiled it, and at length drew it out upon the bank, with several other particulars that lasted all the first course. A dish ⌐f wild-fowl that came afterward furnished conversa-tion for the rest of the dinner, which concluded with a late invention of Will's for improving the quail-pipe.

Upon withdrawing into my room after dinner, I was se-cretly touched with compassion toward the honest gentle-man that had dined with us, and could not but consider, with a great deal of concern, how so good an heart and such busy hands were wholly employed in trifles; that so much humanity should be so little beneficial to others, and so much industry so little advantageous to himself. The same temper of mind and application to affairs might have recommended

him to the public esteem and have raised his fortune in another station of life. What good to his country or himself
might not a trader or merchant have done with such useful
though ordinary qualifications?

Will Wimble's is the case of many a younger brother of
a great family, who had rather see their children starve like
gentlemen than thrive in a trade or profession that is beneath their quality. This humour fills several parts of Europe
with pride and beggary. It is the happiness of a trading
nation, like ours, that the younger sons, though incapable of
any liberal art or profession, may be placed in such a way
of life as may perhaps enable them to vie with the best of their
family. Accordingly, we find several citizens that were
launched into the world with narrow fortunes, rising by an
honest industry to greater estates than those of their elder
brothers. It is not improbable that Will was formerly tried
at divinity, law, or physic; and that, finding his genius did not
lie that way, his parents gave him up at length to his own
inventions. But certainly, however improper he might have
been for studies of a higher nature, he was perfectly well
turned for the occupations of trade and commerce.

VISION OF MIRZA[1]

——*Omnem quæ nunc obducta tuenti*
Mortales hebetat visus tibi, et humida circum
Caligat, nubem eripiam——[2]
                              Virg. Æn. ii. 604.

WHEN I was at Grand Cairo, I picked up several Oriental
manuscripts, which I have still by me. Among others I
met with one entitled The Visions of Mirza, which I have
read over with great pleasure. I intend to give it to the
public when I have no other entertainment for them; and

[1]*Spectator*, No. 159. Saturday, September 1, 1711.
[2]The cloud, which, intercepting the clear light,
Hangs o'er thy eyes, and blunts thy mortal sight,
I will remove——

shall begin with the first vision, which I have translated word for word as follows:—

"On the fifth day of the moon, which according to the custom of my forefathers I always keep holy, after having washed myself, and offered up my morning devotions, I ascended the high hills of Bagdad, in order to pass the rest of the day in meditation and prayer. As I was here airing myself on the tops of the mountains, I fell into a profound contemplation on the vanity of human life; and passing from one thought to another, 'Surely,' said I, 'man is but a shadow, and life a dream.' Whilst I was thus musing, I cast my eyes towards the summit of a rock that was not far from me, where I discovered one in the habit of a shepherd, with a musical instrument in his hand. As I looked upon him he applied it to his lips, and began to play upon it. The sound of it was exceedingly sweet, and wrought into a variety of tunes that were inexpressibly melodious, and altogether different from anything I had ever heard. They put me in mind of those heavenly airs that are played to the departed souls of good men upon their first arrival in Paradise, to wear out the impressions of their last agonies, and qualify them for the pleasures of that happy place. My heart melted away in secret raptures.

"I had been often told that the rock before me was the haunt of a Genius; and that several had been entertained with music who had passed by it, but never heard that the musician had before made himself visible. When he had raised my thoughts by those transporting airs which he played to taste the pleasures of his conversation, as I looked upon him like one astonished, he beckoned to me, and by the waving of his hand directed me to approach the place where he sat. I drew near with that reverence which is due to a superior nature; and as my heart was entirely subdued by the captivating strains I had heard, I fell down at his feet and wept. The Genius smiled upon me with a look of compassion and affability that familiarized him to my imagination, and at once dispelled all the fears and apprehensions with which I approached him. He lifted me from the ground, and taking me by the hand, 'Mirza,' said he, 'I have heard thee in thy soliloquies; follow me.'

"He then led me to the highest pinnacle of the rock, and placing me on the top of it, 'Cast thy eyes eastward,' said he, 'and tell me what thou seest.' 'I see,' said I, 'a huge valley, and a prodigious tide of water rolling through it.' 'The valley that thou seest,' said he, 'is the Vale of Misery, and the tide of water that thou seest is part of the great Tide of Eternity.' 'What is the reason,' said I, 'that the tide I see rises out of a thick mist at one end, and again loses itself in a thick mist at the other?' 'What thou seest,' said he, 'is that portion of eternity which is called time, measured out by the sun, and reaching from the beginning of the world to its consummation. Examine now,' said he, 'this sea that is bounded with darkness at both ends, and tell me what thou discoverest in it.' 'I see a bridge,' said I, 'standing in the midst of the tide.' 'The bridge thou seest,' said he, 'is Human Life: consider it attentively.' Upon a more leisurely survey of it, I found that it consisted of three-score and ten entire arches, with several broken arches, which added to those that were entire, made up the number about a hundred. As I was counting the arches, the Genius told me that this bridge consisted at first of a thousand arches; but that a great flood swept away the rest, and left the bridge in the ruinous condition I now beheld it. 'But tell me farther,' said he, 'what thou discoverest on it.' 'I see multitudes of people passing over it,' said I, 'and a black cloud hanging on each end of it.' As I looked more attentively, I saw several of the passengers dropping through the bridge into the great tide that flowed underneath it; and upon farther examination, perceived there were innumerable trap-doors that lay concealed in the bridge, which the passengers no sooner trod upon, but they fell through them into the tide, and immediately disappeared. These hidden pitfalls were set very thick at the entrance of the bridge, so that throngs of people no sooner broke through the cloud, but many of them fell into them. They grew thinner towards the middle, but multiplied and lay closer together towards the end of the arches that were entire.

"There were indeed some persons, but their number was very small, that continued a kind of hobbling march on the broken arches, but fell through one after another, being quite tired and spent with so long a walk.

"I passed some time in the contemplation of this wonderful structure, and the great variety of objects which it presented. My heart was filled with a deep melancholy to see several dropping unexpectedly in the midst of mirth and jollity, and catching at everything that stood by them to save themselves. Some were looking up towards the heavens in a thoughtful posture, and in the midst of a speculation stumbled and fell out of sight. Multitudes were very busy in the pursuit of bubbles that glittered in their eyes and danced before them; but often when they thought themselves within the reach of them, their footing failed and down they sunk. In this confusion of objects, I observed some with scimitars in their hands, and others with urinals, who ran to and fro upon the bridge, thrusting several persons on trap-doors which did not seem to lie in their way, and which they might have escaped had they not been thus forced upon them.

"The Genius seeing me indulge myself on this melancholy prospect, told me I had dwelt long enough upon it. 'Take thine eyes off the bridge,' said he, 'and tell me if thou yet seest anything thou dost not comprehend.' Upon looking up, 'What mean,' said I, 'those great flights of birds that are perpetually hovering about the bridge, and settling upon it from time to time? I see vultures, harpies, ravens, cormorants, and among many other feathered creatures several little winged boys, that perch in great numbers upon the middle arches.' 'These,' said the Genius, 'are Envy, Avarice, Superstition, Despair, Love, with the like cares and passions that infest human life.'

"I here fetched a deep sigh. 'Alas,' said I, 'Man was made in vain! how is he given away to misery and mortality!

tortured in life, and swallowed up in death!' The Genius being moved with compassion towards me, bid me quit so uncomfortable a prospect. 'Look no more,' said he, 'on man in the first stage of his existence, in his setting out for eternity; but cast thine eye on that thick mist into which the tide bears the several generations of mortals that fall into it.' I directed my sight as I was ordered, and (whether or no the good Genius strengthened it with any supernatural force, or dissipated part of the mist that was before too thick for the eye to penetrate) I saw the valley opening at the farther end, and spreading forth into an immense ocean, that had a huge rock of adamant running through the midst of it, and dividing it into two equal parts. The clouds still rested on one half of it, insomuch that I could discover nothing in it; but the other appeared to me a vast ocean planted with innumerable islands, that were covered with fruits and flowers, and interwoven with a thousand little shining seas that ran among them. I could see persons dressed in glorious habits with garlands upon their heads, passing among the trees, lying down by the sides of fountains, or resting on beds of flowers; and could hear a confused harmony of singing birds, falling waters, human voices, and musical instruments. Gladness grew in me upon the discovery of so delightful a scene. I wished for the wings of an eagle, that I might fly away to those happy seats; but the Genius told me there was no passage to them, except through the gates of death that I saw opening every moment upon the bridge. 'The islands,' said he, 'that lie so fresh and green before thee, and with which the whole face of the ocean appears spotted as far as thou canst see, are more in number than the sands on the seashore: there are myriads of islands behind those which thou here discoverest, reaching farther than thine eye, or even thine imagination can extend itself. These are the mansions of good men after death, who, according to the degree and kinds of virtue in which they excelled, are distributed among these several islands, which abound with pleasures of different kinds and degrees, suitable to the relishes and perfections of those who are settled in them: every island is a paradise accommodated to its respective inhabitants. Are not these, O Mirza, habitations worth contending for? Does life appear miserable that gives thee opportunities of earning such a reward? Is death to be feared that will convey thee to so happy an existence? Think not man was made in vain, who has such an eternity reserved for him.' I gazed with inexpressible pleasure on these happy islands. At length, said I, 'Show me now, I beseech thee, the secrets that lie hid under those dark clouds which cover the ocean on the other side of the rock of adamant.' The Genius making me no answer, I turned me about to address myself to him a second time, but I found that he had left me; I then turned again to the vision which I had been so long contemplating; but instead of the rolling tide, the arched bridge, and the happy islands, I saw nothing but the long hollow valley of Bagdad, with oxen, sheep, and camels grazing upon the sides of it."

CRIES OF LONDON[1]

——Linguæ centum sunt, oraque centum,
Ferrea vox——[2]
Virg. *Æn.* VI, 625.

THERE is nothing which more astonishes a foreigner, and frights a country squire, than the Cries of London. My good friend Sir Roger often declares that he cannot get them out of his head, or go to sleep for them, the first week that he is in town. On the contrary, Will Honeycomb calls them the *Ramage de la Ville*, and prefers them to the sounds of larks and nightingales, with all the music of the fields and woods. I have lately received a letter from some very odd fellow upon this subject, which I shall leave with my reader, without saying anything farther of it.

---

[1]*Spectator*, No. 251. Tuesday, December 18, 1711.
[2]——A hundred mouths, a hundred tongues,
And throats of brass inspir'd with iron lungs. **Dryden.**

"Sir,

"I am a man out of all business, and would willingly turn my hand to anything for an honest livelihood. I have invented several projects for raising many millions of money without burdening the subject, but I cannot get the parliament to listen to me, who look upon me, forsooth, as a crack and a projector; so that, despairing to enrich either myself or my country by this public-spiritedness, I would make some proposals to you relating to a design which I have very much at heart, and which may procure me a handsome subsistence, if you will be pleased to recommend it to the cities of London and Westminster.

"The post I would aim at, is to be Comptroller-General of the London Cries, which are at present under no manner of rules and discipline. I think I am pretty well qualified for this place, as being a man of very strong lungs, of great insight into all the branches of our British trades and manufactures, and of a competent skill in music.

"The Cries of London may be divided into vocal and instrumental. As for the latter, they are at present under a very great disorder. A freeman of London has the privilege of disturbing a whole street for an hour together, with the twanking of a brass kettle or frying-pan. The watchman's thump at midnight startles us in our beds, as much as the breaking in of a thief. The sowgelder's horn has indeed something musical in it, but this is seldom heard within the liberties. I would therefore propose, that no instrument of this nature should be made use of, which I have not tuned and licensed, after having carefully examined in what manner it may affect the ears of her Majesty's liege subjects.

"Vocal cries are of a much larger extent, and indeed so full of incongruities and barbarisms, that we appear a distracted city to foreigners, who do not comprehend the meaning of such enormous outcries. Milk is generally sold in a note above E-la, and in sounds so exceedingly shrill, that it often sets our teeth on edge. The chimney-sweeper is confined to no certain pitch; he sometimes utters himself in the deepest base, and sometimes in the sharpest treble; sometimes in the highest, and sometimes in the lowest note of the gamut. The same observation might be made on the retailers of small-coal, not to mention broken glasses or brick-dust. In these, therefore, and the like cases, it should be my care to sweeten and mellow the voices of these itinerant tradesmen, before they make their appearance in our streets, as also to accommodate their cries to their respective wares: and to take care in particular, that those may not make the most noise who have the least to sell, which is very observable in the vendors of card-matches, to whom I cannot but apply the old proverb of 'Much cry but little wool.'

"Some of these last-mentioned musicians are so very loud in the sale of these trifling manufactures, that an honest splenetic gentleman of my acquaintance bargained with one of them never to come into the street where he lived. But what was the effect of this contract? Why, the whole tribe of card match-makers, which frequent that quarter, passed by his door the very next day, in hopes of being bought off after the same manner.

"It is another great imperfection in our London Cries, that there is no just time nor measure observed in them. Our news should indeed be published in a very quick time, because it is a commodity that will not keep cold. It should not, however, be cried with the same precipitation as fire. Yet this is generally the case. A bloody battle alarms the town from one end to another in an instant. Every motion of the French is published in so great a hurry, that one would think the enemy were at our gates. This likewise I would take upon me to regulate in such a manner, that there should be some distinction made between the spreading of a victory, a march, or an encampment, a Dutch, a Portugal, or a Spanish mail. Nor must I omit under this head those excessive alarms with which several boisterous rustics infest our streets in turnip-season; and which are more inexcusable, because these are wares which are in no danger of cooling upon their hands.

"There are others who affect a very slow time, and are in my opinion much more tuneable than the former. The cooper in particular swells his last note in an hollow voice, that is not without its harmony; nor can I forbear being inspired with a most agreeable melancholy, when I hear that sad and solemn air with which the public are very often asked, if they have any chairs to mend? Your own memory may suggest to you many other lamentable ditties of the same nature, in which the music is wonderfully languishing and melodious.

"I am always pleased with that particular time of the year which is proper for the pickling of dill and cucumbers; but, alas! this cry, like the song of the nightingale, is not heard above two months. It would therefore be worth while to consider, whether the same air might not in some cases be adapted to other words.

"It might likewise deserve our most serious consideration, how far, in a well-regulated city, those humorists are to be tolerated, who, not contented with the traditional cries of their forefathers, have invented particular songs and tunes of their own: such as was, not many years since, the pastryman, commonly known by the name of the Colly-Molly-Puff; and such as is at this day the vendor of powder and wash-balls, who, if I am rightly informed, goes under the name of Powder-Wat.

"I must not here omit one particular absurdity which runs through this whole vociferous generation, and which renders their cries very often not only incommodious, but altogether useless to the public. I mean that idle accomplishment, which they all of them aim at, of crying so as not to be understood. Whether or not they have learned this from several of our affected singers, I will not take upon me to say; but most certain it is, that people know the wares they deal in rather by their tunes than by their words; insomuch that I have sometimes seen a country boy run out to buy apples of a bellows-mender, and ginger-bread from a grinder of knives and scissors. Nay, so strangely infatuated are some very eminent artists of this particular grace in a cry, that none but their acquaintance are able to guess at their profession; for who else can know, that 'work if I had it,' should be the signification of a corn-cutter.

"Forasmuch, therefore, as persons of this rank are seldom men of genius or capacity, I think it would be proper that some man of good sense and profound judgment should preside over these public cries, who should permit none to lift up their voices in our streets, that have not tuneable throats, and are not only able to overcome the noise of the crowd, and the rattling of coaches, but also to vend their respective merchandise in apt phrases, and in the most distinct and agreeable sounds. I do therefore humbly recommend myself as a person rightly qualified for this post; and, if I meet with fitting encouragement, shall communicate some other projects which I have by me, that may no less conduce to the emolument of the public.

"I am, Sir, &c.
"RALPH CROTCHET"

THE LANGUAGE OF *PARADISE LOST*[1]

Ne, quicunque Deus, quicunque adhibebitur heros
Regali conspectus in auro nuper et ostro,
Migret in obscuras humili sermone tabernas:
Aut, dum vitat humum, nubes et inania captet.[2]
Hor. *Ars. Poet.* 227.

HAVING already treated of the fable, the characters, and sentiments in the *Paradise Lost*, we are in the last place to consider the language; and as the learned world is very much divided upon Milton, as to this point, I hope they will excuse

---

[1]*Spectator*, No. 285. Saturday, January 26, 1712.

[2]But then they did not wrong themselves so much,
To make a god, a hero, or a king,
(Stript of his golden crown, and purple robe)
Descend to a mechanic dialect;
Nor (to avoid such meanness) soaring high,
With empty sound, and airy notions, fly. Roscommon.

me if I appear particular in any of my opinions, and incline to those who judge the most advantageously of the author.

It is requisite that the language of an heroic poem should be both perspicuous and sublime. In proportion as either of these two qualities is wanting, the language is imperfect. Perspicuity is the first and most necessary qualification; insomuch, that a good-natured reader sometimes overlooks a little slip even in the grammar or syntax, where it is impossible for him to mistake the poet's sense. Of this kind is that passage in Milton, wherein he speaks of Satan.

> ——God and his Son except,
> created thing nought valu'd he nor shunn'd.

And that in which he describes Adam and Eve.

> Adam the goodliest man of men since born
> His sons, the fairest of her daughters Eve.

It is plain, that in the former of these passages, according to the natural syntax, the Divine Persons mentioned in the first line are represented as created beings; and that in the other, Adam and Eve are confounded with their sons and daughter. Such little blemishes as these, when the thought is great and natural, we should, with Horace, impute to a pardonable inadvertency, or to the weakness of human nature, which cannot attend to each minute particular, and give the last finishing to every circumstance in so long a work. The ancient critics, therefore, who are actuated by a spirit of candour, rather than that of cavilling, invented certain figures of speech, on purpose to palliate little errors of this nature in the writings of those authors, who had so many greater beauties to atone for them.

If clearness and perspicuity only were to be consulted, the poet would have nothing else to do but to clothe his thoughts in the most plain and natural expressions. But, since it often

happens that the most obvious phrases, and those which are
used in ordinary conversation, become too familiar to the
ear, and contract a kind of meanness by passing through the
mouths of the vulgar, a poet should take particular care to
guard himself against idiomatic ways of speaking. Ovid and
Lucian have many poornesses of expression upon this account, as taking up with the first phrases that offered, without
putting themselves to the trouble of looking after such as
would not only have been natural, but also elevated and sublime. Milton has but few failings in this kind, of which,
however, you may meet with some instances, as in the following passages:

> Embrios and Idiots, Eremites and Fryars
> White, black, and grey, with all their trumpery,
> Here Pilgrims roam—
> . . . A while discourse they hold,
> No fear lest dinner cool; when thus began
> Our Author . . .
> Who of all ages to succeed, but feeling
> The evil on him brought by me, will curse
> My head, ill fare our ancestor impure,
> For this we may thank Adam. . . .

The great masters in composition know very well that
many an elegant phrase becomes improper for a poet or an
orator, when it has been debased by common use. For this
reason the works of ancient authors, which are written in
dead languages, have a great advantage over those which are
written in languages that are now spoken. Were there any
mean phrases or idioms in Virgil and Homer, they would not
shock the ear of the most delicate modern reader, so much as
they would have done that of an old Greek or Roman, because we never hear them pronounced in our streets, or in
ordinary conversation.

It is not therefore sufficient, that the language of an
epic poem be perspicuous, unless it be also sublime. To this

end it ought to deviate from the common forms and ordinary phrases of speech. The judgment of a poet very much discovers itself in shunning the common roads of expression, without falling into such ways of speech as may seem stiff and unnatural; he must not swell into a false sublime, by endeavouring to avoid the other extreme. Among the Greeks, Eschylus, and sometimes Sophocles, were guilty of this fault; among the Latins, Claudian and Statius; and among our own countrymen, Shakespeare and Lee. In these authors the affectation of greatness often hurts the perspicuity of the style, as in many others the endeavour after perspicuity prejudices its greatness.

Aristotle has observed, that the idiomatic style may be avoided, and the sublime formed, by the following methods. First, by the use of metaphors, like those in Milton.

> Imparadised in one another's arms,
> . . . And in his hand a reed
> Stood waving tipt with fire; . . .
> The grassie clods now calv'd. . . .

In these and innumerable other instances, the metaphors are very bold, but beautiful: I must however observe, that the metaphors are not thick sown in Milton, which always savours too much of wit; that they never clash with one another, which as Aristotle observes, turns a sentence into a kind of an enigma or riddle; and that he seldom makes use of them where the proper and natural words will do as well.

Another way of raising the language, and giving it a poetical turn, is to make use of the idioms of other tongues. Virgil is full of the Greek forms of speech, which the critics call Hellenisms, as Horace in his Odes abounds with them much more than Virgil. I need not mention the several dialects which Homer has made use of for this end. Milton in conformity with the practice of the ancient poets, and with Aristotle's rule, has infused a great many Latinisms, as well as Græcisms, and sometimes Hebraisms, into the language of his poem, as towards the beginning of it.

Nor did they not perceive the evil plight
In which they were, or the fierce pains not feel.
Yet to their gen'ral's voice they soon obey'd.
. . . Who shall tempt with wand'ring feet
The dark unbottom'd infinite abyss,
And through the palpable obscure find out his way,
His uncouth way, or spread his airy flight
Upborn with indefatigable wings
Over the vast abrupt! . . .
. . . So both ascend
In the visions of God. . . .

Under this head may be reckoned the placing the adjective after the substantive, the transposition of words, the turning the adjective into a substantive, with several other foreign modes of speech, which this poet has naturalized to give his verse the greater sound, and throw it out of prose.

The third method mentioned by Aristotle, is what agrees with the genius of the Greek language more than with that of any other tongue, and is therefore more used by Homer than by any other poet. I mean the length'ning of a phrase by the addition of words, which may either be inserted or omitted, as also by the extending or contracting of particular words by the insertion or omission of certain syllables. Milton has put in practice this method of raising his language, as far as the nature of our tongue will permit, as in the passage above-mentioned, *Eremite*, for what is *Hermit* in common discourse. If you observe the measure of his verse, he has with great judgment suppressed a syllable in several words, and shortened those of two syllables into one, by which method, besides the above mentioned advantage, he has given a greater variety to his numbers. But this practice is more particularly remarkable in the names of persons and of countries, as Beelzebub, Hessebon, and in many other particulars, wherein he has either changed the name, or made use of that which is not the most commonly known, that he might the better deviate from the language of the vulgar.

The same reason recommended to him several old words,

which also makes his poem appear the more venerable, and gives it a greater air of antiquity.

I must likewise take notice, that there are in Milton several words of his own coining, as *Cerberean*, *miscreated*, *Hell-doom'd*, *embryon atoms*, and many others. If the reader is offended at this liberty in our English poet, I would recommend him to a discourse in Plutarch, which shows us how frequently Homer has made use of the same liberty.

Milton, by the above mentioned helps, and by the choice of the noblest words and phrases which our tongue would afford him, has carried our language to a greater height than any of the English poets have ever done before or after him, and made the sublimity of his style equal to that of his sentiments.

I have been the more particular in these observations of Milton's style, because it is that part of him in which he appears the most singular. The remarks I have here made upon the practice of other poets, with my observations out of Aristotle, will perhaps alleviate the prejudice which some have taken to his poem upon this account; tho' after all, I must confess, that I think his style, tho' admirable in general, is in some places too much stiffened and obscured by the frequent use of those methods, which Aristotle has prescribed for the raising of it.

This redundancy of those several ways of speech which Aristotle calls foreign language, and with which Milton has so very much enriched, and in some places darkened the language of his poem, was the more proper for his use, because his poem is written in blank verse; rhyme, without any other assistance, throws the language off from prose, and very often makes an indifferent phrase pass unregarded; but where the verse is not built upon rhymes, there pomp of sound, and energy of expression, are indispensably necessary to support the style, and keep it from falling into the flatness of prose.

Those who have not a taste for this elevation of style, and are apt to ridicule a poet when he departs from the common forms of expression, would do well to see how Aristotle has treated an ancient author, called Euclid, for his insipid mirth upon this occasion. Mr. Dryden used to call this sort of men his prose-critics.

I should, under this head of the language, consider Milton's numbers, in which he has made use of several elisions, that are not customary among other English poets, as may be particularly observed in his cutting off the letter "Y," when it precedes a vowel. This, and some other innovations in the measure of his verse, have varied his numbers in such a manner, as makes them incapable of satiating the ear, and cloying the reader, which the same uniform measure would certainly have done, and which the perpetual returns of rhyme never fail to do in long narrative poems. I shall close these reflections upon the language of *Paradise Lost*, with observing that Milton has copied after Homer, rather than Virgil, in the length of his periods, the copiousness of his phrases, and the running of his verses into one another.

SIR ROGER AT THE PLAY[1]

Respicere exemplar vitæ morumque jubebo
Doctum imitatorem, et vivas hinc ducere voces.[2]
Hor. *Ars. Poet.* 327.

My FRIEND Sir Roger de Coverley, when we last met together at the Club, told me, that he had a great mind to see the new tragedy with me, assuring me at the same time, that he had not been at a play these twenty years. "The last I saw," says Sir Roger, "was the *Committee*, which I should not have gone to neither had not I been told before-hand that it was a good Church of England comedy." He then proceeded to enquire of me who this distress'd mother was, and upon hearing that she was Hector's widow, he told me, that her husband was a brave man, and that when he was a school-

---

[1]*Spectator*, No. 335. Tuesday, March 25, 1712.
[2]Keep Nature's great original in view
And thence the living images pursue. Francis.

boy, he had read his life at the end of the dictionary. My friend asked me, in the next place, if there would not be some danger in coming home late, in case the Mohocks should be abroad. "I assure you," says he, "I thought I had fallen into their hands last night, for I observed two or three lusty black men that followed me half way up Fleet-street, and mended their pace behind me, in proportion as I put on to get away from them. You must know," continued the knight with a smile, "I fancied they had a mind to hunt me; for I remember an honest gentleman in my neighbourhood, who was served such a trick in King Charles the Second's time; for which reason he has not ventured himself in town ever since. I might have shown them very good sport, had this been their design, for as I am an old fox-hunter, I should have turned and dodged, and have play'd them a thousand tricks they had never seen in their lives before." Sir Roger added, that if these gentlemen had any such intention, they did not succeed very well in it; "for I threw them out," says he, "at the end of Norfolk-street, where I doubled the corner, and got shelter in my lodgings before they could imagine what was become of me. However," says the knight, "if Captain Sentry will make one with us to-morrow night, and if you will both of you call upon me about four o'clock, that we may be at the house before it is full, I will have my own coach in readiness to attend you, for John tells me he has got the fore-wheels mended."

The Captain, who did not fail to meet me there at the appointed hour, bid Sir Roger fear nothing, for that he had put on the same sword which he made use of at the Battle of Steen-kirk. Sir Roger's servants, and among the rest my old friend the butler, had, I found, provided themselves with good oaken plants, to attend their master upon this occasion. When we had plac'd him in his coach, with myself at his left hand, the Captain before him, and his butler at the head of his footmen in the rear, we convoy'd him in safety to the play-house; where, after having march'd up the entry in good order, the Captain and I went in with him, and seated him

betwixt us in the pit.   As soon as the house was full, and the
candles lighted, my old friend stood up and looked about him
with that pleasure, which a mind seasoned with humanity
naturally feels in itself, at the sight of a multitude of people
who seem pleased with one another, and partake of the
same common entertainment.   I could not but fancy to
myself, as the old man stood up in the middle of the pit,
that he made a very proper centre to a tragic audience.
Upon the entering of Pyrrhus, the knight told me, that he
did not believe the King of France himself had a better strut.
I was indeed very attentive to my old friend's remarks, because I looked upon them as a piece of natural criticism, and
was well pleased to hear him at the conclusion of almost
every scene, telling me that he could not imagine how the
play would end.   One while he appear'd much concerned
for Andromache; and a little while after as much for Hermione; and was extremely puzzled to think what would
become of Pyrrhus.

When Sir Roger saw Andromache's obstinate refusal to her
lover's importunities, he whispered me in the ear, that he was
sure she would never have him; to which he added, with a
more than ordinary vehemence, "You can't imagine, sir,
what 'tis to have to do with a widow."   Upon Pyrrhus his
threatening afterwards to leave her, the knight shook his
head, and muttered to himself, "Ay, do if you can."   This
part dwelt so much upon my friend's imagination, that at
the close of the third act, as I was thinking of something
else, he whispered in my ear, "These widows, sir, are the most
perverse creatures in the world.   But pray," says he, "you
that are a critic, is the play according to your dramatic
rules, as you call them?   Should your people in tragedy always talk to be understood?   Why, there is not a single sentence in this play that I do not know the meaning of."

The fourth act very luckily began before I had time to
give the old gentleman an answer: "Well," says the knight,
sitting down with great satisfaction, "I suppose we are now
to see Hector's ghost."   He then renewed his attention, and,

from time to time, fell a praising the widow. He made, indeed, a little mistake as to one of her pages, whom, at his first entering, he took for Astyanax; but he quickly set himself right in that particular, though, at the same time, he owned he should have been very glad to have seen the little boy, who, says he, must needs be a very fine child by the account that is given of him. Upon Hermione's going off with a menace to Pyrrhus, the audience gave a loud clap, to which Sir Roger added, "On my word, a notable young baggage."

As there was a very remarkable silence and stillness in the audience during the whole action, it was natural for them to take the opportunity of these intervals between the acts, to express their opinion of the players, and of their respective parts. Sir Roger hearing a cluster of them praise Orestes, struck in with them, and told them, that he thought his friend Pylades was a very sensible man; as they were afterwards applauding Pyrrhus, Sir Roger put in a second time, "and let me tell you," says he, "though he speaks but little, I like the old fellow in whiskers as well as any of them." Captain Sentry, seeing two or three wags who sat near us lean with an attentive ear towards Sir Roger, and fearing lest they should smoke the knight, pluck'd him by the elbow, and whispered something in his ear, that lasted till the opening of the fifth act. The knight was wonderfully attentive to the account which Orestes gives of Pyrrhus his death, and at the conclusion of it, told me it was such a bloody piece of work, that he was glad it was not done upon the stage. Seeing afterwards Orestes in his raving fit, he grew more than ordinary serious, and took occasion to moralize (in his way) upon an evil conscience, adding, that Orestes, in his madness, looked as if he saw something.

As we were the first that came into the house, so we were the last that went out of it; being resolved to have a clear passage for our old friend, whom we did not care to venture among the justling of the crowd. Sir Roger went out fully satisfied with his entertainment, and we guarded him to his lodgings in the same manner that we brought him to the play-house; being highly pleased, for my own part, not only with the performance of the excellent piece which had been presented, but with the satisfaction which it had given to the good old man.

DEATH OF SIR ROGER[1]

Heu pietas ! heu prisca fides !——.[2]
Virg. Æn. VI, 879.

WE LAST night received a piece of ill news at our club which very sensibly afflicted every one of us. I question not but my readers themselves will be troubled at the hearing of it. To keep them no longer in suspense, Sir Roger de Coverley *is dead*. He departed this life at his house in the country, after a few weeks' sickness. Sir Andrew Freeport has a letter from one of his correspondents in those parts, that informs him the old man caught a cold at the county-sessions, as he was very warmly promoting an address of his own penning, in which he succeeded according to his wishes. But this particular comes from a Whig justice of peace, who was always Sir Roger's enemy and antagonist. I have letters both from the chaplain and Captain Sentry which mention nothing of it, but are filled with many particulars to the honour of the good old man. I have likewise a letter from the butler, who took so much care of me last summer when I was at the knight's house. As my friend the butler mentions, in the simplicity of his heart, several circumstances the others have passed over in silence, I shall give my reader a copy of his letter without any alteration or diminution.

"HONORED SIR,
"Knowing that you was my old Master's good Friend, I could not forbear sending you the melancholy News of his Death, which has afflicted the whole Country as well as his

---

[1]*Spectator*, No. 517. Thursday, October 23, 1712.
[2]Mirror of ancient faith!
Undaunted worth! Inviolable truth! Dryden.

poor Servants, who loved him, I may say, better than we did our Lives.   I am afraid he caught his Death the last County Sessions, where he would go to see Justice done to a poor Widow Woman and her Fatherless Children, that had been wronged by a neighbouring Gentleman; for you know, Sir, my good Master was always the poor Man's Friend.   Upon his coming home, the first Complaint he made was, that he had lost his Roast-Beef Stomach, not being able to touch a Sirloin, which was served up according to Custom; and you know he used to take great Delight in it.   From that time forward he grew worse and worse, but still kept a good Heart to the last.   Indeed, we were once in great Hope of his Recovery, upon a kind Message that was sent him from the Widow Lady whom he had made love to the Forty last Years of his Life; but this only proved a Light'ning before Death. He has bequeathed to this Lady, as a token of his Love, a great Pearl Necklace, and a Couple of Silver Bracelets set with Jewels, which belonged to my good old Lady his Mother: He has bequeathed the fine white Gelding, that he used to ride a-hunting upon, to his Chaplain, because he thought he would be kind to him, and has left you all his Books.   He has, moreover, bequeathed, to the Chaplain a very pretty Tenement with good Lands about it.   It being a very cold Day when he made his Will, he left for Mourning, to every Man in the Parish, a great Frize-Coat, and to every Woman a black Riding-hood.   It was a most moving Sight to see him take leave of his poor Servants, commending us all for our Fidelity, whilst we were not able to speak a Word for weeping.   As we most of us are grown Gray-headed in our Dear Master's Service, he has left us Pensions and Legacies, which we may live very comfortably upon, the remaining part of our Days: He has bequeathed a great deal more in Charity, which is not yet come to my Knowledge, and it is peremptorily said in the Parish, that he has left Mony to build a Steeple to the Church; for he was heard to say some time ago, that if he lived two Years longer, Coverley Church should have a Steeple to it.   The Chaplain tells everybody that he made a very good

End, and never speaks of him without Tears. He was buried according to his own Directions, among the Family of the Coverlies, on the Left Hand of his Father, Sir Arthur. The Coffin was carried by Six of his Tenants, and the Pall held up by Six of the Quorum: The whole Parish follow'd the Corps with heavy Hearts, and in their Mourning Suits, the Men in Frize, and the Women in Riding-Hoods. Captain Sentry, my Master's Nephew, has taken Possession of the Hall-House, and the whole Estate. When my old Master saw him a little before his Death, he shook him by the Hand, and wished him Joy of the Estate which was falling to him, desiring him only to make good Use of it, and to pay the several Legacies, and the Gifts of Charity which he told him he had left as Quit-rents upon the Estate. The Captain truly seems a courteous Man, though he says but little. He makes much of those whom my Master loved, and shows great Kindness to the old House-dog, that you know my poor Master was so fond of. It would have gone to your Heart to have heard the Moans the dumb Creature made on the Day of my Master's Death. He has ne'er joyed himself since; no more has any of us. 'Twas the melancholiest Day for the poor People that ever happened in Worcestershire. This being all from,

"Honored Sir,
"Your most Sorrowful Servant,
"EDWARD BISCUIT"

"P. S. My Master desired, some Weeks before he died, that a Book which comes up to you by the Carrier should be given to Sir Andrew Freeport, in his Name."

This letter, notwithstanding the poor butler's manner of writing it, gave us such an idea of our good old friend that upon the reading of it there was not a dry eye in the club. Sir Andrew, opening the book, found it to be a collection of Acts of Parliament. There was in particular the Act of Uniformity, with some passages in it marked by Sir

Roger's own hand. Sir Andrew found that they related to two or three points which he had disputed with Sir Roger the last time he appeared at the club. Sir Andrew, who would have been merry at such an incident on another occasion, at the sight of the old man's handwriting burst into tears, and put the book into his pocket. Captain Sentry informs me that the knight has left rings and mourning for every one in the club.

SIR RICHARD STEELE

1672 Was born in Dublin, the son of an attorney.
1684 Entered Charterhouse School, where he formed a friendship with Joseph Addison.
1690 Entered Christ Church College, Oxford, where he remained until 1694 and then withdrew without taking a degree.
1694 Entered the army.
1700 Fought a duel with a Captain Kelley, the occurrence influencing him, partly, to write later the essays against dueling.
1701 Published *The Christian Hero*.
      Produced his first play, *The Funeral*.
1703 Produced *The Lying Lover*.
1705 Produced *The Tender Husband*.
1705 Married a widow, Mrs. Margaret Stretch.
1706 Occurred the death of his wife.
1707 Married Mary Scurlock ("Prue").
      Became official gazetteer.
1709 Founded the *Tatler*.
1710 Lost position as gazetteer.
1711 Discontinued the *Tatler*; founded with Addison, the *Spectator*.
1712 Discontinued the *Spectator*.
1713 Edited the *Guardian*.
      Founded the *Englishman*.
      Became involved in a political controversy with Swift.
1714 Entered Parliament, but was expelled by political enemies.
      Became manager of Drury Lane Theatre.
      Founded the *Toner*.
1715 Was re-elected to Parliament and knighted
1718 Occurred the death of his second wife.
1719 Became involved in a political controversy with Addison.
1720 Edited the *Theatre*.
1722 Produced *The Conscious Lovers*.
1724 Retired to Wales because of financial difficulties.
1729 Died, and was buried at Carmarthen.

ON DUELLING[1]

Quicquid agunt homines—
Nostri est farrogo libelle.[2]
Juv. *Sat.* I, 85, 86.

A LETTER from a young lady, written in the most passionate terms, wherein she laments the misfortune of a gentleman, her lover, who was lately wounded in a duel, has turned my thoughts to that subject, and inclined me to examine into the causes which precipitate men into so fatal a folly. And as it has been proposed to treat of subjects of gallantry in the article from hence, and no one point in nature is more proper to be considered by the company who frequent this place than that of duels, it is worth our consideration to examine into this chimerical groundless humour, and to lay every other thought aside, until we have stripped it of all its false pretences to credit and reputation amongst men.

But I must confess, when I consider what I am going about, and run over in my imagination all the endless crowd of men of honour who will be offended at such a discourse; I am undertaking, methinks, a work worthy an invulnerable hero in romance, rather than a private gentleman with a single rapier: but as I am pretty well acquainted by great opportunities with the nature of man, and know of a truth that all men fight against their will, the danger vanishes, and resolution rises upon this subject. For this reason, I shall talk very freely on a custom which all men wish exploded, though no man has courage enough to resist it.

But there is one unintelligible word, which I fear will extremely perplex my dissertation, and I confess to you I find very hard to explain, which is the term "satisfaction." An honest country gentleman had the misfortune to fall

---

[1]*Tatler*, No. 25. Tuesday, June 7, 1709.

[2]What e'er men do, or say, or think, or dream,
Our motley paper seizes for its theme.

into company with two or three modern men of honour, where he happened to be very ill-treated; and one of the company, being conscious of his offense, sends a note to him in the morning, and tells him, he was ready to give him satisfaction. "This is fine doing," says the plain fellow; "last night he sent me away cursedly out of humour, and this morning he fancies it would be a satisfaction to be run through the body."

As the matter at present stands, it is not to do handsome actions denominates a man of honour; it is enough if he dares to defend ill ones. Thus you often see a common sharper in competition with a gentleman of the first rank; though all mankind is convinced, that a fighting gamester is only a pickpocket with the courage of an highwayman. One cannot with any patience reflect on the unaccountable jumble of persons and things in this town and nation, which occasions very frequently, that a brave man falls by a hand below that of a common hangman, and yet his executioner escapes the clutches of the hangman for doing it. I shall therefore hereafter consider, how the bravest men in other ages and nations have behaved themselves upon such incidents as we decide by combat; and show, from their practice, that this resentment neither has its foundation from true reason or solid fame; but is an imposture, made of cowardice, falsehood, and want of understanding. For this work, a good history of quarrels would be very edifying to the public, and I apply myself to the town for particulars and circumstances within their knowledge, which may serve to embellish the dissertation with proper cuts. Most of the quarrels I have ever known, have proceeded from some valiant coxcomb's persisting in the wrong, to defend some prevailing folly, and preserve himself from the ingenuousness of owning a mistake.

By this means it is called "giving a man satisfaction," to urge your offense against him with your sword; which puts me in mind of Peter's order to the keeper, in The Tale of a Tub: "if you neglect to do all this, damn you and your generation for ever: and so we bid you heartily farewell." If the contradiction in the very terms of one of our challenges were as well explained and turned into downright English, would it not run after this manner?

"Sir,

"Your extraordinary behaviour last night, and the liberty you were pleased to take with me, makes me this morning give you this, to tell you, because you are an ill-bred puppy, I will meet you in Hyde-park, an hour hence; and because you want both breeding and humanity, I desire you would come with a pistol in your hand, on horseback, and endeavour to shoot me through the head, to teach you more manners. If you fail of doing me this pleasure, I shall say, you are a rascal, on every post in town: and so, sir, if you will not injure me more, I shall never forgive what you have done already. Pray, sir, do not fail of getting everything ready; and you will infinitely oblige, sir, your most obedient humble servant, etc."

OLD AGE AND CONVERSATION[1]

Habeo senectuti magnam gratiam, quæ mihi sermonis avid itatem auxit, potionis et cibi sustulit.[2]

Cicero, *De Sen.*

AFTER having applied my mind with more than ordinary attention to my studies, it is my usual custom to relax and unbend it in the conversation of such, as are rather easy than shining companions. This I find particularly necessary for me before I retire to rest, in order to draw my slumbers upon me by degrees, and fall asleep insensibly. This is the particular use I make of a set of heavy honest men, with whom I have passed many hours with much indolence, though not with great pleasure. Their conversation is a kind of preparative for sleep: it takes the mind down from its abstractions, leads it into the familiar traces of thought, and

---

[1] *Tatler*, No. 132. Saturday, February 11, 1710.

[2] I am much beholden to old age, which has increased my eagerness for conversation, in proportion as it has lessened my appetites of hunger and thirst.

lulls it into that state of tranquillity which is the condition of a thinking man, when he is but half awake. After this, my reader will not be surprised to hear the account, which I am about to give of a club of my own contemporaries, among whom I pass two or three hours every evening. This I look upon as taking my first nap before I go to bed. The truth of it is, I should think myself unjust to posterity, as well as to the society at the Trumpet, of which I am a member, did not I in some part of my writings give an account of the persons among whom I have passed almost a sixth part of my time for these last forty years. Our club consisted originally of fifteen; but, partly by the severity of the law in arbitrary times, and partly by the natural effects of old age, we are at present reduced to a third part of that number: in which, however, we hear this consolation, that the best company is said to consist of five persons. I must confess, besides the aforementioned benefit which I meet with in the conversation of this select society, I am not the less pleased with the company, in that I find myself the greatest wit among them, and am heard as their oracle in all points of learning and difficulty.

Sir Jeoffrey Notch, who is the oldest of the club, has been in possession of the right-hand chair time out of mind, and is the only man among us that has the liberty of stirring the fire. This our foreman is a gentleman of an ancient family, that came to a great estate some years before he had discretion, and run it out in hounds, horses, and cock-fighting; for which reason he looks upon himself as an honest, worthy gentleman, who has had misfortunes in the world, and calls every thriving man a pitiful upstart.

Major Matchlock is the next senior, who served in the last civil wars, and has all the battles by heart. He does not think any action in Europe worth talking of since the fight of Marston Moor; and every night tells us of his having been knocked off his horse at the rising of the London apprentices; for which he is in great esteem among us.

Honest old Dick Reptile is the third of our society. He

is a good-natured indolent man, who speaks little himself, but laughs at our jokes; and brings his young nephew along with him, a youth of eighteen years old, to show him good company, and give him a taste of the world. This young fellow sits generally silent; but whenever he opens his mouth, or laughs at anything that passes, he is constantly told by his uncle, after a jocular manner, "Ay, ay, Jack, you young men think us fools; but we old men know you are."

The greatest wit of our company, next to myself, is a Bencher of the neighbouring Inn, who in his youth frequented the ordinaries about Charing Cross, and pretends to have been intimate with Jack Ogle. He has about ten distichs of Hudibras without book, and never leaves the club until he has applied them all. If any modern wit be mentioned, or any town-frolic spoken of, he shakes his head at the dullness of the present age, and tells us a story of Jack Ogle.

For my own part, I am esteemed among them, because they see I am something respected by others; though at the same time I understand by their behaviour, that I am considered by them as a man of a great deal of learning, but no knowledge of the world; insomuch, that the Major sometimes, in the height of his military pride, calls me the Philosopher: and Sir Jeoffrey, no longer ago than last night, upon a dispute what day of the month it was then in Holland, pulled his pipe out of his mouth, and cried, "What does the scholar say to it?"

Our club meets precisely at *six o'clock in the evening;* but I did not come last night until half an hour after seven, by which means I escaped the battle of Naseby, which the Major usually begins at about three-quarters after six: I found also, that my good friend the Bencher had already spent three of his distichs; and only waited an opportunity to hear a sermon spoken of, that he might introduce the couplet where "a stick" rhymes to "ecclesiastic." At my entrance into the room, they were naming a red petticoat and a cloak, by which I found that the Bencher had been diverting them with a story of Jack Ogle.

I had no sooner taken my seat, but Sir Jeoffrey, to show his good-will towards me, gave me a pipe of his own tobacco, and stirred up the fire. I look upon it as a point of morality, to be obliged by those who endeavour to oblige me; and therefore, in requital for his kindness, and to set the conversation a-going, I took the best occasion I could to put him upon telling us the story of old Gantlett, which he always does with very particular concern. He traced up his descent on both sides for several generations, describing his diet and manner of life, with his several battles, and particularly that in which he fell. This Gantlett was a gamecock, upon whose head the knight, in his youth, had won five hundred pounds, and lost two thousand. This naturally set the Major upon the account of Edge Hill fight, and ended in a duel of Jack Ogle's.

Old Reptile was extremely attentive to all that was said, though it was the same he had heard every night for these twenty years, and, upon all occasions, winked upon his nephew to mind what passed.

This may suffice to give the world a taste of our innocent conversation, which we spun out until about ten of the clock, when my maid came with a lantern to light me home. I could not but reflect with myself, as I was going out, upon the talkative humour of old men, and the little figure which that part of life makes in one who cannot employ his natural propensity in discourses which would make him venerable. I must own, it makes me very melancholy in company, when I hear a young man begin a story; and have often observed, that one of a quarter of an hour long in a man of five-and-twenty, gathers circumstances every time he tells it, until it grows into a long Canterbury tale of two hours by that time he is threescore.

The only way of avoiding such a trifling and frivolous old age is, to lay up in our way to it such stores of knowledge and observation, as may make us useful and agreeable in our declining years. The mind of man in a long life will become a magazine of wisdom or folly, and will consequently discharge itself in something impertinent or improving. For which reason, as there is nothing more ridiculous than an old trifling story-teller, so there is nothing more venerable, than one who has turned his experience to the entertainment and advantage of mankind.

In short, we, who are in the last stage of life, and are apt to indulge ourselves in talk, ought to consider, if what we speak be worth being heard, and endeavour to make our discourse like that of Nestor, which Homer compares to the flowing of honey for its sweetness.

I am afraid I shall be thought guilty of this excess I am speaking of when I cannot conclude without observing that Milton certainly thought of this passage in Homer, when, in his description of an eloquent spirit, he says:

"His tongue dropped Manna."

SPECTATOR CLUB[1]

——*Haec alii sex,*
Vel plures, uno conclamant ore.[2]
Juv. *Sat.* VII, 167.

THE first of our society is a gentleman of Worcestershire, of ancient descent, a baronet, his name Sir Roger de Coverley. His great-grandfather was inventor of that famous country-dance which is called after him. All who know that shire are very well acquainted with the parts and merits of Sir Roger. He is a gentleman that is very singular in his behaviour, but his singularities proceed from his good sense, and are contradictions to the manners of the world only as he thinks the world is in the wrong. However, this humour creates him no enemies, for he does nothing with sourness of obstinacy; and his being unconfined to modes and forms, makes him but the readier and more capable to please and oblige all who know him. When he is in town, he lives in Soho Square. It is

---

[1]*Spectator*, No. 2. Friday, March 2, 1711.

[2]Six more at least join their assenting voice.

said he keeps himself a bachelor by reason he was crossed in love by a perverse, beautiful widow of the next county to him. Before this disappointment, Sir Roger was what you call a fine gentleman, had often supped with my Lord Rochester and Sir George Etherege, fought a duel upon his first coming to town, and kicked Bully Dawson in a public coffee-house for calling him "youngster." But being ill-used by the above-mentioned widow, he was very serious for a year and a half; and though, his temper being naturally jovial, he at last got over it, he grew careless of himself, and never dressed afterward. He continues to wear a coat and doublet of the same cut that were in fashion at the time of his repulse, which, in his merry humours, he tells us, has been in and out twelve times since he first wore it. 'Tis said Sir Roger grew humble in his desires after he had forgot this cruel beauty; but this is looked upon by his friends rather as matter of raillery than truth. He is now in his fifty-sixth year, cheerful, gay, and hearty; keeps a good house in both town and country; a great lover of mankind; but there is such a mirthful cast in his behaviour that he is rather beloved than esteemed. His tenants grow rich, his servants look satisfied, all the young women profess love to him, and the young men are glad of his company; when he comes into a house he calls the servants by their names, and talks all the way up stairs to a visit. I must not omit that Sir Roger is a justice of the quorum; that he fills the chair at a quarter-session with great abilities; and, three months ago, gained universal applause by explaining a passage in the Game Act.

The gentleman next in esteem and authority among us is another bachelor, who is a member of the Inner Temple; a man of great probity, wit, and understanding; but he has chosen his place of residence rather to obey the direction of an old humoursome father, than in pursuit of his own inclinations. He was placed there to study the laws of the land, and is the most learned of any of the house in those of the stage. Aristotle and Longinus are much better understood by him than Littleton or Coke. The father sends up, every post, questions relating to marriage-articles, leases, and tenures, in the neighbourhood; all which questions he agrees with an attorney to answer and take care of in the lump. He is studying the passions themselves, when he should be inquiring into the debates among men which arise from them. He knows the argument of each of the orations of Demosthenes and Tully, but not one case in the reports of our own courts. No one ever took him for a fool, but none, except his intimate friends, know he has a great deal of wit. This turn makes him at once both disinterested and agreeable; as few of his thoughts are drawn from business, they are most of them fit for conversation. His taste of books is a little too just for the age he lives in; he has read all, but approves of very few. His familiarity with the customs, manners, actions, and writings of the ancients makes him a very delicate observer of what occurs to him in the present world. He is an excellent critic, and the time of the play is his hour of business; exactly at five he passes through New Inn, crosses through Russell Court, and takes a turn at Will's till the play begins; he has his shoes rubbed and his periwig powdered at the barber's as you go into the Rose. It is for the good of the audience when he is at a play, for the actors have an ambition to please him.

The person of next consideration is Sir Andrew Freeport, a merchant of great eminence in the city of London, a person of indefatigable industry, strong reason, and great experience. His notions of trade are noble and generous, and (as every rich man has usually some sly way of jesting which would make no great figure were he not a rich man) he calls the sea the British Common. He is acquainted with commerce in all its parts, and will tell you that it is a stupid and barbarous way to extend dominion by arms; for true power is to be got by arts and industry. He will often argue that if this part of our trade were well cultivated, we should gain from one nation; and if another, from another. I have heard him prove that diligence makes more lasting acquisitions than valour, and that sloth has ruined more nations than the sword.

He abounds in several frugal maxims, among which the greatest favourite is, "A penny saved is a penny got." A general trader of good sense is pleasanter company than a general scholar; and Sir Andrew having a natural unaffected eloquence, the perspicuity of his discourse gives the same pleasure that wit would in another man. He has made his fortunes himself, and says that England may be richer than other kingdoms by as plain methods as he himself is richer than other men; though at the same time I can say this of him, that there is not a point in the compass but blows home a ship in which he is an owner.

Next to Sir Andrew in the club-room sits Captain Sentry, a gentleman of great courage, good understanding, but invincible modesty. He is one of those that deserve very well, but are very awkward at putting their talents within the observation of such as should take notice of them. He was some years a captain, and behaved himself with great gallantry in several engagements and at several sieges; but having a small estate of his own, and being next heir to Sir Roger, he has quitted a way of life in which no man can rise suitably to his merit who is not something of a courtier as well as a soldier. I have heard him often lament that in a profession where merit is placed in so conspicuous a view, impudence should get the better of modesty. When he has talked to this purpose I never heard him make a sour expression, but frankly confess that he left the world because he was not fit for it. A strict honesty and an even, regular behaviour are in themselves obstacles to him that must press through crowds who endeavour at the same end with himself, —the favour of a commander. He will, however, in this way of talk, excuse generals for not disposing according to men's desert, or inquiring into it, "For," says he, "that great man who has a mind to help me, has as many to break through to come at me as I have to come at him"; therefore he will conclude that the man who would make a figure, especially in a military way, must get over all false modesty, and assist his patron against the importunity of other pretenders by a proper assurance in his own vindication. He says it is a civil cowardice to be backward in asserting what you ought to expect, as it is a military fear to be slow in attacking when it is your duty. With this candour does the gentleman speak of himself and others. The same frankness runs through all his conversation. The military part of his life has furnished him with many adventures, in the relation of which he is very agreeable to the company; for he is never overbearing, though accustomed to command men in the utmost degree below him; nor ever too obsequious from an habit of obeying men highly above him.

But that our society may not appear a set of humorists unacquainted with the gallantries and pleasures of the age, we have among us the gallant Will Honeycomb, a gentleman who, according to his years, should be in the decline of his life, but having ever been very careful of his person, and always had a very easy fortune, time has made but very little impression either by wrinkles on his forehead or traces in his brain. His person is well turned and of a good height. He is very ready at that sort of discourse with which men usually entertain women. He has all his life dressed very well, and remembers habits as others do men. He can smile when one speaks to him, and laughs easily. He knows the history of every mode, and can inform you from which of the French king's wenches our wives and daughters had this manner of curling their hair, that way of placing their hoods; whose frailty was covered by such a sort of petticoat, and whose vanity to show her foot made that part of the dress so short in such a year. In a word, all his conversation and knowledge have been in the female world. As other men of his age will take notice to you what such a minister said upon such and such an occasion, he will tell you when the Duke of Monmouth danced at court such a woman was then smitten, another was taken with him at the head of his troop in the Park. In all these important relations, he has ever about the same time received a kind glance or a blow of a fan from some celebrated beauty, mother of the present Lord Such-a-one. If you speak of a young commoner that said a lively thing in the House, he starts up: "He has good blood in his veins; Tom Mirabell, the rogue, cheated me in that affair; that young fellow's mother used me more like a dog than any woman I ever made advances to." This way of talking of his very much enlivens the conversation among us of a more sedate turn; and I find there is not one of the company but myself, who rarely speak at all, but speaks of him as of that sort of man who is usually called a well-bred, fine gentleman. To conclude his character, where women are not concerned, he is an honest, worthy man.

I cannot tell whether I am to account him whom I am next to speak of as one of our company, for he visits us but seldom; but when he does, it adds to every man else a new enjoyment of himself. He is a clergyman, a very philosophic man, of general learning, great sanctity of life, and the most exact good breeding. He has the misfortune to be of a very weak constitution, and consequently cannot accept of such cares and business as preferments in his function would oblige him to; he is therefore among divines what a chamber-counselor is among lawyers. The probity of his mind and the integrity of his life create him followers, as being eloquent or loud advances others. He seldom introduces the subject he speaks upon; but we are so far gone in years that he observes, when he is among us, an earnestness to have him fall on some divine topic, which he always treats with much authority, as one who has no interest in this world, as one who is hastening to the object of all his wishes and conceives hope from his decays and infirmities. These are my ordinary companions.

COFFEE-HOUSES[1]

——*Hominem pagina nostra sapit.*[2]
Mart. *Epigr.* X, iv.

It is very natural for a man who is not turned for mirthful meetings of men, or assemblies of the fair sex, to delight in that sort of conversation which we find in coffee-houses. Here a man of my temper is in his element; for, if he cannot talk, he can still be more agreeable to his company, as well as pleased in himself, in being only a hearer. It is a secret known but to few, yet of no small use in the conduct of life, that when you fall into a man's conversation, the first thing you should consider is, whether he has a greater inclination to hear you, or that you should hear him. The latter is the more general desire, and I know very able flatterers that never speak a word in praise of the persons from whom they obtain daily favours, but still practise a skilful attention to whatever is uttered by those with whom they converse. We are very curious to observe the behaviour of great men and their clients; but the same passions and interests move men in lower spheres; and I (that have nothing else to do but make observations) see in every parish, street, lane, and alley of this populous city, a little potentate that has his court and his flatterers, who lay snares for his affection and favour, by the same arts that are practised upon men in higher stations.

In the place I most usually frequent, men differ rather in the time of day in which they make a figure, than in any real greatness above one another. I, who am at the coffee-house at six in the morning, know that my friend Beaver, the haberdasher, has a levee of more undissembled friends and admirers than most of the courtiers or generals of Great Britain. Every man about him has, perhaps, a newspaper in his hand; but none can pretend to guess what step will be taken in any one court of Europe till Mr. Beaver has thrown down his

---

[1]*Spectator,* No. 49. Thursday, April 26, 1711.
[2]Men and their manners I describe.

pipe, and declares what measures the allies must enter into
upon this new posture of affairs. Our coffee-house is near one
of the inns of court, and Beaver has the audience and admiration of his neighbours from six till within a quarter of
eight, at which time he is interrupted by the students of the
house; some of whom are ready dressed for Westminster at
eight in the morning, with faces as busy as if they were retained in every cause there; and others come in their night-
gowns to saunter away their time as if they never designed
to go thither. I do not know that I meet in any of my walks,
objects which move both my spleen and laughter so effectually as those young fellows at the Grecian, Squire's, Searle's,
and all other coffee-houses adjacent to the law, who rise
early for no other purpose but to publish their laziness. One
would think that these young virtuosos take a gay cap and
slippers, with a scarf and party-colored gown, to be ensigns of
dignity; for the vain things approach each other with an
air which shows they regard one another for their vestments.
I have observed that the superiority among these proceeds
from an opinion of gallantry and fashion. The gentleman in
the strawberry sash, who presides so much over the rest, has,
it seems, subscribed to every opera this last winter, and is
supposed to receive favours from one of the actresses.

When the day grows too busy for these gentlemen to enjoy
any longer the pleasures of their deshabille, with any manner of confidence, they give place to men who have business
or good sense in their faces, and come to the coffee-house
either to transact affairs, or enjoy conversation. The persons
to whose behaviour and discourse I have most regard, are
such as are between these two sorts of men; such as have not
spirits too active to be happy, and well pleased in a private
condition; nor complexions too warm to make them neglect
the duties and relations of life. Of these sort of men consist
the worthier part of mankind; of these are all good fathers,
generous brothers, sincere friends, and faithful subjects.
Their entertainments are derived rather from reason than
imagination; which is the cause that there is no impatience

or instability in their speech or action. You see in their countenances they are at home, and in quiet possession of the present instant as it passes, without desiring to quicken it by gratifying any passion, or prosecuting any new design. These are the men formed for society, and those little communities which we express by the word neighbourhoods.

The coffee-house is the place of rendezvous to all that live near it, who are thus turned to relish calm and ordinary life. Eubulus presides over the middle hours of the day, when this assembly of men meet together. He enjoys a great fortune handsomely, without launching into expense; and exerts many noble and useful qualities, without appearing in any public employment. His wisdom and knowledge are serviceable to all that think fit to make use of them; and he does the office of a counsel, a judge, an executor, and a friend to all his acquaintance, not only without the profits which attend such offices, but also without the deference and homage which are usually paid to them. The giving of thanks is displeasing to him. The greatest gratitude you can show him, is to let him see you are the better man for his services; and that you are as ready to oblige others, as he is to oblige you.

In the private exigencies of his friends he lends, at legal value, considerable sums, which he might highly increase by rolling in the public stocks. He does not consider in whose hands his money will improve most, but where it will do most good.

Eubulus has so great an authority in his little diurnal audience, that when he shakes his head at any piece of public news, they all of them appear dejected; and, on the contrary, go home to their dinners with a good stomach and cheerful aspect when Eubulus seems to intimate that things go well. Nay, their veneration towards him is so great, that when they are in other company they speak and act after him; are wise in his sentences, and are no sooner sat down at their own tables, but they hope or fear, rejoice or despond, as they saw him do at the coffee-house. In a word, every man is Eubulus as soon as his back is turned.

Having here given an account of the several reigns that succeed each other from daybreak till dinner-time, I shall mention the monarchs of the afternoon on another occasion, and shut up the whole series of them with the history of Tom the Tyrant; who, as first minister of the coffee-house, takes the government upon him between the hours of eleven and twelve at night, and gives his orders in the most arbitrary manner to the servants below him, as to the disposition of liruors, coal, and cinders.

SIR ROGER'S ANCESTORS[1]

——*Abnormis sapiens*——.[2]
Hor. *Sat.* II, ii, 3.

I was this morning walking in the gallery, when Sir Roger enter'd at the end opposite to me, and advancing towards me, said, he was glad to meet me among his relations the De Coverleys, and hoped I liked the conversation of so much good company, who were as silent as myself. I knew he alluded to the pictures, and as he is a gentleman who does not a little value himself upon his ancient descent, I expected he would give me some account of them. We were now arrived at the upper end of the gallery, when the knight faced towards one of the pictures, and as we stood before it, he entered into the matter, after his blunt way of saying things, as they occur to his imagination, without regular introduction, or care to preserve the appearance of chain of thought.

. "It is," said he, "worth while to consider the force of dress; and how the persons of one age differ from those of another, merely by that only. One may observe also that the general fashion of one age has been follow'd by one particular set of people in another, and by them preserved from one generation to another. Thus the vast jetting coat and small

---

[1]*Spectator*, No. 109. Thursday, July 5, 1711.
[2]Of plain good sense, untutor'd in the schools.

bonnet, which was the habit in Harry the Seventh's time, is kept on in the Yeomen of the Guard; not without a good and politic view, because they look a foot taller, and a foot and a half broader; besides that, the cap leaves the face expanded, and consequently more terrible, and fitter to stand at the entrance of palaces.

"This predecessor of ours, you see, is dressed after this manner, and his cheeks would be no larger than mine were he in a hat as I am. He was the last man that won a prize in the tilt-yard (which is now a common street before White-hall). You see the broken lance that lies there by his right foot: he shivered that lance of his adversary all to pieces; and bearing himself, look you, sir, in this manner, at the same time he came within the target of the gentleman who rode against him, and taking him with incredible force before him on the pummel of his saddle, he in that manner rid the tournament over, with an air that showed he did it rather to perform the rule of the lists, than expose his enemy; however, it appeared he knew how to make use of a victory, and with a gentle trot he marched up to a gallery where their mistress sat (for they were rivals) and lèt him down with laudable courtesy and pardonable insolence. I don't know but it might be exactly where the coffee-house is now.

"You are to know this my ancestor was not only of a military genius but fit also for the arts of peace, for he play'd on the base-viol as well as any gentleman at court; you see where his viol hangs by his basket-hilt sword. The action at the tilt-yard you may be sure won the fair lady, who was a maid of honour, and the greatest beauty of her time; here she stands, the next picture. You see, sir, my great-great-great-grandmother has on the new-fashioned petticoat, except that the modern is gathered at the waist; my grandmother appears as if she stood in a large drum, whereas the ladies now walk as if they were in a go-cart. For all the lady was bred at court, she became an excellent country-wife, she bore ten children, and when I show you the library, you shall see in her own hand (allowing for the difference of the language) the best receipt now in England both for an hasty-pudding and a whitepot.

"If you please to fall back a little, because it is necessary to look at the three next pictures at one view; these are three sisters. She on the right hand, who is so very beautiful, died a maid; the next to her, still handsomer, had the same fate, against her will; this homely thing in the middle had both their portions added to her own, and was stolen by a neighbouring gentleman, a man of stratagem and resolution, for he poisoned three mastiffs to come at her, and knocked down two deer-stealers in carrying her off. Misfortunes happen in all families: the theft of this romp and so much money, was no great matter to our estate. But the next heir that possessed it was this soft gentleman, whom you see there: observe the small buttons, the little boots, the laces, the slashes about his clothes, and above all the posture he is drawn in (which to be sure was his own choosing); you see he sits with one hand on a desk writing, and looking as it were another way, like an easy writer, or a sonneteer: he was one of those that had too much wit to know how to live in the world; he was a man of no justice, but great good manners; he ruined everybody that had anything to do with him, but never said a rude thing in his life; the most indolent person in the world, he would sign a deed that passed away half his estate with his gloves on, but would not put on his hat before a lady if it were to save his country. He is said to be the first that made love by squeezing the hand. He left the estate with ten thousand pounds debt upon it, but, however, by all hands I have been informed that he was every way the finest gentleman in the world. That debt lay heavy on our house for one generation, but it was retrieved by a gift from that honest man you see there, a citizen of our name, but nothing at all akin to us. I know Sir Andrew Freeport has said behind my back, that this man was descended from one of the ten children of the maid of honour I showed you above. But it was never made out; we winked at the thing indeed, because money was wanting at that time."

Here I saw my friend a little embarrassed, and turned my face to the next portraiture.

Sir Roger went on with his account of the gallery in the following manner. "This man" (pointing to him I look'd at) "I take to be the honour of our house. Sir Humphrey de Coverley; he was in his dealings as punctual as a tradesman, and as generous as a gentleman. He would have thought himself as much undone by breaking his word, as if it were to be followed by bankruptcy. He served his country as knight of this shire to his dying day: he found it no easy matter to maintain an integrity in his words and actions, even in things that regarded the offices which were incumbent upon him, in the care of his own affairs and relations of life, and therefore dreaded (tho' he had great talents) to go into employments of state, where he must be exposed to the snares of ambition. Innocence of life and great ability were the distinguishing parts of his character; the latter, he had often observed, had led to the destruction of the former, and used frequently to lament that great and good had not the same signification. He was an excellent husbandman, but had resolved not to exceed such a degree of wealth; all above it he bestowed in secret bounties many years after the sum he aimed at for his own use was attained. Yet he did not slacken his industry, but to a decent old age spent the life and fortune which was superfluous to himself in the service of his friends and neighbours."

Here we were called to dinner, and Sir Roger ended the discourse of this gentleman, by telling me, as we followed the servant, that this his ancestor was a brave man, and narrowly escaped being killed in the civil wars; "for," said he, "he was sent out of the field upon a private message the day before the battle of Worcester." The whim of narrowly escaping, by having been within a day of danger; with other matters above-mentioned, mixed with good sense, left me at a loss whether I was more delighted with my friend's wisdom or simplicity.

A STAGE–COACH JOURNEY[1]

Qui aut tempus quid postulet non videt, aut plura loquitur, aut se ostentat, aut eorum quibuscum est rationem non habet, is ineptus esse dicitur.[2]
Cicero, *De Oratore*, II, 4.

HAVING notified to my good friend Sir Roger that I should set out for London the next day, his horses were ready at the appointed hour in the evening; and attended by one of his grooms, I arrived at the country-town at twilight, in order to be ready for the stage-coach the day following. As soon as we arrived at the inn, the servant who waited upon me, inquired of the chamberlain, in my hearing, what company he had for the coach. The fellow answered, "Mrs. Betty Arable, the great fortune, and the widow, her mother; a recruiting officer (who took a place because they were to go); young Squire Quickset, her cousin (that her mother wished her to be married to); Ephraim, the Quaker, her guardian; and a gentleman that had studied himself dumb from Sir Roger de Coverley's." I observed, by what he said of myself, that according to his office, he dealt much in intelligence; and doubted not but there was some foundation for his reports of the rest of the company as well as for the whimsical account he gave of me.

The next morning at daybreak we were all called; and I, who know my own natural shyness, and endeavour to be as little liable to be disputed with as possible, dressed immediately, that I might make no one wait. The first preparation for our setting out was, that the captain's half-pike was placed near the coachman, and a drum behind the coach. In the meantime the drummer, the captain's equipage, was very loud that none of the captain's things should be placed so as to be spoiled; upon which his cloak bag was fixed in the

---

[1]*Spectator*, No. 132. Wednesday, August 1, 1711.

[2]That man may be called impertinent, who considers not the circumstances of time, or engrosses the conversation, or makes himself the subject of his discourse, or pays no regard to the company he is in.

seal of the coach; and the captain himself, according to a frequent though invidious behaviour of military men, ordered his man to look sharp that none but one of the ladies should have the place he had taken fronting to the coach-box.

We were in some little time fixed in our seats, and sat with that dislike which people not too good-natured usually conceive of each other at first sight. The coach jumbled us insensibly into some sort of familiarity, and we had not moved above two miles when the widow asked the captain what success he had in his recruiting. The officer, with a frankness he believed very graceful, told her that indeed he had but very little luck and had suffered much by desertion, therefore should be glad to end his warfare in the service of her or her fair daughter. "In a word," continued he, "I am a soldier, and to be plain is my character; you see me, madam, young, sound, and impudent; take me yourself, widow, or give me to her; I will be wholly at your disposal. I am a soldier of fortune, ha!" This was followed by a vain laugh of his own, and a deep silence of all the rest of the company. I had nothing left for it but to fall fast asleep, which I did with all speed. "Come," said he, "resolve upon it, we will make a wedding at the next town; we will wake this pleasant companion who has fallen asleep, to be the brideman, and," giving the Quaker a clap on the knee, he concluded, "this sly saint, who, I'll warrant, understands what's what as well as you or I, widow, shall give the bride as father."

The Quaker, who happened to be a man of smartness, answered, "Friend, I take it in good part, that thou hast given me the authority of a father over this comely and virtuous child; and I must assure thee that, if I have the giving her, I shall not bestow her on thee. Thy mirth, friend, savoureth of folly; thou art a person of a light mind; thy drum is a type of thee—it soundeth because it is empty. Verily, it is not from thy fulness but thy emptiness that thou hast spoken this day. Friend, friend, we have hired this coach in partnership with thee, to carry us to a great city;

we cannot go any other way. This worthy mother must hear thee if thou wilt needs utter thy follies; we cannot help it, friend, I say—if thou wilt, we must hear thee; but, if thou wert a man of understanding, thou wouldst not take advantage of thy courageous countenance to abash us children of peace. Thou art, thou sayest, a soldier; give quarter to us, who cannot resist thee. Why didst thou fleer at our friend, who feigned himself asleep? He said nothing, but how dost thou know what he containeth? If thou speakest improper things in the hearing of this virtuous young virgin, consider it is an outrage against a distressed person that cannot get from thee: to speak indiscreetly what we are obliged to hear, by being hasped up with thee in this public vehicle, is in some degree assaulting on the high road."

Here Ephraim paused, and the captain, with an happy and uncommon impudence, which can be convicted and support itself at the same time, cries, "Faith, friend, I thank thee; I should have been a little impertinent if thou hadst not reprimanded me. Come, thou art, I see, a smoky old fellow, and I'll be very orderly the ensuring part of the journey. I was going to give myself airs, but, ladies, I beg pardon."

The captain was so little out of humour, and our company was so far from being soured by this little ruffle, that Ephraim and he took a particular delight in being agreeable to each other for the future, and assumed their different provinces in the conduct of the company. Our reckonings, apartments, and accommodation fell under Ephraim; and the captain looked to all disputes on the road, as the good behaviour of our coachman, and the right we had of taking place, as going to London, of all vehicles coming from thence.

The occurrences we met with were ordinary, and very little happened which could entertain by the relation of them; but when I considered the company we were in, I took it for no small good fortune that the whole journey was not spent in impertinences, which to one part of us might be an entertainment, to the other a suffering.

What, therefore, Ephraim said when we were almost ar-

rived at London, had to me an air not only of good understanding but good breeding. Upon the young lady's expressing her satisfaction in the journey, and declaring how delightful it had been to her, Ephraim declared himself as
follows: "There is no ordinary part of human life which ex-
presseth so much a good mind, and a right inward man, as
his behaviour upon meeting with strangers, especially such
as may seem the most unsuitable companions to him; such
a man, when he falleth in the way with persons of simplicity
and innocence, however knowing he may be in the ways of
men, will not vaunt himself thereof; but will the rather hide
his superiority to them, that he may not be painful unto
them. My good friend," continued he, turning to the officer,
"thee and I are to part by and by, and peradventure we may
never meet again; but be advised by a plain man: modes and
apparel are but trifles to the real man, therefore do not think
such a man as thyself terrible for thy garb, nor such a one as
me contemptible for mine. When two such as thee and I
meet, with affections as we ought to have toward each other,
thou shouldst rejoice to see my peaceable demeanour, and I
should be glad to see thy strength and ability to protect me
in it."

THE CARTOONS AT HAMPTON COURT[1]

Mutum est pictura poema.[2]
Hor. *Ars. Poet.* 361.

I HAVE very often lamented and hinted my sorrow in several speculations, that the art of painting is made so little use
of to the improvement of our manners. When we consider
that it places the action of the person represented in the
most agreeable aspect imaginable, that it does not only express the passion or concern as it sits upon him who is drawn,

---

[1]*Spectator*, No. 226. Monday, November 19, 1711.
[2]A picture is a poem without words.

but has under those features the height of the painter's imagination, what strong images of virtue and humanity might we not expect would be instilled into the mind from the labours of the pencil? This is a poetry which would be understood with much less capacity, and less expense of time, than what is taught by writings; but the use of it is generally perverted, and that admirable skill prostituted to the basest and most unworthy ends. Who is the better man for beholding the most beautiful Venus, the best wrought Bacchanal, the images of sleeping Cupids, languishing nymphs, or any of the representations of gods, goddesses, demigods, satyrs, Polyphemes, sphinxes or fauns? But if the virtues and vices which are sometimes pretended to be represented under such draughts, were given us by the painter in the characters of real life, and the persons of men and women whose actions have rendered them laudable or infamous; we should not see a good history-piece without receiving an instructive lecture. There needs no other proof of this truth, than the testimony of every reasonable creature who has seen the cartoons in her majesty's gallery at Hampton Court: these are representations of no less actions than those of our blessed Saviour and his Apostles. As I now sit and recollect the warm images which the admirable Raphael has raised, it is impossible, even from the faint traces in one's memory of what one has not seen these two years, to be unmoved at the horror and reverence which appears in the whole assembly when the mercenary man fell down dead; at the amazement of the man born blind, when he first receives sight; or at the graceless indignation of the sorcerer, when he is struck blind The lame, when they first find strength in their feet, stand doubtful of their new vigour. The heavenly Apostles appear acting these great things, with a deep sense of the infirmities which they relieve, but no value of themselves who administer to their weakness. They know themselves to be but instruments; and the generous distress they are painted in when divine honours are offered to them, is a representation in the most exquisite degree of the beauty of holiness. When St. Paul is preaching to the Athenians, with what wonderful art are almost all the different tempers of mankind represented in that elegant audience? You see one credulous of all that is said, another wrapt up in deep suspense, another saying there is some reason in what he says, another angry that the Apostle destroys a favourite opinion which he is unwilling to give up, another wholly convinced and holding out his hands in rapture; while the generality attend, and wait for the opinion of those who are of leading characters in the assembly. I will not pretend so much as to mention that chart on which is drawn the appearance of our blessed Lord after his resurrection. Present authority, late suffering, humility and majesty, despotic command and divine love, are at once seated in his celestial aspect. The figures of the eleven Apostles are all in the same passion of admiration, but discover it differently according to their characters. Peter receives his Master's orders on his knees with an admiration mixed with a more particular attention: the two next with a more open extasie, though still constrained by the awe of the divine presence: the beloved Disciple, whom I take to be the right of the two first figures, has in his countenance wonder drowned in love; and the last personage, whose back is towards the spectator and his side towards the presence, one would fancy to be St. Thomas, as abashed by the conscience of his former diffidence; which perplexed concern it is possible Raphael thought too hard a task to draw but by this acknowledgment of the difficulty to describe it.

The whole work is an exercise of the highest piety in the painter; and all the touches of a religious mind are expressed in a manner much more forcible than can possibly be performed by the most moving eloquence. These invaluable pieces are very justly in the hands of the greatest and most pious sovereign in the world; and cannot be the frequent object of every one at their own leisure: but as an engraver is to the painter, what a printer is to an author, it is worthy her majesty's name, that she has encouraged that noble artist,

Monsieur Dorigny, to publish these works of Raphael. We have of this gentleman a piece of the transfiguration, which is held a work second to none in the world.

Methinks it would be ridiculous in our people of condition, after their large bounties to foreigners of no name or merit, should they overlook this occasion of having, for a trifling subscription, a work which it is impossible for a man of sense to behold, without being warmed with the noblest sentiments that can be inspired by love, admiration, compassion, contempt of this world, and expectation of a better.

It is certainly the greatest honour we can do our country, to distinguish strangers of merit who apply to us with modesty and diffidence, which generally accompanies merit. No opportunity of this kind ought to be neglected; and a modest behaviour should alarm us to examine whether we do not lose something excellent under that disadvantage in the possessor of that quality. My skill in paintings, where one is not directed by the passion of the pictures, is so inconsiderable, that I am in very great perplexity when I offer to speak of any performances of painters of landskips, buildings, or single figures. This makes me at a loss how to mention the pieces which Mr. Boul exposes to sale by auction on Wednesday next in Shandois Street: but having heard him commended by those who have bought of him heretofore for great integrity in his dealing, and overheard him himself (tho' a laudable painter) say nothing of his own was fit to come into the room with those he had to sell, I feared I should lose an occasion of serving a man of worth in omitting to speak of his auction.

THE INQUISITIVE MAN[1]

Percunctatorem fugito, nam garrulus idem est.[2]
Hor. *Epist.* I, xviii, 69.

THERE is a creature who has all the organs of speech, a tolerable good capacity for conceiving what is said to it, together with a pretty proper behaviour in all the occurrences of common life; but naturally very vacant of thought in itself, and therefore forced to apply itself to foreign assistances. Of this make is that man who is very inquisitive: you may often observe, that though he speaks as good sense as any man upon any thing with which he is well acquainted, he cannot trust to the range of his own fancy to entertain himself upon that foundation, but goes on to still new inquiries. Thus, though you know he is fit for the most polite conversation, you shall see him very well contented to sit by a jockey giving an account of the many revolutions in his horse's health, what potion he made him take, how that agreed with him, how afterwards he came to his stomach and his exercise, or any the like impertinence; and be as well pleased as if you talked to him on the most important truths.   This humour is far from making a man unhappy, though it may subject him to raillery; for he generally falls in with a person who seems to be born for him, which is your talkative fellow. It is so ordered that there is a secret bent, as natural as the meeting of different sexes, in these two characters, to supply each other's wants.   I had the honour the other day to sit in a public room, and saw an inquisitive man look with an air of satisfaction upon the approach of one of these talkers. The man of ready utterance sat down by him; and rubbing his head, leaning on his arm, and making an uneasy countenance, he began: "There is no manner of news to-day.   I

[1]*Spectator*, No. 228. Wednesday, November 21, 1711.
[2]Th' inquisitive will blab; from such refrain:
Their leaky ears no secret can retain. Shard.

cannot tell what is the matter with me, but I slept very ill last night; whether I caught cold or no I know not, but I fancy I do not wear shoes thick enough for the weather, and I have coughed all this week: it must be so, for the custom of washing my head winter and summer with cold water, prevents any injury from the season entering that way; so it must come in at my feet: but I take no notice of it, as it comes so it goes. Most of our evils proceed from too much tenderness; and our faces are naturally as little able to resist the cold as other parts. The Indian answered very well to an European, who asked him how he could go naked; I am all face."

I observed this discourse was as welcome to my general inquirer as any other of more consequence could have been; but somebody calling our talker to another part of the room, the inquirer told the next man who sat by him, that Mr. Such a One, who was just gone from him, used to wash his head in cold water every morning; and so repeated almost verbatim all that had been said to him. The truth is, the inquisitive are the funnels of conversation; they do not take in anything for their own use, but merely to pass it to another: they are the channels thro' which all the good and evil that is spoken in town are conveyed. Such as are offended at them, or think they suffer by their behaviour, may themselves mend that inconvenience; for they are not a malicious people, and if you will supply them, you may contradict any thing they have said before by their own mouths. A further account of a thing is one of the gratefullest goods that can arrive to them; and it is seldom that they are more particular than to say, the town will have it, or, I have it from a good hand: so that there is room for the town to know the matter more particularly, and for a better hand to contradict what was said by a good one.

I have not known this humour more ridiculous than in a father, who has been earnestly solicitous to have an account how his son has passed his leisure hours; if it be in a way

thoroughly insignificant, there cannot be a greater joy than
an inquirer discovers in seeing him follow so hopefully his own
steps: but this humour among men is most pleasant when
they are saying something which is not wholly proper for a
third person to hear, and yet is in itself indifferent. The
other day there came in a well-dressed young fellow, and
two gentlemen of this species immediately fell a whispering
his pedigree. I could overhear, by breaks, "she was his
aunt"; then an answer, "ay, she was of the mother's side";
then again in a little lower voice, "his father wore generally
a darker wig"; answer, "not much. But this gentleman
wears higher heels to his shoes."

As the inquisitive, in my opinion, are such merely from a
vacancy in their own imaginations, there is nothing, methinks, so dangerous as to communicate secrets to them; for
the same temper of inquiry makes them as impertinently com-
municative: but no man though he converses with them
need put himself in their power, for they will be contented
with matters of less moment as well. When there is full fuel
enough, no matter what it is—Thus the ends of sentences in
the newspapers, as "This wants confirmation," "This occasions many speculations," and "Time will discover the event,"
are read by them, and considered not as mere expletives.

One may see now and then this humour accompanied with
an insatiable desire of knowing what passes, without turning
it to any use in the world but merely their own entertainment.
A mind which is gratified this way is adapted to humour and
pleasantry, and formed for an unconcerned character in the
world; and like myself to be a mere spectator. This curiosity,
without malice or self-interest, lays up in the imagination a
magazine of circumstances which cannot but entertain when
they are produced in conversation. If one were to know from
the man of the first quality to the meanest servant, the different intrigues, sentiments, pleasures and interests of mankind,
would it not be the most pleasing entertainment imaginable to
enjoy so constant a farce, as the observing mankind much
more different from themselves in their secret thoughts

and public actions, than in their night-caps and long peri-
wigs?

"MR. SPECTATOR,

"Plutarch tells us, that Caius Gracchus, the Roman, was
frequently hurried by his passion into so loud and tumultuous
a way of speaking, and so strained his voice as not to be able
to proceed. To remedy this excess, he had an ingenious
servant, by name Licinius, always attending him with a pitch
pipe, or instrument, to regulate the voice; who, whenever he
heard his master begin to be high, immediately touched a soft
note; at which, 'tis said, Caius would presently abate and
grow calm.

"Upon recollecting this story, I have frequently wondered
that this useful instrument should have been so long discontinued; especially since we find that this good office of
Licinius has preserved his memory for many hundred years,
which, methinks, should have encouraged some one to have
revived it, if not for the public good, yet for his own credit.
It may be objected, that our loud talkers are so fond of their
own noise, that they would not take it well to be checked by
their servants: but granting this to be true, surely any of
their hearers have a very good title to play a soft note in their
own defence. To be short, no Licinius appearing, and the
noise increasing, I was resolved to give this late long vacation
to the good of my country; and I have at length, by the assistance of an ingenious artist, (who works to the Royal
Society) almost completed my design, and shall be ready in
a short time to furnish the public with what number of these
instruments they please, either to lodge at coffee-houses, or
carry for their own private use. In the mean time I shall
pay that respect to several gentlemen who I know will be in
danger of offending against this instrument, to give them
notice of it by private letters, in which I shall only write,
'Get a Licinius.'

"I should now trouble you no longer, but that I must not
conclude without desiring you to accept one of these pipes,

which shall be left for you with Buckley; and which I hope will be serviceable to you, since as you are silent yourself, you are most open to the insults of the noisy.

"I am, Sir, &c. W. B.

"I had almost forgot to inform you, that as an improvement in this instrument there will be a particular note which I call a hush-note; and this is to be made use of against a long story, swearing, obsceneness, and the like."

DICK EASTCOURT[1]

Erat homo ingeniosus, acutus, acer, et qui plurimum . . . et salis haberet et fellis, nec candoris minus.[2]

Plin. Epist. III, xxi, 1.

MY PAPER is in a kind a letter of news, but it regards rather what passes in the world of conversation than that of business. I am very sorry that I have at present a circumstance before me which is of very great importance to all who have a relish for gaiety, wit, mirth, or humour; I mean the death of poor Dick Eastcourt. I have been obliged to him for so many hours of jollity, that it is but a small recompence, tho' all I can give him, to pass a moment or two in sadness for the loss of so agreeable a man. Poor Eastcourt! the last time I saw him, we were plotting to show the town his great capacity for acting in its full light, by introducing him as dictating to a set of young players, in what manner to speak this sentence, and utter t'other passion—he had so exquisite a discerning of what was defective in any object before him, that in an instant he could show you the ridiculous side of what would pass for beautiful and just, even to men of no ill judgment, before he had pointed at the failure. He was no less skillful in the knowledge of beauty; and, I dare say, there is no one who knew him well, but can repeat more well-

---

[1]*Spectator*, No. 468. Wednesday, August 27, 1712.

[2]He was an ingenious, pleasant fellow, and one who had a great deal of wit and satire, with an equal share of good humour.

turned compliments, as well as smart repartees of Mr. Eastcourt's, than of any other man in England. This was easily
to be observed in his inimitable faculty of telling a story, in
which he would throw in natural and unexpected incidents
to make his court to one part, and rally the other
part of the company. Then he would vary the usage
he gave them according as he saw them bear kind or sharp
language. He had the knack to raise up a pensive temper,
and mortify an impertinently gay one, with the most agreeable skill imaginable. There are a thousand things which
crowd into my memory, which make me too much concerned
to tell on about him. Hamlet holding up the skull which
the grave-digger threw to him, with an account that it was
the head of the king's jester, falls into very pleasing reflections, and cries out to his companion:

"Alas, poor Yorick! I knew him, Horatio, a fellow of
infinite jest, of most excellent fancy; he hath borne me on his
back a thousand times; and how abhorred my imagination
is now, my gorge rises at it. Here hung those lips that I
have kiss'd I know not how oft. Where be your gibes now,
your gambols, your songs, your flashes of merriment, that
were wont to set the table on a roar: not one now to mock
your own jeerings, quite chop-fallen! Now get you to my
lady's chamber, and tell her, let her paint an inch thick, to
this favour she must come. Make her laugh at that."

It is an insolence natural to the wealthy to affix, as much
as in them lies, the character of a man to his circumstances.
Thus it is ordinary with them to praise faintly the good qualities of those below them, and say it is very extraordinary in
such a man as he is, or the like, when they are forced to
acknowledge the value of him whose lowness upbraids their
exaltation. It is to this humour only, that it is to be ascribed
that a quick wit in conversation, a nice judgment upon any
emergency that could arise, and a most blameless inoffensive
behaviour, could not raise this man above being received
only upon the foot of contributing to mirth and diversion.
But he was as easy under that condition, as a man of so excel-

lent talents was capable; and since they would have it, that to divert was his business, he did it with all the seeming alacrity imaginable, tho' it stung him to the heart that it was his business. Men of sense, who could taste his excellencies, were well satisfied to let him lead the way in conversation, and play after his own manner; but fools who provoked him to mimicry, found he had the indignation to let it be at their expense who called for it, and he would show the form of conceited heavy fellows as jests to the company at their own request, in revenge for interrupting him from being a companion to put on the character of a jester.

What was peculiarly excellent in this memorable companion, was, that in the accounts he gave of persons and sentiments, he did not only hit the figure of their faces, and manner of their gestures, but he would in his narration fall into their very way of thinking, and this when he recounted passages, wherein men of the best wit were concerned, as well as such wherein were represented men of the lowest rank of understanding. It is certainly as great an instance of self-love to a weakness, to be impatient of being mimick'd, as any can be imagined. There were none but the vain, the formal, the proud, or those who were incapable of amending their faults, that dreaded him; to others he was in the highest degree pleasing; and I do not know any satisfaction of any indifferent kind I ever tasted so much, as having got over an impatience of my seeing myself in the air he could put me when I have displeased him. It is indeed to his exquisite talent this way, more than any philosophy I could read on the subject, that my person is very little of my care; and it is indifferent to me what is said of my shape, my air, my manner, my speech, or my address. It is to poor Eastcourt I chiefly owe, that I am arrived at the happiness of thinking nothing a diminution to me, but what argues a depravity of my will.

It has as much surprised me as anything in nature, to have it frequently said, that he was not a good player: but that must be owing to a partiality for former actors in the parts in which he succeeded them, and judging by comparison of what was liked before, rather than by the nature of the thing. When a man of his wit and smartness could put on an utter absence of common sense in his face, as he did in the character of Bullfinch in the *Northern Lass*, and an air of insipid cunning and vivacity in the character of Pounce in the *Tender Husband*, it is folly to dispute his capacity and success as he was an actor.

Poor Eastcourt! let the vain and proud be at rest; they will no more disturb their admiration of their dear selves, and thou art no longer to drudge in raising the mirth of stupids, who know nothing of thy merit, for thy maintenance.

It is natural for the generality of mankind to run into reflections upon our mortality, when disturbers of the world are laid at rest, but to take no notice when they who can please and divert are pulled from us: but for my part, I cannot but think the loss of such talents as the man of whom I am speaking was master of, a more melancholy instance of mortality, than the dissolution of persons of never so high characters in the world, whose pretensions were that they were noisy and mischievous.

But I must grow more succinct, and, as a Spectator, give an account of this extraordinary man, who, in his way, never had an equal in any age before him, or in that wherein he lived. I speak of him as a companion, and a man qualified for conversation. His fortune exposed him to an obsequiousness towards the worst sort of company, but his excellent qualities rendered him capable of making the best figure in the most refined. I have been present with him among men of the most delicate taste a whole night, and have known him (for he saw it was desired) keep the discourse to himself the most part of it, and maintain his good humour with a countenance, in a language so delightful, without offence to any person or thing upon earth, still preserving the distance his circumstances obliged him to; I say I have seen him do all this in such a charming manner, that I am sure none of those I hint at will read this, without giving him some sorrow for their abundant mirth, and one gush of tears for so many bursts

of laughter.   I wish it were any honour to the pleasant creature's memory, that my eyes are too much suffused to let me
go on———

A GENTLEMAN[1]

Mores hominum multorum vidit.[2]
Hor. *Ars. Poet.* V, 142.

IT IS a most vexatious thing to an old man, who endeavours
to square his notions by reason, and to talk from reflection
and experience, to fall in with a circle of young ladies at their
afternoon tea-table.   This happened very lately to be my
fate.   The conversation, for the first half-hour, was so very
rambling, that it is hard to say what was talked of, or who
spoke least to the purpose.   The various motions of the fan,
the tossings of the head, intermixed with all the pretty kinds
of laughter, made up the greatest part of the discourse.   At
last, this modish way of shining, and being witty, settled into
something like conversation, and the talk ran upon fine
gentlemen.   From the several characters that were given,
and the exceptions that were made, as this or that gentleman
happened to be named, I found that a lady is not difficult to
be pleased, and that the town swarms with fine gentlemen.
A nimble pair of heels, a smooth complexion, a full-bottom
wig, a laced shirt, an embroidered suit, a pair of fringed
gloves, a hat and feather; any one or more of these and the
like accomplishments ennobles a man, and raises him above
the vulgar, in a female imagination.   On the contrary, a
modest, serious behaviour, a plain dress, a thick pair of shoes,
a leathern belt, a waistcoat not lined with silk, and such like
imperfections, degrade a man, and are so many blots in his
escutcheon.   I could not forbear smiling at one of the pret-
tiest and liveliest of this gay assembly, who excepted to the
gentility of Sir William Harty, because he wore a frieze
coat, and breakfasted upon toast and ale.   I pretended to

---

[1]*Guardian*, No. 34. Monday, April 30, 1713.

[2]He many men and many manners saw.

admire the fineness of her taste; and to strike in with her in
ridiculing those awkward healthy gentlemen, that seem to
make nourishment the chief end of eating. I gave her
an account of an honest Yorkshire gentleman, who, when I
was a traveller, used to invite his acquaintance at Paris to
break their fast with him upon cold roast beef and mum.
There was, I remember, a little French marquis, who was
often pleased to rally him unmercifully upon beef and
pudding, of which our countryman would despatch a pound
or two with great alacrity, while his antagonist was piddling
at a mushroom, or the haunch of a frog. I could perceive
the lady was pleased with what I said, and we parted very
good friends by virtue of a maxim I always observe, "Never
to contradict or reason with a sprightly female." I went
home, however, full of a great many serious reflections upon
what had passed: and though, in complaisance, I disguised
my sentiments, to keep up the good humour of my fair companions, and to avoid being looked upon as a testy old fellow,
yet out of the good-will I bear to the sex, and to prevent
for the future their being imposed upon by counterfeits, I
shall give them the distinguishing marks of "a true fine
gentleman."

When a good artist would express any remarkable character in sculpture, he endeavours to work up his figure into all
the perfection his imagination can form; and to imitate not
so much what is, as what may or ought to be. I shall follow
their example, in the idea I am going to trace out of a fine
gentleman, by assembling together such qualifications as
seem requisite to make the character complete. In order to
do this I shall premise in general, that by a fine gentleman I
mean a man completely qualified as well for the service and
good, as for the ornament and delight, of society. When I
consider the frame of mind peculiar to a gentleman, I suppose
it graced with all the dignity and elevation of spirit that
human nature is capable of. To this I would have joined a
clear understanding, a reason free from prejudice, a steady
judgment, and an extensive knowledge. When I think of

the heart of a gentleman, I imagine it firm and intrepid, void of all inordinate passions, and full of tenderness, compassion, and benevolence. When I view the fine gentleman with regard to his manner, methinks I see him modest without bashfulness, frank and affable without impertinence, obliging and complaisant without servility, cheerful and in good humour without noise. These amiable qualities are not easily obtained; neither are there many men that have a genius to excel this way. A finished gentleman is perhaps the most uncommon of all the great characters in life. Besides the natural endowments with which this distinguished man is to be born, he must run through a long series of education. Before he makes his appearance and shines in the world, he must be principled in religion, instructed in all the moral virtues, and led through the whole course of the polite arts and sciences. He should be no stranger to courts and to camps; he must travel to open his mind, to enlarge his views, to learn the policies and interests of foreign states, as well as to fashion and polish himself, and to get clear of national prejudices; of which every country has its share. To all these more essential improvements, he must not forget to add the fashionable ornaments of life, such as are the languages and the bodily exercises, most in vogue: neither would I have him think even dress itself beneath his notice.

It is no very uncommon thing in the world to meet with men of probity; there are likewise a great many men of honour to be found. Men of courage, men of sense, and men of letters are frequent: but a true fine gentleman is what one seldom sees. He is properly a compound of the various good qualities that embellish mankind. As the great poet animates all the different parts of learning by the force of his genius, and irradiates all the compass of his knowledge by the lustre and brightness of his imagination; so all the great and solid perfections of life appear in the finished gentleman, with a beautiful gloss and varnish; every thing he says or does is accompanied with a manner, or rather a charm, that draws the admiration and good-will of every beholder.

WILLIAM PULTENEY
EARL OF BATH

1684   Was born in London, the son of William Pulteney, of an ancient Leicestershire family.
      Was educated at Westminster School and at Christ Church College, Oxford.

1705–1734   Served in Parliament.

1714   Married Anna Marcia Gumley.

1726–1729   Contributed to the *Craftsman,* a periodical conducted for the purpose of discrediting the prime minister, Sir Robert Walpole.

1742   Was created Earl of Bath, as a means of removing him as an influence in the House of Commons.

1753   Contributed to the *World.*

1757   Sat to Sir Joshua Reynolds for his portrait.

1764   Died, and was buried in Westminster Abbey.

NEWMARKET[1]

TWICE in every year are solemnized those grand diversions, with which our nobility, gentry, and others, entertain themselves at Newmarket; and as this is the vernal season for the celebration of those curious sports and festivals, and as they are, at this time, likely to be held with the utmost splendour and magnificence, I think it may not be improper to amuse my town readers with one single paper upon the subject.

In this I will endeavour to set forth the usefulness of these anniversary meetings, describing the manner and method of exhibiting such games; and then show what benefit may arise to the kingdom, by horse-races in general, on the one hand; and what detriment may happen from them to the public, on the other, by their spreading too widely over the whole kingdom.

---

[1] *World*, No. 17. Thursday, April 26, 1753.

I read in one of the news-papers of last week the following article: "'Tis said that garrets at Newmarket are let at four guineas each, for the time of the meeting." What, said I to myself, are our principal nobility content to lie in garrets, at such an exorbitant price, for the sake of such amusements? Or are our jockey-gentry, and tradesmen, extravagant enough to throw away their loose corn (as I may properly call it on this occasion) so idly and ridiculously? To be sure there is not a more noble diversion than this. In its original, it was of royal institution, and carried on in the beginning with much honour and integrity, but as the best constitution will always degenerate, I am fearful this may be grown too much into a science, wherein the adepts may have carried matters to a nicety, not altogether reconcilable to the strictest notions of integrity; and which may by degrees, by their affecting to become notable in the profession, corrupt the morals of our young nobility. The language of the place is generally to be understood by the rule of contraries. If anyone says his horse is a pretty good one, but as slow as a town-top (for similes are much in use) you may conclude him to be an exceeding speedy one, but not so good at bottom. If he mentions his design of throwing a particular horse soon out of training, you may be assured he has a mind to match that horse as soon as he can; and so it is in everything else they throw out. Foreigners who come here for curiosity, cannot be shown a finer sight than these races, which are almost peculiar to this country: but I must confess that I have been sometimes put a little to the blush at incidents that are pretty pregnant in the place. Everybody is dressed so perfectly alike, that it is extremely difficult to distinguish between his grace and his groom. I have heard a stranger ask a man of quality how often he dressed, and watered his horses? how much corn, and bread, and hay, he gave them? how many miles he thought they could run in such a number of minutes? and how long he had lived with his master? Those who have been at the place will not be surprised at these mistakes: for a pair of boots, and buckskin breeches, a fustian frock, with a leather belt about it, and a black velvet cap, is the common covering of the whole town: so that if the inside does not differ, the outside of my lord and his rider are exactly the same. There is another most remarkable affectation, which is this: those who are known to have the most, and perhaps best horses of the place, always appear themselves on the very worst, and go to the turf on some ordinary scrub tit, scarce worth five pounds. From persons thus mounted and accoutred, what a surprise must it be to hear a bet offered of an hundred pounds to fifty, and sometimes three hundred pounds to two, when you would imagine the rider to be scarce worth a groat! In that circular convention before the race begins, at the Devil's Ditch, all are hail fellows well met, and every one is at liberty, tailor, distiller, or otherwise, to offer and take such bets, as he thinks proper: and many thousand pounds are usually laid on a side. When the horses are in sight, and come near Choak-Jade, immediately the company all disperse, as if the devil rose out of his ditch and drove them, to get to the turning of the lands, the rest-post, or some other station, they choose, for seeing the push made. Now the contention becomes animating. 'Tis delightful to see two, or sometimes more, of the most beautiful animals of the creation, struggling for superiority, stretching every muscle and sinew to obtain the prize, and reach the goal! to observe the skill and address of the riders, who are all distinguished by different colours, of white, blue, green, red, and yellow, sometimes spurring or whipping, sometimes checking or pulling to give fresh breath and courage! and it is often observed that the race is won, as much by the dexterity of the rider, as by the vigour and fleetness of the animal.

When the sport is over, the company saunter away towards the Warren-Hill, before the other horses, left at the several stables in the town, are rode out to take their evening exercise and their water. On this delightful spot you may see at once, above a hundred of the most beautiful horses in the universe, all led out in strings, with the grooms and boys upon them, in their several liveries, distinguishing each person of rank they belong to. This is indeed a noble sight; it is a piece of grandeur, and an expensive one, too, which no nation can boast of, but our own. To this the crown contributes, not only by a very handsome allowance for keeping horses, but also by giving plates to be run for by horses and mares at different ages, in order to encourage the breed, by keeping up the price of them, and to make the breeders extremely careful of their race and genealogy.

The pedigree of these horses is more strictly regarded and carefully looked into, than that of a knight of Malta. They must have no blemished quarter in the family on either side for many generations; their blood must have run pure and untainted from the great, great, five times great grand-father and grandam, to be attested in the most authentic and solemn manner by the hand of the breeder. It is the care of the breed, and particularly with an eye to their strength, that makes all the world so fond of our horses. Many thousands are carried out of England every year; so that it is become a trade of great consequence, and brings a vast balance of money to this country annually. The French monarch rides no other horses but ours, in his favourite diversion of hunting. You may at any time see two or three hundred beautiful English geldings in those great and noble stables at Chantilli. Most of the German princes, and many of their nobility, are desirous of having English horses; and, I dare say, his present M——y of P——a, however military his genius may be, had rather mount an English horse at a review of his troops, than a breach at any siege in Europe.

The country races over the whole kingdom, are what I confess give me some little disrelish to the sport. Every county, and almost the whole of it, is mad during the time of the races. Many substantial farmers go to them with thirty or forty pounds in their pockets, and return without one single farthing. Here they drink and learn to be vicious, and the whole time is spent in riot and disorder. An honest butcher, that is taken in at a horse-race, is tempted perhaps.

in his return, to borrow an ox, or a few sheep of his neighbour, to make up his losses. An industrious tradesman, or a good farmer, has sometimes turned highway man, to be even with the rogue that bubbled him at the races. Upon the whole, if I consider only how much time is lost to all the labouring men in this kingdom, by county races, the damage they occasion is immense. Let us suppose it but a week's labour all over England; and (we consider the number of plates in the different metropolises, besides the lesser country plates) this must be allowed a very moderate computation: and then let those two ingenious gentlemen, Mr. Pond and Mr. Heber, however they may be at variance with each other, join to compute how much the loss must be to the whole kingdom. I dare answer for it, that it must amount to many hundred thousands of pounds.—But as my paper was principally designed in honour of horses, I will not be led to urge any thing against them. Horses of all kinds have ever been held in the highest esteem. Darius was chosen king of Persia by the neighing of his horse. I question if Alexander himself had pushed his conquests half so far, if Bucephalus had not stooped to take him on his back. An emperor of Rome made his horse a consul; and it will be readily owned that the dignity was as properly conferred upon the beast, as the imperial diadem upon his master.

GEORGE BERKELEY

1685 Was born in Kilkenny, the son of William Berkeley, a kinsman of Lord Berkeley of Stratton.

1696 Attended Kilkenny School.

1700 Entered Trinity College, Dublin.

1705 Formed a philosophical society among his friends.

1707 Received the M.A. degree and was admitted to a fellowship.

1709 Published *Essay Towards a New Theory of Vision*, the first statement of his doctrine that vision only represents sensation.

1710 Published *Treatise Concerning the Principles of Human Knowledge*.

1713–1715 Published *Dialogues Between Hylas and Philonous*.
Went to London, and formed acquaintanceships with Addison, Steele, Swift, and other distinguished literary men.
Went abroad in the suite of Lord Peterborough.
Contributed to the *Guardian*.

1716–1720 Traveled abroad as the tutor of St. George Ashe.

1721 Published *Essay Toward Preventing the Ruin of Great Britain*, an argument against the influence of the South Sea speculations.

1723 Inherited half the property left by Hester Vanhomrigh (Swift's "Vanessa"), a fortune popularly supposed to have been destined for Swift.

1724 Became Dean of Derry.

1728 Married Anne Forster.

1728–1731 Visited America.

1734 Published *Alciphron*, a re-statement of his philosophical doctrines, and *The Analyst*.
Became Bishop of Cloyne.

1735–1737 Published *The Querist*, in three parts, a philosophical work which anticipated, more or less, the work of Hume and of Adam Smith.

1744 Published *Siris*, at the time the most popular of his writings.

1752 Retired to Oxford to be near his son, George, in residence at Christ Church College.

1753 Died, and was buried in Christ Church.

PLEASURES[1]

Quae possit facere et servare beatum.[2]
Hor. *Epist.* I, 6, 2.

IT IS of great use to consider the pleasures which constitute human happiness, as they are distinguished into natural and fantastical. Natural pleasure I call those, which, not depending on the fashion and caprice of any particular age or nation, are suited to human nature in general, and were intended by Providence as rewards for the using our faculties agreeably to the ends for which they were given us. Fantastical pleasures are those, which, having no natural fitness to delight our minds, presuppose some particular whim or taste accidentally prevailing in a set of people, to which it is owing that they please.

Now, I take it, that the tranquillity and cheerfulness with which I have passed my life, are the effect of having ever since I came to years of discretion, continued my inclinations to the former sort of pleasures. But as my experience can be a rule only to my own actions, it may probably be a stronger motive to induce others to the same scheme of life, if they would consider that we are prompted to natural pleasures by an instinct impressed on our minds by the Author of our nature, who best understands our frames, and consequently best knows what those pleasures are, which will give us the least uneasiness in the pursuit, and the greatest satisfaction in the enjoyment of them. Hence it follows that the objects of our natural desires are cheap or easy to be obtained, it being a maxim that holds throughout the whole system of created beings, "that nothing is made in vain," much less the instincts and appetites of animals, which the benevolence as well as wisdom of the Deity, is concerned to provide for. Nor is the fruition of those objects less pleasing, than the acquisition is easy; and the pleasure is heightened

---

[1]*Guardian*, No. 49. Thursday, May 7, 1713.

[2]To make men happy, and to keep them so.

by the sense of having answered some natural end, and the
consciousness of acting in concert with the Supreme Governor
of the universe.

Under natural pleasures, I comprehend those which are
universally suited, as well to the rational as the sensual part
of our nature. And of the pleasures which affect our senses,
those only are to be esteemed natural that are contained
within the rules of reason, which is allowed to be as necessary
an ingredient of human nature as sense. And, indeed, excesses of any kind are hardly to be esteemed pleasures, much
less natural pleasures.

It is evident, that a desire terminated in money is fantastical; so is the desire of outward distinctions; which bring
no delight of sense, nor recommend us as useful to mankind;
and the desire of things merely because they are new or
foreign. Men, who are indisposed to a due exertion of their
higher parts, are driven to such pursuits as these from the
restlessness of the mind, and the sensitive appetites being
easily satisfied. It is, in some sort, owing to the bounty of
Providence, that, disdaining a cheap and vulgar happiness,
they frame to themselves imaginary goods, in which there is
nothing can raise desire, but the difficulty of obtaining them.
Thus men become the contrivers of their own misery, as a
punishment on themselves for departing from the measures
of nature. Having by an habitual reflection on these truths
made them familiar, the effect is, that I, among a number
of persons who have debauched their natural taste, see things
in a peculiar light, which I have arrived at, not by any uncommon force of genius, or acquired knowledge, but only by
unlearning the false notions instilled by custom and education.

The various objects that compose the world were by nature
formed to delight our senses, and as it is this alone that makes
them desirable to an uncorrupted taste, a man may be said
naturally to possess them, when he possesseth those enjoyments which they are fitted by nature to yield. Hence, it is
usual with me to consider myself as having a natural property
in every object that administers pleasures to me. When I

am in the country, all the fine seats near the place of my residence, and to which I have access, I regard as mine. The same I think of the groves and fields where I walk, and muse on the folly of the civil landlord in London, who has the fantastical pleasure of draining dry rent into his coffers, but is a stranger to fresh air and rural enjoyments. By these principles, I am possessed of half a dozen of the finest seats in England, which in the eye of the law belong to certain of my acquaintance, who being men of business choose to live near the court.

In some great families, where I choose to pass my time, a stranger would be apt to rank me with the other domestics; but in my own thoughts, and natural judgment, I am master of the house, and he who goes by that name is my steward, who eases me of the care of providing for myself the conveniences and pleasures of life.

When I walk the streets, I use the foregoing natural maxim, *viz.:* That he is the true possessor of a thing who enjoys it, and not he that owns it without the enjoyment of it, to convince myself that I have a property in the gay part of all the gilt chariots that I meet, which I regard as amusements designed to delight my eyes, and the imagination of those kind people who sit in them gayly attired only to please me. I have a real, and they only an imaginary, pleasure from their exterior embellishments. Upon the same principle, I have discovered that I am the natural proprietor of all the diamond necklaces, the crosses, stars, brocades, and embroidered clothes, which I see at a play or birthnight, as giving more natural delight to the spectator than to those that wear them. And I look on the beaux and ladies as so many paroquets in an aviary, or tulips in a garden, designed purely for my diversion. A gallery of pictures, a cabinet, or library, that I have free access to, I think my own. In a word, all that I desire is the use of things, let who will have the keeping of them. By which maxim I am grown one of the richest men in Great Britain; with this difference, that I am not a prey to my own cares, or the envy of others.

The same principles I find of great use in my private economy. As I cannot go to the price of history-painting, I have purchased at easy rates several beautifully-designed pieces of landscape and perspective, which are much more pleasing to a natural taste than unknown faces or Dutch gambols, though done by the best masters; my couches, bed, and window-curtains are of Irish stuff, which those of that nation work very fine, and with a delightful mixture of colours. There is not a piece of china in my house; but I have glasses of all sorts, and some tinged with the finest colours, which are not the less pleasing, because they are domestic, and cheaper than foreign toys. Every thing is neat, entire, and clean, and fitted to the taste of one who had rather be happy, than thought rich.

Every day, numberless innocent and natural gratifications occur to me, while I behold my fellow-creatures labouring in a toilsome and absurd pursuit of trifles; one, that he may be called by a particular appellation; another, that he may wear a particular ornament, which I regard as a bit of riband that has an agreeable effect on my sight, but is so far from supplying the place of merit where it is not, that it serves only to make the want of it more conspicuous. Fair weather is the joy of my soul; about noon, I behold a blue sky with rapture, and receive great consolation from the rosy dashes of light which adorn the clouds of the morning and evening. When I am lost among green trees, I do not envy a great man with a great crowd at his levee. And I often lay aside thoughts of going to an opera, that I may enjoy the silent pleasure of walking by moonlight, or viewing the stars sparkle in their azure ground; which I look upon as part of my possessions; not without a secret indignation at the tastelessness of mortal men, who, in their race through life, overlook the real enjoyments of it.

But the pleasure which naturally affects a human mind with the most lively and transporting touches, I take to be the sense that we act in the eye of infinite Wisdom, Power, and Goodness, that will crown our virtuous endeavours here, with a happiness hereafter, large as our desires, and lasting as our immortal souls. This is a perpetual spring of gladness in the mind. This lessens our calamities, and doubles our joys. Without this the highest state of life is insipid, and with it the lowest is a paradise. What unnatural wretches, then, are those who can be so stupid as to imagine a merit, in endeavouring to rob virtue of her support, and man of his present as well as future bliss? But as I have frequently taken occasion to animadvert on that species of mortals, so I propose to repeat my animadversions on them till I see some symptoms of amendment.

FRIENDSHIP AND BENEVOLENCE[1]

Homo sum, humani nihil a me alienum puto.[2]
Ter. *Heaut.* Act. 1, Sc. 1, 25.

IF WE consider the whole scope of the creation that lies within our view, the moral and intellectual, as well as the natural and corporeal, we shall perceive throughout, a certain correspondence of the parts, a similitude of operation, and unity of design, which plainly demonstrate the universe to be the work of one infinitely good and wise Being; and that the system of thinking beings is actuated by laws derived from the same divine power, which ordained those by which the corporeal system is upheld.

From the contemplation of the order, motion, and cohesion of natural bodies, philosophers are now agreed, that there is a mutual attraction between the most distant parts at least of this solar system. All those bodies that revolve round the sun are drawn towards each other, and towards the sun, by some secret, uniform, and never-ceasing principle. Hence it is, that the earth, as well as the other planets, without flying off in a tangent line, constantly rolls about the sun, and the moon about the earth, without deserting her com-

---

[1] *Guardian*, No. 126. Wednesday, August 5, 1713.
[2] I am a man, and have a fellow feeling with everything belonging to man.

panion in so many thousand years. And as the larger systems of the universe are held together by this cause, so likewise the particular globes derive their cohesion and consistence from it.

Now if we carry our thoughts from the corporeal to the moral world, we may observe in the spirits or minds of men, a like principle of attraction, whereby they are drawn together into communities, clubs, families, friendships, and all the various species of society. As in bodies, where the quantity is the same, the attraction is strongest between those which are placed nearest to each other; so it is likewise in the minds of men, *cæteris paribus*,[1] between those which are most nearly related. Bodies that are placed at the distance of many millions of miles, may nevertheless attract and constantly operate on each other, although this action do not show itself by an union or approach of those distant bodies so long as they are withheld by the contrary forces of other bodies, which, at the same time, attract them in different ways; but would, on the supposed removal of all other bodies, mutually approach and unite with each other. The like holds with regard to the human soul, whose affection towards the individuals of the same species, who are distantly related to it, is rendered inconspicuous by its more powerful attraction towards those who have a nearer relation to it. But as those are removed, the tendency which before lay concealed doth gradually disclose itself.

A man who has no family is more strongly attracted towards his friends and neighbours; and if absent from these, he naturally falls into an acquaintance with those of his own city or country who chance to be in the same place. Two Englishmen meeting at Rome or Constantinople, soon run into a familiarity. And in China or Japan, Europeans would think their being so, a good reason for their uniting in particular converse. Farther, in case we suppose ourselves translated into Jupiter or Saturn, and there to meet a Chinese or

---

[1]Other things being equal.

other most distant native of our own planet, we should look on him as a near relation, and readily commence a friendship with him. These are natural reflections, and such as may convince us that we are linked by an imperceptible chain to every individual of the human race.

The several great bodies which compose the solar system are kept from joining together at the common centre of gravity, by the rectilinear motions the Author of nature has impressed on each of them; which, concurring with the attractive principle, form their respective orbits round the sun; upon the ceasing of which motions, the general law of gravitation, that is now thwarted, would show itself by drawing them all into one mass. After the same manner, in the parallel case of society, private passions, and motions of the soul do often obstruct the operation of that benevolent uniting instinct implanted in human nature; which, notwithstanding, doth still exert, and will not fail to show itself when those obstructions are taken away.

The mutual gravitation of bodies cannot be explained any other way than by resolving it into the immediate operation of God, who never ceases to dispose and actuate his creatures in a manner suitable to their respective beings. So neither can that reciprocal attraction in the minds of men be accounted for by any other cause. It is not the result of education, law, or fashion, but it is a principle originally ingrafted in the very first formation of the soul by the Author of our nature.

And as the attractive power in bodies is the most universal principle which produceth innumerable effects, and is a key to explain the various phenomena of nature; so the corresponding social appetite in human souls is the great spring and source of moral actions. This it is that inclines each individual to an intercourse with his species, and models every one to that behaviour which best suits with the common well-being. Hence that sympathy in our nature whereby we feel the pains and joys of our fellow creatures. Hence that prevalent love in parents towards their children, which is neither founded on the merit of the object, nor yet on self-interest. It is this that makes us inquisitive concerning the affairs of distant nations, which can have no influence on our own. It is this that extends our care to future generations, and excites us to acts of beneficence towards those who are not yet in being, and consequently from whom we can expect no recompense. In a word, hence arises that diffusive sense of humanity so unaccountable to the selfish man, who is un-touched with it, and is, indeed, a sort of monster, or anoma-lous production.

These thoughts do naturally suggest the following particu-lars. First, that as social inclinations are absolutely neces-sary to the well-being of the world, it is the duty and interest of each individual to cherish and improve them to the benefit of mankind; the duty, because it is agreeable to the intention of the Author of our being, who aims at the common good of his creatures, and, as an indication of his will, hath implanted the seeds of mutual benevolence in our souls; the interest, because the good of the whole is inseparable from that of the parts; in promoting, therefore, the common good, every one doth at the same time promote his own private interest. Another observation I shall draw from the premises is, that it makes a signal proof of the divinity of the Christian religion, that the main duty which it inculcates above all others is charity. Different maxims and precepts have distinguished the different sects of philosophy and religion; our Lord's peculiar precept is, "Love thy neighbour as thyself. By this shall all men know that you are my disciples, if you love one another."

I will not say, that what is a most shining proof of our religion, is not often a reproach to its professors; but this I think very plain, that whether we regard the analogy of nature, as it appears in the mutual attraction or gravitations of the mundane system, in the general frame and constitu-tion of the human soul; or, lastly, in the ends and aptness which are discoverable in all parts of the visible and intel-lectual world; we shall not doubt but the precept, which is the characteristic of our religion, came from the Author of nature. Some of our modern free-thinkers would, indeed, insinuate the Christian morals to be defective, because, say they, there is no mention made in the gospel of the virtue of friendship. These sagacious men, if I might be allowed the use of that vulgar saying, "cannot see the wood for the trees." That a religion, whereof the main drift is to inspire its professors with the most noble and disinterested spirit of love, charity, and beneficence, to all mankind, or, in other words, with a friendship to every individual man, should be taxed with the want of that very virtue, is surely a glaring evidence of the blindness and prejudice of its adversaries.

EUSTACE BUDGELL

1686 Was born in Exeter, the son of a clergyman, and the cousin of Joseph Addison.

1705 Entered Trinity College, Oxford, afterward entering the Inner Temple and being called to the bar.

1709 Became clerk to Addison as secretary to the Lord Lieutenant of Ireland.

1711 Contributed thirty-seven papers to the *Spectator*.
Inherited nine hundred and fifty pounds a year upon the death of his father.

1715-1727 Served as a member of Parliament.

1717 Became under-secretary to Addison as Secretary of State.

1717-1718 Served as Accountant-General.

1719 Published a pamphlet against the peerage bill, thus siding with Steele against Addison in their political controversy.

1719-1728 Published various pamphlets of political or financial import.
Traveled abroad.
Lost £20,000 in the South Sea Bubble.
Became involved in various law suits.
Became affected mentally, thinking himself the victim of persecution.

1728 Spent £6,000 in an attempt to re-enter Parliament.
Published a complimentary poem upon the accession of George III.

1732 Published *Liberty and Property*, a pamphlet dealing with his litigations.
Published *Life and Character of the Earl of Orrery*, issuing a second edition in 1737.

1733-1735 Founded and edited *The Bee*, a weekly periodical.

1737 Was attacked by *The Grub Street Journal* concerning the matter of the Tindal inheritance, in which Budgell is thought to have been dishonest.
Drowned himself in the Thames at Dorset Stairs.

SIR ROGER'S HOUNDS[1]

——Vocat ingenti clamore Cithæron,
Taygetique canes.[2]

Virg. *Georg.* III, 43.

THOSE who have searched into human nature observe that nothing so much shows the nobleness of the soul, as that its felicity consists in action. Every man has such an active principle in him, that he will find out something to employ himself upon, in whatever place or state of life he is posted. I have heard of a gentleman who was under close confinement in the Bastile seven years, during which time he amused himself in scattering a few small pins about his chamber, gathering them up again, and placing them in different figures on the arm of a great chair. He often told his friends afterward, that unless he had found out this piece of exercise, he verily believed he should have lost his senses.

After what has been said, I need not inform my readers that Sir Roger, with whose character I hope they are at present pretty well acquainted, has in his youth gone through the whole course of those rural diversions which the country abounds in; and which seem to be extremely well suited to that laborious industry a man may observe here in a far greater degree than in towns and cities. I have before hinted at some of my friend's exploits: he has in his youthful days taken forty coveys of partridges in a season: and tired many a salmon with a line consisting of but a single hair. The constant thanks and good wishes of the neighbourhood always attended him on account of his remarkable enmity towards foxes; having destroyed more of those vermin in one year, than it was thought the whole country could have produced. Indeed the knight does not scruple to own among his most intimate friends, that in order to establish his reputation this way, he has secretly sent for great numbers of them

---

[1]*Spectator*, No. 116. Friday, July 13, 1711.
[2]The echoing hills and chiding hounds invite.

out of other counties, which he used to turn loose about the
country by night, that he might the better signalize himself
in their destruction the next day. His hunting horses were
the finest and best managed in all these parts. His tenants
are still full of the praises of a grey stone-horse that unhappily
staked himself several years since, and was buried with great
solemnity in the orchard.

Sir Roger being at present too old for fox-hunting, to keep
himself in action, has disposed of his beagles and got a pack
of stop-hounds. What these want in speed, he endeavours to
make amends for by the deepness of their mouths and the
variety of their notes, which are suited in such a manner to
each other, that the whole cry makes up a complete concert.
He is so nice in this particular, that a gentleman having made
him a present of a very fine hound the other day, the knight
returned it by the servant with a great many expressions of
civility; but desired him to tell his master that the dog he
had sent was indeed a most excellent bass, but that at present
he only wanted a counter-tenor. Could I believe my friend
had ever read Shakespeare, I should certainly conclude he
had taken the hint from Theseus in the *Midsummer Night's
Dream:*

> My hounds are bred out of the Spartan kind,
> So flu'd, so sanded; and their heads are hung
> With ears that sweep away the morning dew.
> Crook'd-kneed and dew-lap'd like Thessalian bulls,
> Slow in pursuit, but match'd in mouth like bells,
> Each under each. A cry more tuneable
> Was never halloo'd to, nor cheer'd with horn.

Sir Roger is so keen at this sport, that he has been out
almost every day since I came down; and upon the chaplain's
offering to lend me his easy pad, I was prevailed on yesterday morning to make one of the company. I was extremely
pleased, as we rid along, to observe the general benevolence
of all the neighbourhood towards my friend. The farmers'
sons thought themselves happy if they could open a gate

for the good old knight as he passed by; which he generally requited with a nod or a smile, and a kind inquiry after their fathers or uncles.

After we had rid about a mile from home, we came upon a large heath, and the sportsmen began to beat. They had done so for some time, when, as I was at a little distance from the rest of the company, I saw a hare pop out from a small furze-brake almost under my horse's feet. I marked the way she took, which I endeavoured to make the company sensible of by extending my arm; but to no purpose, till Sir Roger, who knows that none of my extraordinary motions are insignificant, rode up to me and asked me if puss was gone that way? Upon my answering yes, he immediately called in the dogs, and put them upon the scent. As they were going off, I heard one of the country fellows muttering to his companion, "that 'twas a wonder they had not lost all their sport, for want of the silent gentleman's crying, 'Stole away.'"

This, with my aversion to leaping hedges, made me withdraw to a rising ground, from whence I could have the pleasure of the whole chase, without the fatigue of keeping in with the hounds. The hare immediately threw them above a mile behind her; but I was pleased to find that, instead of running straight forwards, or, in hunter's language, "flying the country," as I was afraid she might have done, she wheeled about and described a sort of circle round the hill where I had taken my station, in such a manner as gave me a very distinct view of the sport. I could see her first pass by, and the dogs some time afterward unravelling the whole track she had made, and following her through all her doubles. I was at the same time delighted in observing that deference which the rest of the pack paid to each particular hound, according to the character he had acquired among them. If they were at fault, and an old hound of reputation opened but once, he was immediately followed by the whole cry; while a raw dog, or one who was a noted liar, might have yelped his heart out, without being taken notice of.

The hare now, after having squatted two or three times,

and being put up again as often, came still nearer to the
place where she was at first started.   The dogs pursued her,
and these were followed by the jolly knight, who rode upon a
white gelding, encompassed by his tenants and servants, and
cheering his hounds with all the gaiety of five-and-twenty.
One of the sportsmen rode up to me, and told me, that he was
sure the chase was almost at an end, because the old dogs,
which had hitherto lain behind, now headed the pack.   The
fellow was in the right.   Our hare took a large field just under
us, followed by the full cry in view.   I must confess the brightness of the weather, the cheerfulness of every thing around
me, the chiding of the hounds, which was returned upon us in
a double echo from two neighbouring hills, with the hallooing
of the sportsmen, and the sounding of the horn, lifted my
spirits into a most lively pleasure, which I freely indulged
because I was sure it was innocent.   If I was under any concern, it was on account of the poor hare, that was now quite
spent, and almost within the reach of her enemies; when the
huntsman getting forward, threw down his pole before the
dogs.   They were now within eight yards of that game which
they had been pursuing for almost as many hours; yet on the
signal before-mentioned they all made a sudden stand, and
though they continued opening as much as before, durst
not once attempt to pass beyond the pole.   At the same time
Sir Roger rode forward, and alighting, took up the hare in his
arms; which he soon after delivered up to one of his servants
with an order if she could be kept alive, to let her go in his
great orchard; where it seems he has several of these prisoners
of war, who live together in a very comfortable captivity.   I
was highly pleased to see the discipline of the pack, and the
good-nature of the knight, who could not find in his heart to
murder a creature that had given him so much diversion.

As we were returning home, I remembered that Monsieur
Paschal, in his most excellent discourse on the Misery of
Man, tells us, that all our endeavours after greatness proceed
from nothing but a desire of being surrounded by a multitude
of persons and affairs that may hinder us from looking into

ourselves, which is a view we cannot bear. He afterwards goes on to shew that our love of sports comes from the same reason, and is particularly severe upon hunting. "What," says he, "unless it be to drown thought, can make them throw away so much time and pains upon a silly animal, which they might buy cheaper in the market?" The foregoing reflection is certainly just, when a man suffers his whole mind to be drawn into his sports, and altogether loses himself in the woods; but does not affect those who propose a far more laudable end from this exercise, I mean the preservation of health, and keeping all the organs of the soul in a condition to execute her orders. Had that incomparable person whom I last quoted been a little more indulgent to himself in this point, the world might probably have enjoyed him much longer; whereas, through too great an application to his studies in his youth, he contracted that ill habit of body, which, after a tedious sickness, carried him off in the fortieth year of his age; and the whole history we have of his life till that time is but one continued account of the behaviour of a noble soul struggling under innumerable pains and distempers.

For my own part, I intend to hunt twice a week during my stay with Sir Roger; and shall prescribe the moderate use of this exercise to all my country friends, as the best kind of physic for mending a bad constitution, and preserving a good one.

I cannot do this better, than in the following lines out of Mr. Dryden:

> The first physicians by debauch were made;
> Excess began, and Sloth sustains the trade.
> By chase our long-liv'd fathers earn'd their food;
> Toil strung the nerves, and purify'd the blood;
> But we their sons, a pamper'd race of men,
> Are dwindled down to three-score years and ten.
> Better to hunt in fields for health unbought,
> Than fee the doctor for a nauseous draught.
> The wise for cure on exercise depend:
> God never made His work for man to mend.

ALEXANDER POPE

1688   Born in London, the son of a wealthy merchant. Educated privately.

1709   Published Pastorals, a fragment translated from Homer, and a modernized version of one of Chaucer's "Canterbury Tales" in Tonson's *Miscellany*, work which he claimed to have done at the age of sixteen.

1711   Published *An Essay on Criticism*.
Made the acquaintance of Addison and his circle.

1712   Published first version of *The Rape of the Lock*; second version appeared in 1714.
Published the "Messiah" in the *Spectator*.

1713   Published *Windsor Forest*.
Issued proposals for a translation of the *Iliad*.
Became a member of the Scriblerus Club.
Contributed to the *Guardian*.
Composed, at the request of Addison, a prologue for *Cato*.
Drew away from Addison and his group, having come under the social and political influence of Swift.

1715   Published the first volume of the *Iliad*.

1717   Published collected *Works*.
Declined to renounce the Catholic religion in order to become eligible for political preferment.

1719   Took up his residence at Twickenham, where he built the "Grotto."

1720   Finished translating the *Iliad*, a work which is said to have netted him $30,000.

1725   Issued an edition of Shakespeare.

1726   Finished translating the *Odyssey*.

1728   Published first version of *The Dunciad*; second version appeared in 1742.

1731   Published *Moral Essays*.

1732   Published *An Essay on Man*.

1735   Published *Epistle to Dr. Arbuthnot*.

1733   Published *Imitations of Horace*.

1744   Died, and was buried in Twickenham Church.

ON CRUELTY TO ANIMALS[1]

——Primaque e cæde ferarum
Incaluisse putem maculatum sanguine ferrum.[2]

Ovid. *Met.* XV, 106.

I CANNOT think it extravagant to imagine, that mankind
are no less in proportion accountable for the ill use of their
dominion over creatures of the lower rank of beings, than for
the exercise of tyranny over their own species. The more
entirely the inferior creation is submitted to our power, the
more answerable we should seem for our mismanagement
of it; and the rather, as the very condition of nature renders
these creatures incapable of receiving any recompense in
another life for their ill treatment in this.

It is observable of those noxious animals, which have qualities most powerful to injure us, that they naturally avoid
mankind, and never hurt us unless provoked or necessitated
by hunger. Man, on the other hand, seeks out and pursues
even the most inoffensive animals, on purpose to persecute
and destroy them.

Montaigne thinks it some reflection upon human nature
itself, that few people take delight in seeing beasts caress
or play together, but almost every one is pleased to see them
lacerate and worry one another. I am sorry this temper is
become almost a distinguishing character of our nation,
from the observation which is made by foreigners of our
beloved pastimes, bear-bating, cock-fighting, and the like.
We should find it hard to vindicate the destroying of anything
that has life, merely out of wantonness; yet in this principle
our children are bred up, and one of the first pleasures we
allow them is the license of inflicting pain upon poor animals;
almost as soon as we are sensible what life is ourselves, we
make it our sport to take it from other creatures. I cannot

---

[1] *Guardian*, No. 61. Thursday, May 21, 1713.
[2] Th' essay of bloody feasts on brutes began,
And after forged the sword to murder man. Dryden.

but believe a very good use might be made of the fancy which children have for birds, and insects. Mr. Locke takes notice of a mother who permitted them to her children, but rewarded or punished them as they treated them well or ill. This was no other than entering them betimes into a daily exercise of humanity, and improving their very diversion to a virtue.

I fancy, too, some advantage might be taken of the common notion, that it is ominous or unlucky to destroy some sorts of birds, as swallows and martins; this opinion might possibly arise from the confidence these birds seem to put in us by building under our roofs, so that it is a kind of violation of the laws of hospitality, to murder them. As for robin-redbreasts in particular, it is not improbable they owe their security to the old ballad of the *Children in the Wood*. However it be, I do not know, I say, why this prejudice, well improved and carried as far as it would go, might not be made to conduce to the preservation of many innocent creatures, which are now exposed to all the wantonness of an ignorant barbarity.

There are other animals that have the misfortune, for no manner of reason, to be treated as common enemies wherever found. The conceit that a cat has nine lives, has cost at least nine lives in ten of the whole race of them. Scarce a boy in the streets but has in this point outdone Hercules himself, who was famous for killing a monster that had but three lives. Whether the unaccountable animosity against this useful domestic may be any cause of the general persecution of owls, who are a sort of feathered cats, or whether it be only an unreasonable pique the moderns have taken to a serious countenance, I shall not determine. Though I am inclined to believe the former; since I observe the sole reason alleged for the destruction of frogs, is because they are like toads. Yet amidst all the misfortunes of these unfriended creatures, it is some happiness that we have not yet taken a fancy to eat them; for should our countrymen refine upon the French never so little, it is not to be conceived to what unheard-of torments owls, cats, and frogs may be yet reserved.

When we grow up to men, we have another succession of sanguinary sports; in particular, hunting. I dare not attack a diversion which has such authority and custom to support it; but must have leave to be of opinion, that the agitation of that exercise, with the example and number of the chasers, not a little contribute to resist those checks, which compassion would naturally suggest in behalf of the animal pursued. Nor shall I say with Monsieur Fleury, that this sport is a remain of the Gothic barbarity. But I must animadvert upon a certain custom yet in use with us, and barbarous enough to be derived from the Goths, or even the Scythians; I mean that savage compliment our huntsmen pass upon ladies of quality, who are present at the death of a stag, when they put the knife in their hands to cut the throat of a helpless, trembling, and weeping creature.

——*Questuque cruentus,*
Atque imploranti similis.——[1]
Virg. Æn. VII, 5.

But if our sports are destructive, our gluttony is more so, and in a more inhuman manner. Lobsters roasted alive, pigs whipt to death, fowls sewed up, are testimonies of our outrageous luxury. Those who, as Seneca expresses it, divide their lives betwixt an anxious conscience and a nauseated stomach, have a just reward of their gluttony in the diseases it brings with it; for human savages, like other wild beasts, find snares and poison in the provisions of life, and are allured by their appetite to their destruction. I know nothing more shocking or horrid than the prospect of one of their kitchens covered with blood, and filled with the cries of creatures expiring in tortures. It gives one an image of a giant's-den in a romance, bestrewed with the scattered heads and mangled limbs of those who were slain by his cruelty.

The excellent Plutarch, who has more strokes of goodnature in his writings than I remember in any other author,

[1]——That lies beneath the knife,
Looks up, and from her butcher begs her life.

cites a saying of Cato to this effect: "That it is no easy task to preach to the belly, which has no ears." "Yet if," says he, "we are ashamed to be so out of fashion as not to offend, let us at least offend with some discretion and measure. If we kill an animal for our provision, let us do it with the meltings of compassion, and without tormenting it. Let us consider, that it is in its own nature cruelty to put a living creature to death; we at least destroy a soul that has sense and perception."—In the life of Cato the Censor, he takes occasion, from the severe disposition of that man, to discourse in this manner: "It ought to be esteemed a happiness to mankind, that our humanity has a wider sphere to exert itself in than bare justice. It is no more than the obligation of our very birth to practise equity to our own kind; but humanity may be extended through the whole order of creatures, even to the meanest. Such actions of charity are the overflowings of a mild good-nature on all below us. It is certainly the part of a well-natured man to take care of his horses and dogs, not only in expectation of their labour while they are foals and whelps, but even when their old age has made them incapable of service."

History tells us of a wise and polite nation that rejected a person of the first quality, who stood for a judiciary office, only because he had been observed in his youth to take pleasure in tearing and murdering of birds. And of another that expelled a man out of the senate, for dashing a bird against the ground which had taken shelter in his bosom. Every one knows how remarkable the Turks are for their humanity in this kind. I remember an Arabian author, who has written a treatise to show how far a man supposed to have subsisted in a desert island, without any instruction, or so much as the sight of any other man, may, by the pure light of nature, attain the knowledge of philosophy and virtue. One of the first things he makes him observe is, that universal benevolence of nature in the protection and preservation of its creatures. In imitation of which, the first act of virtue he thinks his self-taught philosopher would of course fall into is, to relieve and assist all the animals about him in their wants and distresses.

Ovid has some very tender and pathetic lines applicable to this occasion:

> *Quid meruistis, oves, placidum pecus, inque tegendos*
> *Natum homines, plenu quae fertis in ubere nectar?*
> *Mollia quae nobis vestras velamina lanas*
> *Praebetis; vitaque magis quam morte juvatis.*
> *Quid meruere boves, animal sine fraude dolisque,*
> *Innocuum, simplex, natum tolerare labores?*
> *Immemor est demum, nec frugum munere dignus,*
> *Qui potuit, curvi dempto modo pondere aratri,*
> *Ruricolam mactare suum.——*
>
> Met. XV, 116.

* * * * * * * * *

> *Quam male consuevit, quam se parat ille curori*
> *Impius humano, vituli qui guttura cultro*
> *Rumpit, et immotas praebet mugitibus aures!*
> *Aut qui vagitus similes puerilibus haedum*
> *Edentem jugulare potest!——*[1]
>
> Ib. 463.

Perhaps that voice or cry so nearly resembling the human, with which Providence has endued so many different animals, might purposely be given them to move our pity, and prevent those cruelties we are too apt to inflict on our fellow-creatures.

There is a passage in the book of Jonas, when God declares his unwillingness to destroy Nineveh, where methinks that

---

[1] The sheep was sacrificed on no pretence,
But meek and unresisting innocence.
A patient, useful creature, born to bear
The warm and woolly fleece, that clothed her murderer;
And daily to give down the milk she bred,
A tribute for the grass on which she fed,
Living, both food and raiment she supplies,
And is of least advantage when she dies.
How did the toiling ox his death deserve;
A downright simple drudge, and born to serve?

compassion of the Creator, which extends to the meanest rank of his creatures, is expressed with wonderful tenderness.—"Should I not spare Nineveh, that great city, wherein are more than six score thousand persons—and also much cattle?" And we have in Deuteronomy a precept of great good-nature of this sort, with a blessing in form annexed to it, in those words: "If thou shalt find a bird's nest in the way, thou shalt not take the dam with the young: But thou shalt in any wise let the dam go; that it may be well with thee, and that thou mayest prolong thy days."

To conclude, there is certainly a degree of gratitude owing to those animals that serve us. As for such as are mortal or noxious, we have a right to destroy them; and for those that are neither of advantage nor prejudice to us, the common enjoyment of life is what I cannot think we ought to deprive them of.

This whole matter with regard to each of these considerations, is set in a very agreeable light in one of the Persian fables of Pilpay, with which I shall end this paper.

A traveller passing through a thicket, and seeing a few sparks of a fire, which some passengers had kindled as they went that way before, made up to it. On a sudden, the sparks

---

O tyrant! with what justice canst thou hope
The promise of the year, a plenteous crop;
When thou destroy'st thy lab'ring steer, who till'd,
And ploughed with pains, thy else ungrateful field!
From his yet reeking neck to draw the yoke,
That neck, with which the surly clods he broke:
And to the hatchet yield thy husbandman,
Who finish'd autumn, and the spring began?

*   *   *   *   *   *   *   *   *

What more advance can mortals make in sin
So near perfection, who with blood begin?
Deaf to the calf that lies beneath the knife,
Looks up, and from her butcher begs her life:
Deaf to the harmless kid, that, ere he dies,
All methods to secure thy mercy tries,
And imitates in vain the children's cries. Dryden.

caught hold of a bush in the midst of which lay an adder, and set it in flames. The adder intreated the traveller's assistance, who, tying a bag to the end of his staff, reached it, and drew him out: he then bid him go where he pleased, but never more be hurtful to men, since he owed his life to a man's compassion. The adder, however, prepared to sting him, and when he expostulated how unjust it was to retaliate good with evil, "I shall do no more," said the adder, "than what you men practise every day, whose custom it is to requite benefits with ingratitude. If you cannot deny this truth, let us refer it to the first we meet." The man consented, and seeing a tree, put the question to it, in what manner a good turn was to be recompensed? "If you mean according to the usage of men," replied the tree, "by its contrary: I have been standing here these hundred years to protect them from the scorching sun, and in requital they have cut down my branches, and are going to saw my body into planks." Upon this, the adder insulting the man, he appealed to a second evidence, which was granted, and immediately they met a cow. The same demand was made, and much the same answer given, that among men it was certainly so. "I know it," said the cow, "by woeful experience; for I have served a man this long time with milk, butter, and cheese, and brought him besides a calf every year; but now I am old, he turns me into this pasture with design to sell me to a butcher, who will shortly make an end of me." The traveller upon this stood confounded, but desired, of courtesy, one trial more, to be finally judged by the next beast they should meet. This happened to be a fox, who, upon hearing the story in all its circumstances, could not be persuaded it was possible for the adder to enter into so narrow a bag. The adder, to convince him, went in again; when the fox told the man he had now his enemy in his power, and with that he fastened the bag, and crushed him to pieces.

THE SHORT CLUB[1]

——Inest sua gratia parvis.[2]

IT IS the great rule of behaviour "to follow nature." The author of the following letter is so much convinced of this truth, that he turns what would render a man of a little soul exceptious, humorsome, and particular in all his actions, to a subject of raillery and mirth. He is, you must know, but half as tall as an ordinary man, but is contented to be still at his friend's elbow, and has set up a club, by which he hopes to bring those of his own size into a little reputation.

"To NESTOR IRONSIDE, ESQ.,
"SIR,
"I remember a saying of yours concerning persons in low circumstances of stature, that their littleness would hardly be taken notice of, if they did not manifest a consciousness of it themselves in all their behaviour. Indeed, that observation that no man is ridiculous, for being what he is, but only in the affectation of being something more, is equally true in regard to the mind and the body.

"I question not but it will be pleasing to you to hear that a set of us have formed a society, who are sworn to 'dare to be short,' and boldly bear out the dignity of littleness under the noses of those enormous engrossers of manhood, those hyperbolical monsters of the species, the tall fellows that overlook us.

"The day of our institution was the tenth of December, being the shortest of the year, on which we are to hold an annual feast over a dish of shrimps.

"The place we have chosen for this meeting is in the Little Piazza, not without an eye to the neighbourhood of Mr. Powel's opera, for the performers of which we have, as becomes us, a brotherly affection.

---

[1]*Guardian*, No. 91. Thursday, June 25, 1713.
[2]Little things have their value.

"At our first resort hither, an old woman brought her son to the club-room, desiring he might be educated in this school, because she saw here were finer boys than ordinary. However, this accident no way discouraged our designs. We began with sending invitations to those of a stature not exceeding five foot, to repair to our assembly; but the greater part returned excuses, or pretended they were not qualified.

"One said he was, indeed, but five foot at present, but represented that he should soon exceed that proportion, his periwig-maker and shoemaker having lately promised him three inches more betwixt them.

"Another alleged, he was so unfortunate as to have one leg shorter than the other, and whoever had determined his stature to five foot, had taken him at a disadvantage; for when he was mounted on the other leg, he was at least five foot two inches and a half.

"There were some who questioned the exactness of our measures; and others, instead of complying, returned us informations of people yet shorter than themselves. In a word, almost every one recommended some neighbour or acquaintance, whom he was willing we should look upon to be less than he. We were not a little ashamed that those who are past the years of growth, and whose beards pronounce them men, should be guilty of as many unfair tricks in this point, as the most aspiring children when they are measured.

"We therefore proceeded to fit up the club-room, and provide conveniences for our accommodation. In the first place, we caused a total removal of all the chairs, stools, and tables, which had served the gross of mankind for many years. The disadvantages we had undergone while we made use of these, were unspeakable. The president's whole body was sunk in the elbow-chair; and when his arms were spread over it, he appeared, to the great lessening of his dignity, like a child in a go-cart. It was also so wide in the seat, as to give a wag occasion of saying, that, notwithstanding the president sat in it, there was a *sede vacante.*[1]

---

[1] Vacant seat.

"The table was so high, that one who came by chance to the door, seeing our chins just above the pewter dishes, took us for a circle of men that sat ready to be shaved, and sent in half a dozen barbers. Another time, one of the club spoke contumeliously of the president, imagining he had been absent, when he was only eclipsed by a flask of Florence, which stood on the table in a parallel line before his face. We therefore new-furnished the room in all respects proportionably to us, and had the door made lower, so as to admit no man above five foot high, without brushing his foretop, which, whoever does, is utterly unqualified to sit among us.

"Some of the statutes of the club are as follows:—

"I. If it be proved upon any member, though never so duly qualified, that he strives as much as possible to get above his size, by stretching, cocking, or the like; or that he hath stood on tiptoe in a crowd, with design to be taken for as tall a man as the rest; or hath privily conveyed any large book, cricket, or other device under him, to exalt him on his seat; every such offender shall be sentenced to walk in pumps for a whole month.

"II. If any member shall take advantage from the fulness or length of his wig, or any part of his dress, or the immoderate extent of his hat, or otherwise, to seem larger or higher than he is; it is ordered, he shall wear red heels to his shoes, and a red feather in his hat, which may apparently mark and set bounds to the extremities of his small dimension, that all people may readily find him out between his hat and his shoes.

"III. If any member shall purchase a horse for his own riding above fourteen hands and a half in height, that horse shall forthwith be sold, a Scotch galloway bought in its stead for him, and the overplus of the money shall treat the club.

"IV. If any member, in direct contradiction to the fundamental laws of the society, shall wear the heels of his shoes exceeding one inch and a half, it shall be interpreted as an open renunciation of littleness, and the criminal shall instantly be expelled. NOTE: The form to be used in expelling a member shall be in these words: 'Go from among us, and be tall if you can!'

"It is the unanimous opinion of our whole society, that since the race of mankind is granted to have decreased in stature from the beginning to this present, it is the intent of nature itself, that men should be little; and we believe that all human kind shall at last grow down to perfection, that is to say, be reduced to our own measure.

"I am, very literally,

"Your humble servant,

"BOB SHORT"

PHILIP DORMER STANHOPE
EARL OF CHESTERFIELD

1694   Was born in London, the son of Philip Stanhope, third earl of Chesterfield.

1712   Entered Trinity Hall, Cambridge.

1714   Left Cambridge and went abroad.

1715   Was appointed gentleman of the bedchamber to the Prince of Wales. Entered the House of Commons.

1723   Was appointed captain of the gentleman-pensioners. Failed of re-election to Parliament.

1726   Occurred the death of his father and his succession to the peerage.

1728   Became ambassador to The Hague.

1730   Opened negotiations for the marriage of William of Orange with the Princess Anne.

1732   Resigned his embassy because of ill health.
Became the father of Philip Stanhope by Mlle. du Bouchet.

1733   Married a natural daughter of George I.

1733–1745 Served in Parliament as a powerful member of the opposition.

1737   Began the famous series of *Letters* to his son, published by Dodsley in 1774.

1737–1739 Contributed to *Common Sense.*

1745   Sent on an embassy to The Hague.

1746–1748 Served as Secretary of State.

1747   Failed to acknowledge Dr. Johnson's overtures to sponsor the *Dictionary.*

1753–1754 Contributed to the *World* two papers in praise of Johnson among other contributions.

1755   Became the object of Johnson's censure of literary patronage.

1761–1770 Addressed a series of letters, similar in manner and purpose to those addressed to his natural son, to his godson Philip Stanhope.

1768   Occurred the death of Philip Stanhope, his natural son.

1769   Sat to Gainsborough for his portrait.

1773   Died in Chesterfield House, London.

A DRINKING CLUB[1]

I

An old friend and fellow-student of mine at the university called upon me the other morning, and found me reading Plato's *Symposion*. I laid down my book to receive him, which, after the first usual compliments, he took up, saying, "You will give me leave to see what was the object of your studies." "Nothing less than the divine Plato," said I, "that amiable philosopher—" "with whom (interrupted my friend) Cicero declares that he would rather be in the wrong, than in the right way with any other." "I cannot," replied I, "carry my veneration for him to that degree of enthusiasm; but yet, wherever I understand him (for I confess I do not everywhere) I prefer him to all the ancient philosophers. His *Symposion* more particularly engages and entertains me, as I see there the manners and characters of the most eminent men, of the politest times, of the politest city of Greece. And, with all due respect to the moderns, I much question whether an account of a modern Symposion, though written by the ablest hand, could be read with so much pleasure and improvement." "I do not know that," replied my friend, "for though I revere the ancients as much as you possibly can, and look upon the moderns as pigmies, when compared to those giants, yet if we come up to, or near them in any thing, it is the elegancy and delicacy of our convivial intercourse."

I was the more surprized at this doubt of my friend's, because I knew that he implicitly subscribed to, and superstitiously maintained, all the articles of the classical faith. I therefore asked him whether he was serious? He answered me that he was: that in his mind, Plato spun out that silly affair of love too fine and too long; and that if I would but let him introduce me to the club, of which he was an unworthy member, he believed I should at least entertain the same

[1]*World*, No. 90. Thursday, September 19, 1754.

doubt, or perhaps even decide in favour of the moderns. I thanked my friend for his kind offer, but added, that in whatever society he was an unworthy member, I should be still a more unworthy guest. That moreover my retired and domestic turn of life was as inconsistent with the engagements of a club, as my natural taciturnity amongst strangers would be misplaced in the midst of all that festal mirth and gaiety. "You mistake me (answered my friend); every member of our club has the privilege of bringing one friend along with him, who is by no means thereby engaged to become a member of it; and as for your taciturnity, we have some silent members, who, by the way, are none of our worst. Silent people never spoil company, but on the contrary, by being good hearers, encourage good speakers." "But I have another difficulty (answered I) and that, I doubt, a very solid one, which is, that I drink nothing but water." "So much the worse for you (replied my friend, who, by the by, loves his bottle most academically); you will pay for the claret you do not drink. We use no compulsion; every one drinks as little as he pleases—" "Which I presume (interrupted I) is as much as he can." "That is just as it happens," said he; "sometimes, it is true, we make pretty good sittings; but for my own part I choose to go home always before eleven: for, take my word for it, it is the sitting up late, and not the drink, that destroys the constitution." As I found that my friend would have taken a refusal ill, I told him that for this once I would certainly attend him to the club, but desired him to give me previously the outlines of the characters of the sitting members, that I might know how to behave myself properly. "Your precaution (said he) is a prudent one, and I will make you so well acquainted with them beforehand, that you shall not seem a stranger when among them. You must know then that our club consists of at least forty members when complete. Of these, many are now in the country: and besides, we have some vacancies which cannot be filled up till next winter. Palsies and apoplexies have of late, I don't know why, been pretty rife among us, and carried off a good many. It is not above a week ago, that poor Tom Toastwell fell on a sudden under the table, as we thought only a little in drink, but he was carried home, and never spoke more. Those whom you will probably meet with to-day are, first of all, Lord Feeble, a nobleman of admirable sense, a true fine gentleman, and, for a man of quality, a pretty classic. He has lived rather fast formerly, and impaired his constitution by sitting up late, and drinking your thin sharp wines. He is still what you call nervous, which makes him a little low spirited and reserved at first; but he grows very affable and cheerful as soon as he has warmed his stomach with about a bottle of good claret.

"Sir Tunbelly Guzzle is a very worthy north-country baronet, of a good estate, and one who was beforehand in the world, till being twice chosen knight of the shire, and having in consequence got a pretty employment at court, he ran out considerably. He has left off housekeeping, and is now upon a retrieving scheme. He is the heartiest, honestest fellow living; and though he is a man of very few words, I can assure you he does not want sense. He had a university education, and has a good notion of the classics. The poor man is confined half the year at least with the gout, and has besides an inveterate scurvy, which I cannot account for: no man can live more regularly; he eats nothing but plain meat, and very little of that: he drinks no thin wines, and never sits up late; for he has his full dose by eleven.

"Colonel Culverin is a brave old experienced officer, though but a lieutenant-colonel of foot. Between you and me, he has had great injustice done him, and is now commanded by many who were not born when he first came into the army. He has served in Ireland, Minorca, and Gibralter; and would have been in all the late battles in Flanders, had the regiment been ordered there. It is a pleasure to hear him talk of war. He is the best natured man alive, but a little too jealous of his honour, and too apt to be in a passion; but that is soon over, and then he is sorry for it. I fear he is dropsical, which I impute to his drinking your champaigns and burgundies. He got that ill habit abroad.

"Sir George Plyant is well born, has a genteel fortune, keeps the very best company, and is to be sure one of the best bred men alive: he is so good natured, that he seems to have no will of his own. He will drink as little or as much as you please, and no matter of what. He has been a mighty man with the ladies formerly, and loves the crack of the whip still. He is our news-monger; for being a gentleman of the privy-chamber, he goes to court every day, and consequently knows pretty well what is going forward there. Poor gentleman! I fear we shall not keep him long; for he seems far gone in a consumption, though the doctors say it is only a nervous atrophy.

"Will Sitfast is the best natured fellow living, and an excellent companion, though he seldom speaks; but he is no flincher, and sits every man's hand out at the club. He is a very good scholar, and can write very pretty Latin verses. I doubt he is in a declining way; for a paralytic stroke has lately twitched up one side of his mouth so, that he is now obliged to take his wine diagonally. However, he keeps up his spirits bravely, and never shames his glass.

"Doctor Carbuncle is an honest, jolly, merry parson, well affected to the government, and much of a gentleman. He is the life of our club, instead of being the least restraint upon it. He is an admirable scholar, and I really believe has all Horace by heart; I know he has him always in his pocket. His red face, inflamed nose, and swelled legs, make him generally thought a hard drinker by those who do not know him; but I must do him the justice to say, that I never saw him disguised with liquor in my life. It is true, he is a very large man, and can hold a great deal, which makes the colonel call him, pleasantly enough, a vessel of election.

"The last and least (concluded my friend) is your humble servant, such as I am; and if you please we will go and walk in the park till dinner time." I agreed, and we set out to-

gether. But here the reader will perhaps expect that I
should let him walk on a little, while I give his character.
We were of the same year of St. John's College in Cambridge:
he was a younger brother of a good family, was bred to the
church, and had just got a fellowship in the college, when his
elder brother dying, he succeeded to an easy fortune, and resolved to make himself easy with it, that is, to do nothing.
As he had resided long in college, he had contracted all the
habits and prejudices, the laziness, the soaking, the pride,
and the pedantry of the cloister, which after a certain time
are never to be rubbed off. He considered the critical knowledge of the Greek and Latin words as the utmost effort of
the human understanding, and a glass of good wine in good
company, as the highest pitch of human felicity. Accordingly he passes his mornings in reading the classics, most of
which he has long had by heart, and his evenings in drinking
his glass of good wine, which by frequent filling, amounts at
least to two, and often to three bottles a day. I must not
omit mentioning that my friend is tormented with the stone,
which misfortune he imputes to his once having drank water
for a month, by the prescription of the late Doctor Cheyne,
and by no means to at least two quarts of claret a day, for
these last thirty years. To return to my friend: "I am very
much mistaken," said he, as we were walking in the park,
"if you do not thank me for procuring this day's entertainment: for a set of worthier gentlemen to be sure never lived."
"I make no doubt of it," said I, "and am therefore the more
concerned when I reflect that this club of worthy gentlemen
might, by your own account, be not improperly called an
hospital of incurables, as there is not one among them who
does not labour under some chronical and mortal distemper."
"I see what you would be at," answered my friend, "you
would insinuate that it is all owing to wine: but let me assure
you, Mr. Fitz-Adam, *that wine, especially claret, if neat and
good, can hurt no man.*" I did not reply to this aphorism of
my friend's, which I knew would draw on too long a discussion, especially as we were just going into the clubroom,

where I took it for granted that it was one of the great con-
stitutional principles. The account of this modern Symposion shall be the subject of my next paper.

II[1]

My friend presented me to the company, in what he
thought the most obliging manner; but which, I confess, put
me a little out of countenance. "Give me leave, gentlemen,"
said he, "to present to you my old friend Mr. Fitz-Adam,
the ingenious author of the *World*." The word author instantly excited the attention of the whole company, and drew
all their eyes upon me: for people who are not apt to write
themselves, have a strange curiosity to see a live author.
The gentlemen received me in common, with those gestures
that intimate welcome; and I on my part respectfully muttered some of those nothings, which stand instead of the
something one should say, and perhaps do full as well.

The weather being hot, the gentlemen were refreshing
themselves before dinner, with what they called a cool
tankard; in which they successively drank to me. When it
came to my turn, I thought I could not decently decline
drinking the gentlemen's healths, which I did aggregately:
but how was I surprized, when upon the first taste I discovered that this cooling and refreshing draught was composed of the strongest mountain wine, lowered indeed with a
very little lemon and water, but then heightened again, by a
quantity of those comfortable aromatics, nutmeg and ginger!
Dinner, which had been called for more than once with some
impatience, was at last brought up, upon the colonel's threatening perdition to the master and all the waiters of the house,
if it was delayed two minutes longer. We sat down without ceremony, and we were no sooner sat down than everybody (except myself) drank everybody's health, which made
a tumultuous kind of noise. I observed with surprize, that
the common quantity of wine was put into glasses of an im-

[1]*World*, No. 91. Thursday, September 26, 1754.

mense size and weight; but my surprize ceased when I saw
the tremulous hands that took them, and for which I supposed they were intended as ballast. But even this precaution did not protect the nose of Doctor Carbuncle from a
severe shock, in his attempt to hit his mouth. The colonel,
who observed this accident, cried out pleasantly, "Why,
doctor, I find you are but a bad engineer. While you aim
at your mouth you will never hit it, take my word for it.
A floating battery, to hit the mark, must be pointed something above, or below it. If you would hit your mouth,
direct your four-pounder at your forehead, or your chin."
The doctor good-humouredly thanked the colonel for the
hint, and promised him to communicate it to his friends at
Oxford, where, he owned, that he had seen many a good glass
of port spilt for want of it. Sir Tunbelly almost smiled,
Sir George laughed, and the whole company, some how or
other, applauded this elegant piece of railery. But alas!
things soon took a less pleasant turn; for an enormous but-
tock of boiled salt beef, which had succeeded the soup, proved
not to be sufficiently corned for Sir Tunbelly, who had bespoke it; and at the same time Lord Feeble took a dislike to
the claret, which he affirmed not to be the same which they
had drank the day before; it had no silkiness, went rough off
the tongue, and his lordship shrewdly suspected that it was
mixed with Benecarlo or some of those black wines. This
was a common cause, and excited universal attention. The
whole company tasted it seriously, and every one found a
different fault with it. The master of the house was immediately sent for up, examined, and treated as a criminal.
Sir Tunbelly reproached him with the freshness of the beef,
while at the same time all the others fell upon him for the
badness of his wines, telling him that it was not fit usage for
such good customers as they were, and in fine, threatening
him with a migration of the club to some other house. The
criminal laid the blame of the beef's not being corned enough
upon his cook, whom he promised to turn away; and attested heaven and earth that the wine was the very same

which they had all approved of the day before; and as he had a soul to be saved, was true Château Margàux. "Château devil (said the colonel with warmth) it is your d——d rough Chaos wine." Will Sitfast, who thought himself obliged to articulate upon this occasion, said, he was not sure it was a mixed wine, but that indeed it drank down. "If that is all (interrupted the doctor) let us e'en drink it up then. Or, if that won't do, since we cannot have the true Falernum, let us take up for once with the vile Sabinum. What say you, gentlemen, to good honest port, which I am convinced is a much wholesomer stomach wine?" My friend, who in his heart loves port better than any other wine in the world, willingly seconded the doctor's motion, and spoke very favorably of your Portingal wines in general, if neat. Upon this some was immediately brought up, which I observed my friend and the doctor stuck to the whole evening. I could not help asking the doctor if he really preferred port to lighter wines? To which he answered, "You know, Mr. Fitz-Adam, that use is second to nature; and port is in a manner mother's milk to me; for it is what my *Alma Mater* suckles all her numerous progeny with." I silently assented to the doctor's account, which I was convinced was a true one, and then attended to the judicious animadversions of the other gentlemen upon the claret, which were still continued, though at the same time they continued to drink it. I hinted my surprize at this to Sir Tunbelly, who gravely answered me, and in a moving way, "Why, what can we do?" "Not drink it (replied I) since it is not good." "But what will you have us do? and how shall we pass the evening? (rejoined the baronet). One cannot go home at five o'clock." "That depends a great deal upon use," said I. "It may be so, to a certain degree (said the doctor). But give me leave to ask you, Mr. Fitz-Adam, you who drink nothing but water, and live much at home, how do you keep up your spirits?" "Why, doctor," said I, "as I never lowered my spirits by strong liquor, I do not want it to raise them." Here we were interrupted by the colonel's raising his voice and indignation against the burgundy and champaign, swearing that the former was ropy, and the latter upon the fret, and not without some suspicion of cider and sugar-candy; notwithstanding which, he drank, in a bumper of it, confusion to the town of Bristol and the bottle act. It was a shame, he said, that gentlemen could have no good burgundies and champaigns, for the sake of some increase of the revenue, the manufacture of glass bottles, and such sort of stuff. Sir George confirmed the same, adding that it was scandalous; and the whole company agreed, that the new parliament would certainly repeal so absurd an act the very first session; but if they did not, they hoped they would receive instructions to the purpose from their constituents. "To be sure," said the colonel. "What a d——d rout they made about the repeal of the jew-bill, for which nobody cared one farthing! But by the way (continued he) I think everybody has done eating, and therefore had not we better have the dinner taken away, and the wine set upon the table?" To this the company gave an unanimous Ay. While this was doing, I asked my friend, with seeming seriousness, whether no part of the dinner was to be served up again, when the wine should be set upon the table? He seemed surprized at my question, and asked me if I was hungry? To which I answered, No; but asked him in my turn if he was dry? To which he also answered, No. "Then pray," replied I, "why not as well eat without being hungry, as drink without being dry?" My friend was so stunned with this, that he attempted no reply, but stared at me with as much astonishment, as he would have done at my great ancestor Adam in his primitive state of nature.

The cloth was now taken away, and the bottles, glasses, and dish-clouts put upon the table; when Will Sitfast, who I found was perpetual toastmaker, took the chair, of course, as the man of application to business. He began the King's health in a bumper, which circulated in the same manner, not without some nice examinations of the chairman as to daylight. The bottle standing by me, I was called upon by the chairman, who added, that though a water-drinker, he hoped I would not refuse that health in wine. I begged to be excused, and told him that I never drank his Majesty's health at all, though no one of his subjects wished it more heartily than I did. That hitherto it had not appeared to me, that there could be the least relation between the wine I drank, and the king's state of health; and that till I was convinced that impairing my own health would improve his Majesty's, I was resolved to preserve the use of my faculties and my limbs, to employ both in his service, if he could ever have occasion for them. I had foreseen the consequences of this refusal; and though my friend had answered for my principles, I easily discovered an air of suspicion in the countenances of the company; and I overheard the colonel whisper to Lord Feeble, "This author is a very odd dog."

My friend was ashamed of me; but however, to help me off as well as he could, he said to me aloud, "Mr. Fitz-Adam, this is one of those singularities which you have contracted by living so much alone." From this moment the company gave me up to my oddnesses, and took no farther notice of me. I leaned silently upon the table, waiting for (though to say the truth, without expecting) some of that festal gaiety, that urbanity, and that elegant mirth, of which my friend had promised so large a share. Instead of all which, the conversation ran chiefly into narrative, and grew duller and duller with every bottle. Lord Feeble recounted his former achievements in love and wine; the colonel complained, though with dignity, of hardships and injustice; Sir George hinted at some important discoveries which he had made that day at court, but cautiously avoided naming names; Sir Tunbelly slept between glass and glass; the doctor and my friend talked over college matters, and quoted Latin; and our worthy president applied himself wholly to business, never speaking but to order; as, "Sir, the bottle stands with you; Sir, you are to name a toast; That has been drunk already; Here, more claret! &c." In the height of all this convivial pleasantry, which I plainly saw was come to its zenith,

I stole away at about nine o'clock, and went home; where
reflections upon the entertainment of the day crowded into
my mind, and may perhaps be the subject of some future
paper.

DR. JOHNSON'S DICTIONARY[1]

I HEARD the other day with great pleasure from my worthy
friend Mr. Dodsley, that Mr. Johnson's English Dictionary,
with a grammar and history of our language prefixed, will be
published this winter, in two large volumes in folio.

I had long lamented that we had no lawful standard of
our language set up, for those to repair to, who might choose
to speak and write it grammatically and correctly: and I have
as long wished that either some one person of distinguished
abilities would undertake the work singly, or that a certain
number of gentlemen would form themselves, or be formed
by the government, into a society for that purpose. The
late ingenious Doctor Swift proposed a plan of this nature to
his friend (as he thought him) the Lord Treasurer Oxford,
but without success; precision and perspicuity not being in
general the favourite objects of ministers, and perhaps still
less so of that minister, than of any other.

Many people have imagined that so extensive a work
would have been best performed by a number of persons,
who should have taken their several departments, of examining, sifting, winnowing (I borrow this image from the Italian
Crusca), purifying, and finally fixing our language, by incor-
porating their respective funds into one joint stock. But
whether this opinion be true or false, I think the public in
general, and the republic of letters in particular, greatly
obliged to Mr. Johnson, for having undertaken and executed
so great and desirable a work. Perfection is not to be expected from man; but if we are to judge by the various works
of Mr. Johnson, already published, we have good reason to
believe that he will bring this as near to perfection as any one

[1] *World*, No. 100. Thursday, November 28, 1754.

man could do. The plan of it, which he published some years ago, seems to me to be a proof of it. Nothing can be more rationally imagined, or more accurately and elegantly expressed. I therefore recommend the previous perusal of it to all those who intend to buy the dictionary, and who, I suppose, are all those who can afford it.

The celebrated dictionaries of the Florentine and French academies owe their present size and perfection to very small beginnings. Some private gentlemen of Florence, and some at Paris, had met at each other's houses to talk over and consider their respective language: upon which they published some short essays, which essays, were the embryos of those perfect productions, that now do so much honour to the two nations. Even Spain, which seems not to be the soil where, of late at least, letters have either prospered, or been cultivated, has produced a dictionary, and a good one too, of the Spanish language; in six large volumes in folio.

I cannot help thinking it a sort of disgrace to our nation, that hitherto we have had no such standard of our language; our dictionaries at present being more properly what our neighbours the Dutch and the Germans call theirs, *word-books*, than dictionaries in the superior sense of that title. All words, good and bad, are there jumbled indiscriminately together, insomuch that the injudicious reader may speak, and write as inelegantly, improperly, and vulgarly as he pleases, by and with the authority of one or other of our *word-books*.

It must be owned that our language is at present in a state of anarchy; and hitherto, perhaps, it may not have been the worse for it. During our free and open trade, many words and expressions have been imported, adopted, and naturalized from other languages, which have greatly enriched our own. Let it preserve what real strength and beauty it may have borrowed from others, but let it not, like the Tarpeian maid, be overwhelmed and crushed by unnecessary foreign ornaments. The time for discrimination seems to be now come. Toleration, adoption, and naturalization have run their lengths. Good order and authority are now necessary. But where shall we find them, and at the same time the obedience due to them? We must have recourse to the old Roman expedient in times of confusion, and choose a dictator. Upon this principle I give my vote for Mr. Johnson to fill that great and arduous post. And I hereby declare that I make a total surrender of all my rights and privileges in the English language, as a free-born British subject, to the said Mr. Johnson, during the term of his dictatorship. Nay more; I will not only obey him, like an old Roman, as my dictator, but, like a modern Roman, I will implicitly believe in him as my pope, and hold him to be infallible while in the chair; but no longer. More than this he cannot well require; for I presume that obedience can never be expected when there is neither terror to enforce, nor interest to invite it.

I confess that I have so much honest English pride, or perhaps prejudice about me, as to think myself more considerable for whatever contributes to the honour, the advantage, or the ornament of my native country. I have therefore a sensible pleasure in reflecting upon the rapid progress which our language has lately made, and still continues to make all over Europe. It is frequently spoken, and almost universally understood, in Holland; it is kindly entertained as a relation in the most civilized parts of Germany; and it is studied as a learned language, though yet little spoke, by all those in France and Italy, who either have, or pretend to have, any learning.

The spreading the French language over most parts of Europe, to the degree of making it almost an universal one, was always reckoned among the glories of the reign of Lewis the fourteenth. But be it remembered, that the success of his arms first opened the way to it; though at the same time it must be owned, that a great number of most excellent authors who flourished in this time, added strength and velocity to its progress. Whereas our language has made its way singly by its own weight and merit, under the conduct of those great leaders, Shakespeare, Bacon, Milton, Locke,

Newton, Swift, Pope, Addison, &c. A nobler sort of conquest and a far more glorious triumph, since graced by none but willing captives!

These authors, though for the most part but indifferently translated into foreign languages, gave other nations a sample of the British genius. The copies, imperfect as they were, pleased, and excited a general desire of seeing the originals: and both our authors and our language soon became classical.

But a grammar, a dictionary, and a history of our language, through its several stages, were still wanting at home, and importunately called for from abroad. Mr. Johnson's labours will now, and, I dare say, very fully, supply that want, and greatly contribute to the farther spreading of our language in other countries. Learners were discouraged by finding no standard to resort to, and consequently thought it incapable of any. They will now be undeceived and encouraged.

There are many hints and considerations relative to our language, which I should have taken the liberty of suggesting to Mr. Johnson, had I not been convinced that they have equally occurred to him: but there is one, and a very material one it is, to which perhaps he may not have given all the necessary attention. I mean the genteeler part of our language, which owes both its rise and progress to my fair countrywomen, whose natural turn is more to the copiousness, than to the correctness of diction. I would not advise him to be rash enough to proscribe any of those happy redundancies, and luxuriancies of expression, with which they have enriched our language. They willingly inflict letters, but very unwillingly submit to wear them. In this case his task will be so difficult, that I design, as a common friend, to propose in some future paper, the means which appear to me the most likely to reconcile matters.

P. S. I hope that none of my courteous readers will upon this occasion to be so uncourteous, as to suspect me of being a hired and interested puff of this work; for I most solemnly protest, that neither Mr. Johnson, nor any person employed by him, nor any bookseller or booksellers concerned in the success of it, have ever offered me the usual compliment of a pair of gloves or a bottle of wine; nor has even Mr. Dodsley, though my publisher, and, as I am informed, deeply interested in the sale of this dictionary, so much as invited me to take a bit of mutton with him.

SOAME JENYNS

1704   Was born in London, the son of Sir Roger Jenyns.
1722   Entered St. John's College, Cambridge.
1725   Left Cambridge without taking a degree.
1727   Published *The Art of Dancing: a Poem*, anonymously.
1735   Published *An Epistle to Lord Lovelace*, a poem.
1742–1780 Served as a member of Parliament.
1752   Published *Poems*, a collection of verse previously issued in Dodsley's *Miscellany*.
1755   Contributed to the *World*.
1757   Published *Enquiry into the Nature and Origin of Evil*.
1765   Published *The Objections to the Taxation of Our American Colonies Considered*.
1770   Published *Miscellanies*, consisting of essays previously contributed to the *World*, a number of poems, and the *Enquiry*.
1776   Published *View of the Internal Evidence of the Christian Religion*, a work which reached a tenth edition by 1798, and which was translated into several languages.
1782   Published *Disquisitions on Several Subjects*.
1784   Published *Thoughts on Parliamentary Reform*.
1787   Died in London.

A VISIT TO SIR JOHN JOLLY[1]

HAVING been frequently pressed by Sir John Jolly (an old friend of mine, possessed of a fine estate, a large park, and a plentiful fortune) to pass a few weeks with him in the country, I determined last autumn to accept his invitation, proposing to myself the highest pleasure from changing the noise and hurry of this bustling metropolis, for the agreeable silence, and soothing indolence of a rural retirement. I accordingly set out one morning, and pretty early on the next arrived at the habitation of my friend, situated in a most delicious and

----
[1]*World*, No. 153. Thursday, December 4, 1755.

romantic spot, which (the owner having fortunately no taste) is not yet defaced with improvements. On my approach, I abated a little of my travelling pace, to look round me, and admire the towering hills, and fertile vales, the winding streams, the stately woods, and spacious lawns, which, gilded by the sun-shine of a beautiful morning, on every side afforded a most enchanting prospect: and I pleased myself with the thoughts of the happy hours I should spend amidst these pastoral scenes, in reading, in meditation, or in soft repose, inspired by the lowing of distant herds, the falls of waters, and the melody of birds.

I was received with a hearty welcome, and many shakes of the hand, by my old friend, whom I had not seen for many years, except once, when he was called to town by a prosecution in the King's bench, for misunderstanding the sense of an act of parliament, which, on examination, was found to be nonsense. He is an honest gentleman of a middle age, a hale constitution, good natural parts, and abundant spirits, a keen sportsman, an active magistrate, and a tolerable farmer, not without some ambition of acquiring a seat in parliament, by his interest in a neighbouring borough; so that between his pursuits of game, of justice, and popularity, besides the management of a large quantity of land, which he keeps in his own hands, as he terms it, for amusement, every moment of his time is sufficiently employed. His wife is an agreeable woman, of about the same age, and has been handsome; but though years have somewhat impaired her charms, they have not in the least her relish for company, cards, balls, and all manner of public diversions.

On my arrival I was first conducted into the breakfast room, which, with some surprize, I saw quite filled with genteel persons of both sexes, in dishabille, with their hair in papers; the cause of which I was quickly informed of, by the many apologies of my lady for the meanness of the apartment she was obliged to allot me, "By reason the house was so crowded with company during the time of their races, which she said, began that very day for the whole week, and for which they were immediately preparing." I was instantly attacked by all present with one voice, or rather with many voices at the same time, to accompany them thither; to which I made no opposition, thinking it would be attended with more trouble than the expedition itself.

As soon as the ladies and the equipages were ready, we issued forth in a most magnificent cavalcade; and after travelling five or six miles through bad roads, we arrived at the Red Lion, just as the ordinary was making its appearance upon the table. The ceremonials of this sumptuous entertainment, which consisted of cold fish, lean chickens, rusty hams, raw venison, stale game, green fruit, and grapeless wine, destroyed at least two hours, with five times that number of heads, ruffles, and suits of clothes, by the unfortunate effusion of butter and gravy. From hence we proceeded a few miles farther to the race-ground, where nothing, I think, extraordinary happened, but that amongst much disorder and drunkenness, few limbs, and no necks, were broken: and from these Olympic games, which to the great emolument of pick-pockets, lasted till it was dark, we galloped back to the town through a soaking shower, to dress for the assembly. But this I found no easy task; nor could I possibly accomplish it, before my clothes were quite dried upon my back; my servant staying behind to settle his bets, and having stowed my portmanteau into the boot of some coach, which he could not find, to save himself both the trouble and indignity of carrying it.

Being at last equipped, I entered the ballroom, where the smell of the stable over which it was built, the savour of the neighbouring kitchen, the fumes of tallow-candles, rum-punch and tobacco, dispersed over the whole house, and the balsamic effluvias from many sweet creatures who were dancing, with almost equal strength contended for superiority. The company was numerous and well-drest, and differed not in any respect from that of the most brilliant assembly in London, but in seeming better pleased, and most desirous of pleasing; that is, happier in themselves, and civiller to each other. I observed the door was blocked up the whole night by a few fashionable young men, whose faces I remembered to have seen about town, who would neither dance, drink tea, play at cards, nor speak to any one, except now and then in whispers to a young lady, who sat at the upper end of the room, in a hat and negligée, with her back against the wall, her arms akimbo, her legs thrust out, a sneer on her lips, a scowl on her forehead, and an invincible assurance in her eyes. This lady I had also frequently met with, but could not then recollect where; but have since learnt, that she had been toad-eater to a woman of quality, and turned off for too close and presumptuous an imitation of her betters. Their behaviour affronted most of the company, yet obtained the desired effect: for I overheard several of the country ladies say, "It was pity they were so proud; for to be sure they were prodigious well-bred people, and had an immense deal of wit:" a mistake they could never have fallen into, had these patterns of politeness condescended to have entered into any conversation. Dancing and cards, with the refreshment of cold chickens and negus about twelve, carried us on till day break, when our coaches being ready, with much solicitation and more squeezing, I obtained a place in one, in which no more than six had before artificially seated themselves; and about five in the morning, through many and great perils, we arrived safely at home.

It was now the middle of harvest, which had not a little suffered by our diversions; and therefore our coach-horses were immediately degraded to a cart; and having rested during our fatigues, by a just distribution of things, were now obliged to labour, while we were at rest. I mean not in this number to include myself; for, though I hurried immediately to bed, no rest could I obtain for some time, for the rumbling of the carts, and the conversation of their drivers, just under my window. Fatigue at length got the better of all obstacles, and I fell asleep; but I had scarce closed my eyes, when I was awakened by a much louder noise, which was that of a whole pack of hounds, with their

vociferous attendants, setting out to meet my friend, and
some choice spirits, whom we had just left behind at the
assembly, and who chose this manner of refreshment after a
night's debauch, rather than the usual and inglorious one of
going to bed. These sounds dying away by their distance, I
again composed myself to rest; but was presently again
roused by more discordant tongues, uttering all the grossness
of Drury-lane, and scurrility of Billingsgate. I now waked
indeed with somewhat more satisfaction, at first thinking,
by this unpastoral dialogue, that I was once more returned
safe to London; but I soon found my mistake, and understood
that these were some innocent and honest neighbours of Sir
John's, who were come to determine their gentle disputes before his tribunal, and being ordered to wait till his return
from hunting, were resolved to make all possible use of this
suspension of justice. It being now towards noon, I gave
up all thoughts of sleep, and it was well I did; for I was presently alarmed by a confusion of voices, as loud, though somewhat sweeter than the former. As they proceeded from the
parlour under me, amidst much giggling, laughing, squeaking
and screaming, I could distinguish only the few following inco-
herent words—*horrible—frightful—ridiculous—Friesland hen
—rouge—red lion at Brentford—stays-padded—ram's-horn—
saucy minx—impertinent coxcomb.* I started up, dressed me,
and went down, where I found the same polite company,
who breakfasted there the day before, in the same attitudes
discoursing of their friends, with whom they had so agreeably
spent the last night, and to whom they were again hastening
with the utmost impatience. I was saluted with how-d'ye
from them all at the same instant, and again pressed into the
service of the day.

In this manner I went through the persecutions of the
whole week, with the sufferings and resolution, but not with
the reward of a martyr, as I found no peace at the last: for
at the conclusion of it, Sir John obligingly requested me, to
make my stay with him as long as I possibly could, assuring
me, that though the races were now over, I should not want

diversions; for that next week he expected Lord Rattle, Sir Harry Bumper, and a large fox-hunting party; and that the week after, being the full moon, they should pay and receive all their neighbouring visits, and spend their evenings very sociably together; by which is signified, in the country dialect, eating, drinking, and playing at cards all night. My lady added, with a smile, and much delight in her eyes, that she believed they should not be alone one hour in the whole week, and that she hoped I should not think the country so dull and melancholy a place as I expected. Upon this information I resolved to leave it immediately, and told them I was extremely sorry that I was hindered by particular business from any longer enjoying so much polite and agreeable company; but that I had received a letter, which made it necessary for me to be in town. My friend said, he was not less concerned; but that I must not positively go, till after tomorrow: for that he then expected the mayor and aldermen of his corporation, some of whom were facetious companions, and sung well. This determined me to set out that very evening: which I did with much satisfaction, and made all possible haste, in search of silence and solitude, to my lodgings next door to a brasier's at Charing-cross.

DR. SAMUEL JOHNSON

1709   Was born at Lichfield, Staffordshire, the son of a bookseller.
1728   Entered Pembroke College, Oxford.
1731   Left Oxford without taking a degree.
       Published a Latin translation of Pope's *Messiah*.
1731-1735 Tried to teach school.
1735   Married Elizabeth Porter.
       Published a translation of Lobo's *Voyage to Abyssinia*.
1736   Tried to conduct a school near Lichfield.
1737   Went to London accompanied by David Garrick, the, later,
       famous actor.
1738-1744 Contributed reports of parliamentary debates to the
       Gentlemen's Magazine.
1738   Published *London*.
1744   Published *Life of Savage*.
1747   Began the *Dictionary of the English Language*.
       Sought the patronage of Lord Chesterfield.
1749   Published *The Vanity of Human Wishes*.
       Wrote Irene, a tragedy, produced by David Garrick.
1750-1752 Founded and edited the *Rambler*.
1752-1754 Contributed to the *Adventurer*.
1752   Occurred the death of his wife.
1755   Published the *Dictionary of the English Language;* wrote the
       letter to Lord Chesterfield, which hastened the end of liter-
       ary patronage.
1758-1760 Founded and edited the *Idler*, published in the *Universal*
       Chronicle.
1759   Published *Rasselas*.
1762   Received a pension of £300 from the Crown.
1763   Met James Boswell, who became the author of the *Life of*
       Johnson.
1764   Founded the Literary Club.
1765   Published an edition of Shakespeare.
1775   Published *Journey to the Western Islands*.
1779-1781 Published *The Lives of the Poets*.
1784   Died, and was buried in Westminster Abbey.

THE MISERY OF A MODISH LADY IN SOLITUDE[1]

To the Rambler,

Mr. Rambler,

I am no great admirer of grave writings, and therefore very frequently lay your papers aside before I have read them through; yet I cannot but confess that, by slow degrees, you have raised my opinion of your understanding, and that, though I believe it will be long before I can be prevailed upon to regard you with much kindness, you have, however, more of my esteem than those whom I sometimes make happy with opportunities to fill my teapot, or pick up my fan. I shall therefore choose you for the confident of my distresses, and ask your counsel with regard to the means of conquering or escaping them, though I never expect from you any of that softness and pliancy which constitutes the perfection of a companion for the ladies: as, in the place where I now am, I have recourse to the mastiff for protection, though I have no intention of making him a lapdog.

My mamma is a very fine lady, who has more numerous and more frequent assemblies at our house than any other person in the same quarter of the town. I was bred from my earliest infancy to a perpetual tumult of pleasure, and remember to have heard of little else than messages, visits, playhouses, and balls; of the awkwardness of one woman, and the coquetry of another; the charming convenience of some rising fashion, the difficulty of playing a new game, and the incidents of a masquerade, and the dresses of a court night. I knew before I was ten years old all the rules of paying and receiving visits, and to how much civility every one of my acquaintance was entitled: and was able to return, with the proper degree of reserve or vivacity, the stated and established answer to every compliment; so that I was very soon celebrated as a wit and a beauty, and had heard before I was thirteen all that is ever said to a young lady. My mother

---

[1]*Rambler*, No. 42. Saturday, August 11, 1750.

was generous to so uncommon a degree as to be pleased with my advance into life, and allowed me, without envy or reproof, to enjoy the same happiness with herself; though most women about her own age were very angry to see young girls so forward, and many fine gentlemen told her how cruel it was to throw new chains upon mankind, and to tyrannize over them at the same time with her own charms and those of her daughter.

I have now lived two and twenty years, and have passed of each year nine months in town, and three at Richmond; so that my time has been spent uniformly in the same company and the same amusements, except as fashion has introduced new diversions, or the revolutions of the gay world have afforded new successions of wits and beaux. However, my mother is so good an economist of pleasure that I have no spare hours upon my hands; for every morning brings some new appointment, and every night is hurried away by the necessity of making our appearance at different places, and of being with one lady at the opera, and with another at the card-table.

When the time came of setting our scheme of felicity for the summer, it was determined that I should pay a visit to a rich aunt in a remote county. As you know the chief conversation of all tea-tables, in the spring, arises from a communication of the manner in which time is to be passed till winter, it was a great relief to the barrenness of our topics to relate the pleasures that were in store for me, to describe my uncle's seat, with the park and gardens, the charming walks and beautiful waterfalls; and everyone told me how much she envied me, and what satisfaction she had once enjoyed in a situation of the same kind.

As we are all credulous in our own favour, and willing to imagine some latent satisfaction in anything which we have not experienced, I will confess to you, without restraint, that I had suffered my head to be filled with expectations of some nameless pleasure in a rural life, and that I hoped for the happy hour that should set me free from noise, and flutter, and ceremony, dismiss me to the peaceful shade, and lull me in content and tranquillity. To solace myself under the misery of delay, I sometimes heard a studious lady of my acquaintance read pastorals, I was delighted with scarce any talk but of leaving the town, and never went to bed without dreaming of groves, and meadows, and frisking lambs.

At length I had all my clothes in a trunk, and saw the coach at the door; I sprung in with ecstasy, quarrelled with my maid for being too long in taking leave of the other servants, and rejoiced as the ground grew less which lay between me and the completion of my wishes. A few days brought me to a large old house, encompassed on three sides with woody hills, and looking from the front on a gentle river, the sight of which renewed all my expectations of pleasure, and gave me some regret for having lived so long without the enjoyment which these delightful scenes were now to afford me. My aunt came out to receive me, but in a dress so far removed from the present fashion that I could scarcely look upon her without laughter, which would have been no kind requital for the trouble which she had taken to make herself fine against my arrival. The night and the next morning were driven along with inquiries about our family; my aunt then explained our pedigree, and told me stories of my great grandfather's bravery in the civil wars; nor was it less than three days before I could persuade her to leave me to myself.

At last economy prevailed; she went in the usual manner about her own affairs, and I was at liberty to range in the wilderness, and sit by the cascade. The novelty of the objects about me pleased me for a while, but after a few days they were new no longer, and I soon began to perceive that the country was not my element; that shades, and flowers, and lawns, and waters had very soon exhausted all their power of pleasing, and that I had not in myself any fund of satisfaction with which I could supply the loss of my customary amusements.

I unhappily told my aunt, in the first warmth of our embraces, that I had leave to stay with her ten weeks. Six only are yet gone, and how shall I live through the remaining four? I go out and return; I pluck a flower, and throw it away; I catch an insect, and when I have examined its colours, set it at liberty; I fling a pebble into the water, and see one circle spread after another. When it chances to rain I walk in the great hall, and watch the minute-hand upon the dial, or play with a litter of kittens which the cat happens to have brought in a lucky time.

My aunt is afraid I shall grow melancholy, and therefore encourages the neighbouring gentry to visit us. They came at first with great eagerness to see the fine lady from London, but when we met we had no common topic on which we could converse; they had no curiosity after plays, operas, or music; and I find as little satisfaction from their accounts of the quarrels or alliances of families, whose names, when once I can escape, I shall never hear. The women have now seen me, know how my gown is made, and are satisfied; the men are generally afraid of me, and say little, because they think themselves not at liberty to talk rudely.

Thus am I condemned to solitude; the day moves slowly forward, and I see the dawn with uneasiness, because I consider that night is at a great distance. I have tried to sleep by a brook, but find its murmurs ineffectual; so that I am forced to be awake at least twelve hours, without visits, without cards, without laughter, and without flattery. I walk because I am disgusted with sitting still, and sit down because I am weary with walking. I have no motive to action, nor any object of love, or hate or fear, or inclination. I cannot dress with spirit, for I have neither rival nor admirer. I cannot dance without a partner, nor be kind, or cruel, without a lover.

Such is the life of Euphelia, and such it is likely to continue for a month to come. I have not yet declared against existence, nor called upon the destinies to cut my thread; but I have sincerely resolved not to condemn myself to such another summer, nor too hastily to flatter myself with happiness. Yet I have heard, Mr. Rambler, of those who never thought themselves so much at ease as in solitude, and cannot but suspect it to be some way or other my own fault, that, without great pain, either of mind or body, I am thus weary of myself: that the current of youth stagnates, and that I am languishing in a dead calm for want of some external impulse. I shall, therefore, think you a benefactor to our sex, if you will teach me the art of living alone; for I am confident that a thousand and a thousand and a thousand ladies, who affect to talk with ecstasies of the pleasures of the country, are, in reality, like me, longing for the winter, and wishing to be delivered from themselves by company and diversion.

I am, sir, yours,
EUPHELIA

THE EMPLOYMENTS OF A HOUSEWIFE IN THE COUNTRY[1]

Stultus labor est ineptiorum[2]
Mart. Epig. II, 86, 10.

To THE RAMBLER,
SIR,

As you have allowed a place in your paper to Euphelia's letters from the country, and appear to think no form of human life unworthy of your attention, I have resolved, after many struggles with idleness and diffidence, to give you some account of my entertainment in this sober season of universal retreat, and to describe to you the employments of those who look with contempt on the pleasures and diversions of polite life, and employ all their powers of censure and invective upon the uselessness, vanity, and folly of dress, visits, and conversation.

When a tiresome and vexatious journey of four days had brought me to the house where invitation, regularly sent for

---

[1]*Rambler*, No. 51. Tuesday, September 11, 1750.

[2]How foolish is the toil of trifling cares.

seven years together, had at last induced me to pass the summer, I was surprised, after the civilities of my first reception, to find, instead of the leisure and tranquillity which a rural life always promises, and, if well conducted, might always afford, a confused wildness of care and a tumultuous hurry of diligence, by which every face was clouded and every motion agitated. The old lady, who was my father's relation, was, indeed, very full of the happiness which she received from my visit, and, according to the forms of obsolete breeding, insisted that I should recompense the long delay of my company with a promise not to leave her till winter. But, amidst all her kindness and caresses, she very frequently turned her head aside, and whispered, with anxious earnestness, some order to her daughters, which never failed to send them out with unpolite precipitation. Sometimes her impatience would not suffer her to stay behind; she begged my pardon, she must leave me for a moment; she went, and returned and sat down again, but was again disturbed by some new care, dismissed her daughters with the same trepidation, and followed them with the same countenance of business and solicitude.

However I was alarmed at this show of eagerness and disturbance, and however my curiosity was excited by such busy preparations as naturally promised some great event, I was yet too much a stranger to gratify myself with inquiries; but finding none of the family in mourning, I pleased myself with imagining that I should rather see a wedding than a funeral.

At last we sat down to supper, when I was informed that one of the young ladies, after whom I thought myself obliged to inquire, was under a necessity of attending some affair that could not be neglected: soon afterward my relation began to talk of the regularity of her family and the inconvenience of London hours: and at last let me know that they had purposed that night to go to bed sooner than was usual, because they were to rise early in the morning to make cheesecakes. This hint sent me to my chamber, to which I was accompanied by all the ladies, who begged me to excuse some large sieves of leaves and flowers that covered two-thirds of the floor, for they intended to distil them when they were dry, and they had no other room that so conveniently received the rising sun.

The scent of the plants hindered me from rest, and therefore I rose early in the morning with a resolution to explore my new habitation. I stole unperceived by my busy cousins into the garden, where I found nothing either more great or elegant than in the same number of acres cultivated for the market. Of the gardener I soon learned that his lady was the greatest manager in that part of the country, and that I was come hither at the time in which I might learn to make more pickles and conserves than could be seen at any other house a hundred miles round.

It was not long before her ladyship gave me sufficient opportunities of knowing her character, for she was too much pleased with her own accomplishments to conceal them, and took occasion, from some sweetmeats which she set next day upon the table, to discourse for two long hours upon robs and jellies; laid down the best methods of conserving, reserving, and preserving all sorts of fruit; told us with great contempt of the London lady in the neighbourhood, by whom these terms were very often confounded; and hinted how much she should be ashamed to set before company, at her own house, sweetmeats of so dark a colour as she had often seen at Mistress Sprightly's.

It is, indeed, the great business of her life to watch the skillet on the fire, to see it simmer with the due degree of heat, and to snatch it off at the moment of projection; and the employments to which she has bred her daughters are to turn rose leaves in the shade, to pick out the seeds of currants with a quill, to gather fruit without bruising it, and to extract bean flower water for the skin. Such are the tasks with which every day, since I came hither, has begun and ended, to which the early hours of life are sacrificed, and in which that time is passing away which never shall return.

But to reason or expostulate are hopeless attempts. The

lady has settled her opinions, and maintains the dignity of her own performances with all the firmness of stupidity accustomed to be flattered. Her daughters, having never seen any house but their own, believe their mother's excellence on her own word. Her husband is a mere sportsman, who is pleased to see his table well furnished, and thinks the day sufficiently successful in which he brings home a leash of hares to be potted by his wife.

After a few days I pretended to want books, but my lady soon told me that none of her books would suit my taste; for her part she never loved to see young women give their minds to such follies, by which they would only learn to use hard words; she bred up her daughters to understand a house, and whoever should marry them, if they knew anything of good cookery, would never repent it.

There are, however, some things in the culinary science too sublime for youthful intellects, mysteries into which they must not be initiated till the years of serious maturity, and which are referred to the day of marriage as the supreme qualification for connubial life. She makes an orange pudding, which is the envy of all the neighbourhood, and which she had hitherto found means of mixing and baking with such secrecy, that the ingredient to which it owes its flavour has never been discovered. She, indeed, conducts this great affair with all the caution that human policy can suggest. It is never known beforehand when this pudding will be produced; she takes the ingredients privately in her own closet; employs her maids and daughters in different parts of the house, orders the oven to be heated for a pie, and places the pudding in it with her own hands: the mouth of the oven is then stopped, and all inquiries are vain.

The composition of the pudding she has, however, promised Clarinda, that if she pleases her in marriage, she shall be told without reserve. But the art of making English capers she has not yet persuaded herself to discover, but seems resolved that secret shall perish with her, as some alchemists have obstinately suppressed the art of transmuting metals.

I once ventured to lay my fingers on her book of receipts, which she left upon the table, having intelligence that a vessel of gooseberry wine had burst the hoops. But though the importance of the event sufficiently engrossed her care, to prevent any recollection of the danger to which her secrets were exposed, I was not able to make use of the golden moments; for this treasure of hereditary knowledge was so well concealed by the manner of spelling used by her grandmother, her mother, and herself, that I was totally unable to understand it, and lost the opportunity of consulting the oracle, for want of knowing the language in which its answers were returned.

It is, indeed, necessary, if I have any regard to her ladyship's esteem, that I should apply myself to some of these economical accomplishments; for I overheard her, two days ago, warning her daughters, by my mournful example, against negligence of pastry, and ignorance in carving; for you saw, she said, that, with all her pretensions to knowledge, she turned the partridge the wrong way when she attempted to cut it, and, I believe, scarcely knows the difference between paste raised and paste in a dish.

The reason, Mr. Rambler, why I have laid Lady Bustle's character before you, is a desire to be informed whether in your opinion it is worthy of imitation, and whether I shall throw away the books which I have hitherto thought it my duty to read, for *The Lady's Closet Opened*, *The Complete. Servant-Maid*, and *The Court Cook*, and resign all curiosity after right and wrong for the art of scalding damascenes without bursting them, and preserving the whiteness of pickled mushrooms.

Lady Bustle has, indeed, by this incessant application to fruits and flowers, contracted her cares into a narrow space, and set herself free from many perplexities with which other minds are disturbed. She has no curiosity after the events of a war, or the fate of heroes in distress; she can hear without the least emotion the ravage of a fire, or devastations of a storm; her neighbours grow rich or poor, come into the world or go out of it, without regard, while she is pressing the jelly-bag, or airing the store-room; but I cannot perceive that she is more free from disquiets than those whose understandings take a wider range. Her marigolds, when they are almost cured, are often scattered by the wind, and the rain sometimes falls upon fruit when it ought to be gathered dry. While her artificial wines are fermenting, her whole life is restlessness and anxiety. Her sweetmeats are not always bright, and the maid sometimes forgets the just proportion of salt and pepper, when venison is to be baked. Her conserves mould, her wines sour, and pickles mother; and, like all the rest of mankind, she is every day mortified with the defeat of her schemes and the disappointment of her hopes.

With regard to vice and virtue she seems a kind of neutral being. She has no crime but luxury, nor any virtue but chastity; she has no desire to be praised but for her cookery; nor wishes any ill to the rest of mankind, but that whenever they aspire to a feast, their custards may be wheyish, and their pie-crusts tough.

I am now very impatient to know whether I am to look on these ladies as the great patterns of our sex, and to consider conserves and pickles as the business of my life; whether the censures which I now suffer be just, and whether the brewers of wines, and the distillers of washes, have a right to look with insolence on the weakness of

CORNELIA

THE SCHOLAR'S COMPLAINT OF HIS OWN BASHFULNESS[1]

To the Rambler,
Sir,

THOUGH one of your correspondents has presumed to mention with some contempt that presence of attention and easiness of address, which the polite have long agreed to

---

[1] *Rambler*, No. 157. Tuesday, September 17, 1751.

celebrate and esteem, yet I cannot be persuaded to think
them unworthy of regard of cultivation; but am inclined to
believe that as we seldom value rightly what we have never
known the misery of wanting, his judgment has been vitiated
by this happiness; and that a natural exuberance of assurance
has hindered him from discovering its excellence and use.

This felicity, whether bestowed by constitution, or obtained by early habitudes, I can scarcely contemplate without envy. I was bred under a man of learning in the country,
who inculcated nothing but the dignity of knowledge and the
happiness of virtue. By frequency of admonition and confidence of assertion, he prevailed upon me to believe that the
splendour of literature would always attract reverence, if not
darkened by corruption. I therefore pursued my studies
with incessant industry, and avoided everything which I
had been taught to consider either as vicious or tending to
vice, because I regarded guilt and reproach as inseparably
united, and thought a tainted reputation the greatest calamity.

At the university I found no reason for changing my opinion; for though many among my fellow-students took the
opportunity of a more remiss discipline to gratify their passions, yet virtue preserved her natural superiority, and those
who ventured to neglect, were not suffered to insult her.
The ambition of petty accomplishments found its way into the
receptacles of learning, but was observed to seize commonly
on those who either neglected the sciences or could not attain them; and I was therefore confirmed in the doctrines of
my old master, and thought nothing worthy of my care but
the means of gaining and imparting knowledge.

This purity of manners and intenseness of application soon
extended my renown, and I was applauded by those whose
opinion I then thought unlikely to deceive me, as a young
man that gave uncommon hopes of future eminence. My
performances in time reached my native province, and my
relations congratulated themselves upon the new honours
that were added to their family.

I returned home covered with academical laurels, and fraught with criticism and philosophy. The wit and the scholar excited curiosity, and my acquaintance was solicited by innumerable invitations. To please will always be the wish of benevolence, to be admired must be the constant aim of ambition; and I therefore considered myself as about to receive the reward of my honest labours, and to find the efficacy of learning and of virtue.

The third day after my arrival I dined at the house of a gentleman who had summoned a multitude of his friends to the annual celebration of his wedding day. I set forward with great exultation, and thought myself happy that I had an opportunity of displaying my knowledge to so numerous an assembly. I felt no sense of my own insufficiency, till going upstairs to the dining-room, I heard the mingled roar of obstreperous merriment. I was, however, disgusted rather than terrified, and went forward without dejection. The whole company rose at my entrance; but when I saw so many eyes fixed at once upon me, I was blasted with a sudden imbecility; I was quelled by some nameless power which I found impossible to be resisted. My sight was dazzled, my cheeks glowed, my perceptions were confounded; I was harassed by the multitude of eager salutations, and returned the common civilities with hesitation and impropriety; the sense of my own blunders increased my confusion, and before the exchange of ceremonies allowed me to sit down, I was ready to sink under the oppression of surprise; my voice grew weak, and my knees trembled.

The assembly then resumed their places, and I sat with my eyes fixed upon the ground. To the questions of curiosity, or the appeals of complaisance, I could seldom answer but with negative monosyllables, or professions of ignorance; for the subjects on which they conversed were such as are seldom discussed in books, and were therefore out of my range of knowledge. At length an old clergyman, who rightly conjectured the reason of my conciseness, relieved me by some questions about the present state of natural knowledge, and engaged me, by an appearance of doubt and opposition, in the explication and defence of the Newtonian philosophy.

The consciousness of my own abilities roused me from depression, and long familiarity with my subject enabled me to discourse with ease and volubility; but however I might please myself, I found very little added by my demonstrations to the satisfaction of the company; and my antagonist, who knew the laws of conversation too well to detain their attention long upon an unpleasing topic, after he had commended my acuteness and comprehension, dismissed the controversy, and resigned me to my former insignificance and perplexity.

After dinner I received from the ladies, who had heard that I was a wit, an invitation to the tea table. I congratulated myself upon an opportunity to escape from the company, whose gaiety began to be tumultuous, and among whom several hints had been dropped of the uselessness of universities, the folly of book learning, and the awkwardness of scholars. To the ladies, therefore, I flew as to a refuge from clamour, insult and rusticity; but found my heart sink as I approached their apartment, and was again disconcerted by the ceremonies of entrance, and confounded by the necessity of encountering so many eyes at once.

When I sat down I considered that something pretty was always said to ladies, and resolved to recover my credit by some elegant observation or graceful compliment, I applied myself to the recollection of all I had read or heard in praise of beauty, and endeavoured to accommodate some classical compliment to the present occasion. I sunk into profound meditation, revolved the character of the heroines of old, considered whatever the poets have sung in their praise, and after having borrowed and invented, chosen and rejected a thousand sentiments, which, if I had uttered them, would not have been understood, I was awakened from my dream of learned gallantry by the servant who distributed the tea.

There are not many situations more incessantly uneasy than that in which the man is placed who is watching an opportunity to speak without courage to take it when it is offered, and who, though he resolves to give a specimen of his abilities, always finds some reason or other for delaying it to the next minute. I was ashamed of silence, yet could find nothing to say of elegance or importance equal to my wishes. The ladies, afraid of my learning, thought themselves not qualified to propose any subject to prattle to a man so famous for dispute, and there was nothing on either side but impatience and vexation.

In this conflict of shame, as I was reassembling my scattered sentiments, and, resolving to force my imagination to some sprightly sally, had just found a very happy compliment, by too much attention to my own meditations, I suffered the saucer to drop from my hand, the cup was broken, the lapdog was scalded, a brocaded petticoat was stained, and the whole assembly was thrown into disorder. I now considered all hopes of reputation as at an end, and while they were consoling and assisting one another, stole away in silence.

The misadventures of this unhappy day are not yet at an end; I am afraid of meeting the meanest of them that triumphed over me in this state of stupidity and contempt, and feel the same terrors encroaching upon my heart at the sight of those who have once impressed them. Shame, above any other passion, propagates itself. Before those who have seen me confused I can never appear without new confusion, and the remembrance of the weakness which I formerly discovered hinders me from acting or speaking with my natural force.

But is this misery, Mr. Rambler, never to cease? Have I spent my life in study only to become the sport of the ignorant, and debarred myself from all the common enjoyments of youth to collect ideas which must sleep in silence, and form opinions which I must not divulge? Inform me, dear sir, by what means I may rescue my faculties from these shackles of cowardice, how I may rise to a level with my fellow

beings, recall myself from this languor of involuntary subjection to the free exertion of my intellects, and add to the
power of reasoning the liberty of speech.

I am, sir, etc.,
VERECUNDULUS

THE REVOLUTIONS OF A GARRET[1]

MR. RAMBLER,
SIR,

You have formerly observed that curiosity often terminates
in barren knowledge, and that the mind is prompted to study
and inquiry rather by the uneasiness of ignorance than the
hope of profit. Nothing can be of less importance to any
present interest than the fortune of those who have been
long lost in the grave, and from whom nothing now can be
hoped or feared. Yet to rouse the zeal of a true antiquary,
little more is necessary than to mention a name which mankind have conspired to forget; he will make his way to remote scenes of action through obscurity and contradiction,
as Tully sought amidst bushes and brambles the tomb of
Archimedes.

It is not easy to discover how it concerns him that gathers
the produce, or receives the rent of an estate, to know through
what families the land has passed, who is registered in the
Conqueror's survey as its possessor, how often it has been
forfeited by treason, or how often sold by prodigality. The
power of wealth of the present inhabitants of a country
cannot be much increased by an inquiry after the names of
those barbarians who destroyed one another twenty centuries ago, in contests for the shelter of woods or convenience
of pasturage. Yet we see that no man can be at rest in the
enjoyment of a new purchase till he has learned the history
of his grounds from the ancient inhabitants of the parish,
and that no nation omits to record the actions of their ancestors, however bloody, savage, and rapacious.

[1]*Rambler*, No. 161. Tuesday, October 1, 1751.

The same disposition, as different opportunities call it forth, discovers itself in great or little things. I have always thought it unworthy of a wise man to slumber in total inactivity, only because he happens to have no employment equal to his ambition or genius; it is therefore my custom to apply my attention to the objects before me, and as I cannot think any place wholly unworthy of notice that affords a habitation to a man of letters, I have collected the history and antiquities of the several garrets in which I have resided.

Quantulacunque estis, vos ego magna voco.[1]

Many of these narratives my industry has been able to extend to a considerable length; but the woman with whom I now lodge has lived only eighteen months in the house, and can give no account of its ancient revolutions; the plasterer having at her entrance obliterated, by his whitewash, all the smoky memorials which former tenants had left upon the ceiling, and perhaps drawn the veil of oblivion over politicians, philosophers, and poets.

When I first cheapened my lodgings, the landlady told me that she hoped I was not an author, for the lodgers on the first floor had stipulated that the upper rooms should not be occupied by a noisy trade. I very readily promised to give no disturbance to her family, and soon dispatched a bargain on the usual terms.

I had not slept many nights in my new apartment before I began to inquire after my predecessors, and found my landlady, whose imagination is filled chiefly with her own affairs, very ready to give me information.

Curiosity, like all other desires, produces pain as well as pleasure. Before she began her narrative, I had heated my head with expectations of adventures and discoveries, of elegance in disguise, and learning in distress; and was somewhat mortified when I heard that the first tenant was a tailor, of whom nothing was remembered but that he complained of

---

[1] How small to others, but how great to me!

his room for want of light; and, after having lodged in it a month, and paid only a week's rent, pawned a piece of cloth which he was trusted to cut out, and was forced to make a precipitate retreat from this quarter of the town.

The next was a young woman newly arrived from the country, who lived for five weeks with great regularity, and became, by frequent treats, very much the favourite of the family, but at last received visits so frequently from a cousin in Cheapside, that she brought the reputation of the house into danger, and was therefore dismissed with good advice.

The room then stood empty for a fortnight; my landlady began to think that she had judged hardly, and often wished for such another lodger. At last an elderly man of a grave aspect read the bill, and bargained for the room at the very first price that was asked. He lived in close retirement, seldom went out till evening, and then returned early, sometimes cheerful, and at other times dejected. It was remarkable that, whatever he purchased, he never had small money in his pocket, and, though cool and temperate on other occasions, was always vehement and stormy till he received his change. He paid his rent with great exactness, and seldom failed once a week to requite my landlady's civility with a supper. At last, such is the fate of human felicity, the house was alarmed at midnight by the constable, who demanded to search the garrets. My landlady assuring him that he had mistaken the door, conducted him upstairs, where he found the tools of a coiner; but the tenant had crawled along the roof to an empty house, and escaped; much to the joy of my landlady, who declares him a very honest man, and wonders why anybody should be hanged for making money when such numbers are in want of it. She, however, confesses that she shall for the future always question the character of those who take her garret without beating down the price.

The bill was then placed again in the window, and the poor woman was teased for seven weeks by innumerable passengers, who obliged her to climb with them every hour up five stories, and then disliked the prospect, hated the noise of a

public street, thought the stairs narrow, objected to a low
ceiling, required the walls to be hung with a fresher paper,
asked questions about the neighbourhood, could not think of
living so far from their acquaintance, wished the windows
had looked to the south rather than the west, told how the
door and chimney might have been better disposed, bid her
half the price that she asked, or promised to give her earnest
the next day, and came no more.

At last, a short meagre man, in a tarnished waistcoat,
desired to see the garret, and, when he had stipulated for
two long shelves and a larger table, hired it at a low rate.
When the affair was completed, he looked round him with
great satisfaction, and repeated some words which the woman
did not understand. In two days he brought a great box of
books, took possession of his room, and lived very inoffen-
sively except that he frequently disturbed the inhabitants of
the next floor by unseasonable noises. He was generally
in bed at noon, but from evening to midnight he sometimes
talked aloud with great vehemence, sometimes stamped as in
a rage, sometimes threw down his poker, then clattered his
chairs, then sat down in deep thought, and again burst out
into loud vociferations; sometimes he would sigh, as op-
pressed with misery, and sometimes shake with convulsive
laughter. When he encountered any of the family, he gave
way or bowed, but rarely spoke, except that as he went upstairs he often repeated.

—Ὅς ὑπέρτατα δώματα ναίει[1]

hard words, to which his neighbours listened so often that they
learned them without understanding them. What was his
employment she did not venture to ask him, but at last heard
a printer's boy inquire for "the author." My landlady was
very often advised to beware of this strange man, who,
though he was quiet for the present, might perhaps become
outrageous in the hot months; but as she was punctually

---

[1] This habitant the aërial regions boast.

paid, she could not find any sufficient reason for dismissing him, till one night he convinced her, by setting fire to his curtains, that it was not safe to have an author for her inmate. She had then, for six weeks, a succession of tenants, who left her house on Saturday, and, instead of paying their rent, stormed at their landlady. At last she took in two sisters, one of whom had spent her little fortune in procuring remedies for a lingering disease, and was now supported and attended by the other. She climbed with difficulty to the apartment, where she languished eight weeks without impatience or lamentation, except for the expense and fatigue which her sister suffered, and then calmly and contentedly expired. The sister followed her to the grave, paid the few debts which they had contracted, wiped away the tears of useless sorrow, and, returning to the business of common life, resigned to me the vacant habitation.

Such, Mr. Rambler, are the changes which have happened in the narrow space where my present fortune has fixed my residence. So true it is that amusement and instruction are always at hand for those who have skill and willingness to find them; and so just is the observation of Juvenal, that a single house will show whatever is done or suffered in the world.

I am, Sir, &c.

LOTTERIES[1]

To the Rambler,
Sir,

As I have passed much of life in disquiet and suspense, and lost many opportunities of advantage by a passion which I have reason to believe prevalent in different degrees over a great part of mankind, I cannot but think myself well qualified to warn those, who are yet uncaptivated of the danger which they incur by placing themselves within its influence.

I served an apprenticeship to a linen-draper, with uncom-

---

[1]*Rambler*, No. 181. December 10, 1751.

mon reputation for diligence and fidelity; and at the age of three-and-twenty opened a shop for myself with a large stock, and such credit among all the merchants, who were acquainted with my master, that I could command whatever was imported curious or valuable. For five years I proceeded with success proportionate to close application and untainted integrity; was a daring bidder at every sale; always paid my notes before they were due; and advanced so fast in commercial reputation that I was proverbially marked out as the model of young traders, and every one expected that a few years would make me an alderman.

In this course of even prosperity, I was one day persuaded to buy a ticket in the lottery. The sum was inconsiderable, part was to be repaid though fortune might fail to favour me, and therefore my established maxims of frugality did not restrain me from so trifling an experiment. The ticket lay almost forgotten till the time at which every man's fate was to be determined; nor did the affair even then seem of any importance, till I discovered by the public papers that the number next to mine had conferred the great prize.

My heart leaped at the thoughts of such an approach to sudden riches, which I considered myself, however contrarily to the laws of computation, as having missed by a single chance; and I could not forbear to revolve the consequences which such a bounteous allotment would have produced, if it had happened to me. This dream of felicity, by degrees, took possession of my imagination. The great delight of my solitary hours was to purchase an estate, and form plantations with money which once might have been mine, and I never met my friends but I spoiled all their merriment by perpetual complaints of my ill luck.

At length another lottery was opened, and I had now so heated my imagination with the prospect of a prize, that I should have pressed among the first purchasers, had not my ardour been withheld by deliberation upon the probability of success from one ticket rather than another. I hesitated long between even and odd; considered the square and cubic numbers through the lottery; examined all those to which good luck had been hitherto annexed; and at last fixed upon one, which, by some secret relations to the events of my life, I thought predestined to make me happy. Delay in great affairs is often mischievous; the ticket was sold, and its possessor could not be found.

I returned to my conjectures, and after many arts of prognostication, fixed upon another chance, but with less confidence. Never did captive, heir, or lover, feel so much vexation from the slow pace of time, as I suffered between the purchase of my ticket and the distribution of the prizes. I solaced my uneasiness as well as I could, by frequent contemplations of approaching happiness; when the sun arose I knew it would set, and congratulated myself at night that I was so much nearer to my wishes. At last the day came, my ticket appeared, and rewarded all my care and sagacity with a despicable prize of fifty pounds.

My friends, who honestly rejoiced upon my success, were very coldly received; I hid myself a fortnight in the country, that my chagrin might fume away without observation, and then returning to my shop, began to listen after another lottery.

With the news of a lottery I was soon gratified, and having now found the vanity of conjecture and inefficacy of computation, I resolved to take the prize by violence, and therefore bought forty tickets, not omitting, however, to divide them between the even and odd numbers, that I might not miss the lucky class. Many conclusions did I form, and many experiments did I try to determine from which of those tickets I might most reasonably expect riches. At last, being unable to satisfy myself by any modes of reasoning, I wrote the numbers upon dice, and allotted five hours every day to the amusement of throwing them in a garret; and examining the event by an exact register, found, on the evening before the lottery was drawn, that one of my numbers had been turned up five times more than any of the rest in three hundred and thirty thousand throws.

This experiment was fallacious; the first day presented the hopeful ticket, a detestable blank. The rest came out with different fortune, and in conclusion I lost thirty pounds by this great adventure.

I had now wholly changed the cast of my behaviour and the conduct of my life. The shop was for the most part abandoned to my servants, and if I entered it, my thoughts were so engrossed by my tickets that I scarcely heard or answered a question, but considered every customer as an intruder upon my meditations, whom I was in haste to dispatch. I mistook the price of my goods, committed blunders in my bills, forgot to file my receipts, and neglected to regulate my books. My acquaintances by degrees began to fall away; but I perceived the decline of my business with little emotion, because whatever deficiency there might be in my gains I expected the next lottery to supply.

Miscarriage naturally produced diffidence; I began now to seek assistance against ill luck, by an alliance with those that had been more successful. I inquired diligently at what office any prize had been sold, that I might purchase of a propitious vender; solicited those who had been fortunate in former lotteries, to partake with me in my new tickets, and whenever I met with one that had in any event of his life been eminently prosperous I invited him to take a larger share. I had, by this rule of conduct, so diffused my interest, that I had a fourth part of fifteen tickets, an eighth part of forty, and a sixteenth of ninety.

I waited for the decision of my fate with my former palpitations, and looked upon the business of my trade with the usual neglect. The wheel at last was turned, and its revolutions brought me a long succession of sorrows and disappointments. I indeed often partook of a small prize, and the loss of one day was generally balanced by the gain of the next; but my desires yet remained unsatisfied, and when one of my chances had failed, all my expectations were suspended on those which remained yet undetermined. At last a prize of five thousand pounds was proclaimed; I caught fire at the cry, and inquiring the number, found it to be one of my own tickets, which I had divided among those on whose luck I depended, and of which I had retained only a sixteenth part.

You will easily judge with what detestation of himself a man thus intent upon gain reflected that he had sold a prize which was once in his possession. It was to no purpose that I represented to my mind the impossibility of recalling the past, of the folly of condemning an act, which only its event, an event which no human intelligence could foresee, proved to be wrong. The prize which, though put in my hands, had been suffered to slip from me, filled me with anguish; and knowing that complaint would only expose me to ridicule, I gave myself up silently to grief, and lost by degrees my appetite and my rest.

My indisposition soon became visible: I was visited by my friends, and among them by Eumathes, a clergyman, whose piety and learning, gave him such an ascendant over me that I could not refuse to open my heart. "There are," said he, "few minds sufficiently firm to be trusted in the hands of chance. Whoever finds himself inclined to anticipate futurity, and exalt possibility to certainty, should avoid every kind of casual adventure, since his grief must be always proportionate to his hope. You have long wasted that time which, by a proper application, would have certainly though moderately, increased your fortune, in a laborious and anxious pursuit of a species of gain which no labour or anxiety, no art or expedient, can secure or promote. You are now fretting away your life in repentance of an act against which repentance can give no caution but to avoid the occasion of committing it. Rouse from this lazy dream of fortuitous riches, which if obtained, you could scarcely have enjoyed, because they could confer no consciousness of desert; return to rational and manly industry, and consider the mere gift of luck as below the care of a wise man."

THE STAGE COACH[1]

To the Adventurer,
Sir,

It has been observed, I think, by Sir William Temple, and after him by almost every other writer, that England affords a greater variety of characters than the rest of the world. This is ascribed to the liberty prevailing amongst us, which gives every man the privilege of being wise or foolish his own way, and preserves him from the necessity of hypocrisy or the servility of imitation.

That the position itself is nearly true, I am not completely satisfied. To be nearly acquainted with the people of different countries can happen to very few; and in life, as in everything else beheld at a distance, there appears an even uniformity: the petty discriminations which diversify the natural character, are not discoverable but by a close inspection; we, therefore, find them most at home, because there we have most opportunities of remarking them. Much less am I convinced, that his peculiar diversification, if it be real, is the consequence of peculiar liberty; for where is the government to be found that superintends individuals with so much vigilance, as not to leave their private conduct without restraint? Can it enter into a reasonable mind to imagine that men of every other nation are not equally masters of their own time or houses with ourselves, and equally at liberty to be parsimonious or profuse, frolic or sullen, abstinent or luxurious? Liberty is certainly necessary to the full play of predominant humours; but such liberty is to be found alike under the government of the many or the few, in monarchies or in commonwealths.

How readily the predominant passion snatches an interval of liberty, and how fast it expands itself when the weight of restraint is taken away, I had lately an opportunity to discover, as I took a journey into the country in a stage coach;

[1] *Adventurer*, No. 84. Saturday, August 25, 1753.

which, as every journey is a kind of adventure, may be very
properly related to you, though I can display no such extraordinary assembly as Cervantes has collected at Don
Quixote's inn.

In a stage coach the passengers are for the most part wholly
unknown to one another, and without expectation of ever
meeting again when their journey is at an end; one should,
therefore, imagine, that it was of little importance to any of
them, what conjectures the rest should form concerning him.
Yet so it is, that as all think themselves secure from detection,
all assume that character of which they are most desirous,
and on no occasion is the general ambition of superiority
more apparently indulged.

On the day of our departure, in the twilight of the morning,
I ascended the vehicle with three men and two women, my
fellow travellers. It was easy to observe the affected elevation of mien with which every one entered, and the supercili-
ous civility with which they paid their compliments to each
other. When the first ceremony was dispatched, we sat
silent for a long time, all employed in collecting importance
into our faces, and endeavouring to strike reverence and sub-
mission into our companions.

It is always observable that silence propagates itself, and
that the longer talk has been suspended, the more difficult it
is to find any thing to say. We began now to wish for conversation; but no one seemed inclined to descend from his
dignity, or first to propose a topic of discourse. At last a
corpulent gentleman, who had equipped himself for this
expedition with a scarlet surtout and a large hat with a broad
lace, drew out his watch, looked on it in silence, and then
held it dangling at his finger. This was, I suppose, understood by all the company as an invitation to ask the time
of the day, but nobody appeared to heed his overture; and
his desire to be talking so far overcame his resentment, that
he let us know of his own accord that it was past five, and
that in two hours we should be at breakfast.

His condescension was thrown away; we continued all

obdurate; the ladies held up their heads; I amused myself with watching their behaviour; and of the other two, one seemed to employ himself in counting the trees as we drove by them, the other drew his hat over his eyes and counter-feited a slumber. The man of benevolence, to show that he was not depressed by our neglect, hummed a tune and beat time upon his snuff-box.

Thus universally displeased with one another, and not much delighted with ourselves, we came at last to the little inn appointed for our repast; and all began at once to recom-pense themselves for the constraint of silence, by innumber-able questions and orders to the people that attended us. At last, what every one had called for was got, or declared impossible to be got at that time, and we were persuaded to sit round the same table; when the gentleman in the red sur-tout looked again upon his watch, told us that we had half an hour to spare, but he was sorry to see so little merriment among us; that all fellow travellers were for the time upon the level, and that it was always his way to make himself one of the company. "I remember," says he, "it was on just such a morning as this, that I and my Lord Mumble and the Duke of Tenterden were out upon a ramble: we called at a little house as it might be this; and my landlady, I warrant you, not suspecting to whom she was talking, was so jocular and facetious, and made so many merry answers to our ques-tions, that we were all ready to burst with laughter. At last the good woman happening overhear me whisper the duke and call him by his title, was so surprised and confounded that we could scarcely get a word from her; and the duke never met me from that day to this, but he talks of the little house, and quarrels with me for terrifying the landlady."

He had scarcely had time to congratulate himself on the veneration which this narrative must have procured him from the company, when one of the ladies having reached out for a plate on a distant part of the table, began to remark the inconveniences of travelling, and the difficulty which they who never sat at home without a great number of at-

tendants found in performing for themselves such offices as
the road required; but that people of quality often travelled
in disguise, and might be generally known from the vulgar
by their condescension to poor inn-keepers, and the allowance
which they made for any defect in their entertainment; that
for her part, while people were civil and meant well, it was
never her custom to find fault, for one was not to expect upon
a journey all that one enjoyed at one's own house.

A general emulation seemed now to be excited. One of
the men, who had hitherto said nothing, called for the last
newspaper; and having perused it a while with deep pensive-
ness, "It is impossible," says he, "for any man to guess how
to act with regard to the stocks; last week it was the general
opinion that they would fall; and I sold out twenty thousand
pounds in order to a purchase: they have now risen unexpectedly and I make no doubt but at my return to London I
shall risk thirty thousand pounds amongst them again."

A young man, who had hitherto distinguished himself only
by the vivacity of his look, and a frequent diversion of his
eyes from one object to another, upon this closed his snuff-
box, and told us that "he had a hundred times talked with the
chancellor and the judges on the subject of the stocks; that
for his part he did not pretend to be well acquainted with the
principles on which they were established, but had always
heard them reckoned pernicious to trade, uncertain in their
produce, and unsolid in their foundation; and that he had
been advised by three judges, his most intimate friends,
never to venture his money in the funds, but to put it out
upon land security, till he could light upon an estate in his
own country."

It might be expected that upon these glimpses of latent
dignity, we should all have begun to look around us with
veneration; and have behaved like the princes of romance,
when the enchantment that disguises them is dissolved, and
they discovered the dignity of each other: yet it happened,
that none of these hints made much impression on the company; every one was apparently suspected of endeavouring

to impose false appearances upon the rest; all continued their haughtiness, in hopes to enforce their claims; and all grew every hour more sullen, because they found their representations of themselves without effect.

Thus we travelled on four days with malevolence perpetually increasing, and without any endeavour but to outvie each other in superciliousness and neglect; and when any two of us could separate ourselves for a moment, we vented our indignation at the sauciness of the rest.

At length the journey was at an end; and time and chance, that strip off all disguises, have discovered, that the intimate of lords and dukes is a nobleman's butler, who has furnished a shop with the money he has saved; the man who deals so largely in the funds, is a clerk of a broker on 'Change-alley; the lady who so carefully concealed her quality, keeps a cook-shop behind the Exchange; and the young man, who is so happy in the friendship of the judges, engrosses and transcribes for bread in a garret of the Temple. Of one of the women only I could make no disadvantageous detection, because she had assumed no character, but accommodated herself to the scene before her, without any struggle for distinction or superiority.

I could not forbear to reflect on the folly of practising a fraud, which, as the event shewed, had been already practised too often to succeed, and by the success of which no advantage could have been obtained; of assuming a character, which was to end with the day; and of claiming upon false pretences honours which must perish with the breath that paid them.

But, Mr. Adventurer, let not those who laugh at me and my companions, think this folly confined to a stage coach. Every man in the journey of life takes the same advantage of the ignorance of his fellow travellers, disguises himself in counterfeited merit, and hears those praises with complacency which his conscience reproaches him for accepting. Every man deceives himself, while he thinks he is deceiving others and forgets that the time is at hand when every illusion shall cease, when fictitious excellence shall be torn away, and *all* must be shown to *all* in their real estate.

I am, Sir,
Your humble Servant,
Viator

ON THE ART OF ADVERTISING[1]

The practice of appending to the narratives of public transactions more minute and domestic intelligence, and filling the newspapers with advertisements, has grown up by slow degrees to its present state.

Genius is shown only by invention. The man who first took advantage of the general curiosity that was excited by a siege or battle, to betray the readers of news into the knowledge of the shop where the best puffs and powder were to be sold, was undoubtedly a man of great sagacity and profound skill in the nature of man. But when he had once shown the way, it was easy to follow him; and every man now knows a ready method of informing the public of all that he desires to buy or sell, whether his wares be material or intellectual; whether he makes clothes, or teaches the mathematics; whether he be a tutor that wants a pupil, or a pupil that wants a tutor.

Whatever is common is despised. Advertisements are now so numerous that they are very negligently perused, and it is therefore become necessary to gain attention by magnificence of promises, and by eloquence sometimes sublime and sometimes pathetic.

Promise, large promise, is the soul of an advertisement. I remember a *wash-ball* that had a quality truly wonderful —it gave *an exquisite edge to the razor.* And there are now to be sold, *for ready money only,* some *duvets for bed-coverings of down, beyond comparison, superior to what is called otter-down,* and indeed such, that its *many excellences cannot be here*

---

[1] *Idler,* No. 40. Saturday, January 20, 1759.

set forth. With one excellence we are made acquainted—*it is warmer than four or five blankets, and lighter than one.*

There are some, however, that know the prejudice of mankind in favour of modest sincerity. The vender of the *beautifying fluid* sells a lotion that repels pimples, washes away freckles, smooths the skin, and plumps the flesh, and yet, with a generous abhorrence of ostentation, confesses that it will not *restore the bloom of fifteen to a lady of fifty.*

The true pathos of advertisements must have sunk deep into the heart of every man that remembers the zeal shown by the seller of the *anodyne necklace,* for the ease and safety of *poor teething infants,* and the affection with which he warned every mother that *she would never forgive herself* if her infant should perish without a necklace.

I cannot but remark to the celebrated author who gave, in his notifications of the camel and dromedary, so many specimens of the genuine sublime, that there is now arrived another subject yet more worthy of his pen. *A famous Mohawk Indian warrior, who took Dieskaw, the French General prisoner, dressed in the same manner with the native Indians when they go to war, with his face and body painted, with his scalping-knife, tom-axe, and all other implements of war! a sight worthy the curiosity of every true Briton!* This is a very powerful description; but a critic of great refinement would say that it conveys rather *horror* than *terror.* An Indian, dressed as he goes to war, may bring company together; but if he carries the scalping-knife and tom-axe, there are many true Britons that will never be persuaded to see him but through a grate.

It has been remarked by the severer judges that the salutary sorrow of tragic scenes is too soon effaced by the merriment of the epilogue; the same inconvenience arises from the improper disposition of advertisements. The noblest objects may be so associated as to be made ridiculous. The camel and dromedary themselves might have lost much of their dignity between *the true flour of mustard* and the *original Daffy's elixir;* and I could not but feel some indignation when

I found this illustrious Indian warrior immediately succeeded by *a fresh parcel of Dublin butter.*

The trade of advertising is now so near to perfection, that it is not easy to propose any improvement. But as every art ought to be exercised in due subordination to the public good, I cannot but propose it as a moral question to these masters of the public ear, Whether they do not sometimes play too wantonly with our passions, as when the registrar of lottery tickets invites us to his shop by an account of the prizes which he sold last year; and whether the advertising controvertists do not indulge asperity of language without any adequate provocation; as in the dispute about *straps for razors,* now happily subsided, and in the altercation which at present subsists concerning *eau de luce?*

In an advertisement it is allowed to every man to speak well of himself, but I know not why he should assume the privilege of censuring his neighbour. He may proclaim his own virtue or skill, but ought not to exclude others from the same pretensions.

Every man that advertises his own excellence should write with some consciousness of a character which dares to call the attention of the public. He should remember that his name is to stand in the same paper with those of the King of Prussia and the Emperor of Germany, and endeavour to make himself worthy of such association.

Some regard is likewise to be paid to posterity. There are men of diligence and curiosity who treasure up the papers of the day merely because others neglect them, and in time they will be scarce. When these collections shall be read in another century, how will numberless contradictions be reconciled; and how shall fame be possibly distributed among the tailors and bodice-makers of the present age?

Surely these things deserve consideration. It is enough for me to have hinted my desire that these abuses may be rectified; but such is the state of nature, that what all have the right of doing, many will attempt without sufficient care or due qualifications.

THE MULTIPLICATION OF BOOKS[1]

ONE of the peculiarities which distinguish the present age is the multiplication of books. Every day brings new advertisements of literary undertakings, and we are flattered with repeated promises of growing wise on easier terms than our progenitors.

How much either happiness or knowledge is advanced by this multitude of authors, it is not very easy to decide. He that teaches us anything which we knew not before, is undoubtedly to be reverenced as a master. He that conveys knowledge by more pleasing ways, may very properly be loved as a benefactor; and he that supplies life with innocent amusement will certainly be caressed as a pleasing companion. But few of those who fill the world with books have any pretensions to the hope either of pleasing or instructing. They have often no other task than to lay two books before them, out of which they compile a third, without any new materials of their own, and with very little application of judgment to those which former authors have supplied.

That all compilations are useless, I do not assert. Particles of science are often very widely scattered. Writers of extensive comprehension have incidental remarks upon topics very remote from the principal subject, which are often more valuable than formal treatises, and which yet are not known because they are not promised in the title. He that collects those under proper heads is very laudably employed, for though he exerts no great abilities in the work, he facilitates the progress of others, and, by making that easy of attainment which is already written, may give some mind, more vigorous or more adventurous than his own, leisure for new thoughts and original designs.

But the collections poured lately from the press have been seldom made at any great expense of time or inquiry, and therefore only serve to distract choice without supplying any

---

[1] *Idler*, No. 85. Saturday, December 1, 1759.

real want. It is observed that "a corrupt society has many laws"; I know not whether it is not equally true that an ignorant age has many books. When the treasures of ancient knowledge lie unexamined, and original authors are neglected and forgotten, compilers and plagiaries are encouraged, who give us again what we had before, and grow great by setting before us what our own sloth had hidden from our view.

Yet are not even these writers to be indiscriminately censured and rejected. Truth, like beauty, varies its fashions, and it is best recommended by different dresses to different minds; and he that recalls the attention of mankind to any part of learning which time has left behind it, may be truly said to advance the literature of his own age. As the manners of nations vary, new topics of persuasion become necessary, and new combinations of imagery are produced; and he that can accommodate himself to the reigning taste may always have readers who, perhaps, would not have looked upon better performances. To exact of every man who writes that he should say something new, would be to reduce authors to a small number; to oblige the most fertile genius to say only what is new would be to contract his volumes to a few pages. Yet surely there ought to be some bounds to repetition; libraries ought no more to be heaped for ever with the same thoughts differently expressed, than with the same books differently decorated.

The good or evil which these secondary writers produce is seldom of any long duration. As they owe their existence to change of fashion, they commonly disappear when a new fashion becomes prevalent. The authors that in any nation last from age to age are very few, because there are very few that have any other claim to notice than that they catch hold on present curiosity, and gratify some accidental desire, or produce some temporary conveniency.

But however the writers of the day may despair of future fame, they ought at least to forbear any present mischief. Though they cannot arrive at eminent heights of excellence, they might keep themselves harmless. They might take care to inform themselves, before they attempt to inform others, and exert the little influence which they have for honest purposes.

But such is the present state of our literature, that the ancient sage, who thought "a great book a great evil," would now think the multitude of books a multitude of evils. He would consider a bulky writer who engrossed a year, and a swarm of pamphleteers who stole each an hour, as equal wasters of human life, and would make no other difference between them than between a beast of prey and a flight of locusts.

EDWARD MOORE

1712   Was born in Berkshire, the son of a dissenting minister.
1722–1743 Occurred the death of his father, upon which he became
        the ward of his uncle, a schoolmaster in Somerset.
        Attended his uncle's school and also a school in Dorset.
        Became apprenticed to a merchant in London.
        Spent some time in business in Ireland.
        Went into business in London but failed, and turned to
        literature.
1744   Published *Fables for the Female Sex*, a series of moral com-
        ments.
1748   Produced *The Foundling*, his first play, at Drury Lane.
1749   Married Jenny Hamilton, the daughter of the queen's table-
        decker.
1751   Produced *Gil Blas*, a play founded upon Le Sage's story.
1753   Produced *The Gamester*, a tragedy written in prose, in which
        Garrick played the leading part.
        Was appointed editor of the *World*, and composed sixty-one
        of its 210 numbers, writing under the *nom de plume*, Adam
        FitzAdam.
1757   Died, and was buried in South Lambeth Churchyard.

PRESENT AND PAST[1]

I HAVE hinted more than once in the course of these papers,
that the present age, notwithstanding the vices and follies
with which it abounds, has the happiness of standing as high
in my opinion as any age whatsoever. But it has been always the fashion to believe, that from the beginning of the
world to the present day, men have been increasing in wicked-
ness; and though we have the Bible to turn to, which gives
us the history of mankind before the flood, and of the Jews

---
[1]*World*, No. 75. Thursday, June 6, 1754.

after it, we have still the humility to retain this opinion, and to lament the amazing degeneracy of the present times. But the eye of a philosopher can penetrate into this false humility, and discover it to be mere peevishmess and discontent. The truth is, that the present times, like our wives and our other possessions, are our own, and therefore we have no relish of them.

Many of my readers may possibly object to these encomiums on the times, imagining they may tend to make men satisfied with what they are, instead of inciting them to become what they ought to be. But it was always my opinion (and I believe it to be universally true) that men are more likely to be praised into virtue, than to be railed out of vice. It is a maxim in everybody's mouth, that reputation once lost is never to be recovered. He therefore to whom you give an ill name, will have little or no encouragement to endeavour at a good one, as knowing that if a character of infamy is once fixed, no change of behaviour can have power to redeem it. On the contrary, the man to whom you give a good name, though he should have merited a bad one, will find in his commerce with the world the advantages of such a name, and from conviction of those advantages be so solicitous to deserve it, as to become in reality the good man you have called him. People may reason away the merit of such a person's behaviour if they please, by ascribing it solely to self-love; they may add too, if they choose (and they have my hearty leave), that all virtue whatsoever has its source in that passion: if this be true (though the revealers of such truths cannot be complimented on their intention to promcte virtue) can there be a stronger argument for goodness, than that it is necessary to our happiness? It is said of that sagacious insect the bee, that he extracts honey from poison: and a mind, rightly turned, may draw instruction even from these gentlemen. But to return to my subject.

If people, when they are railing against the present times, instead of asserting in the gross that they are more wicked than the past, would content themselves with pointing out

what are really the vices that have gathered head amongst
us; if, for instance, they were to say that luxury and gaming
are at present at a much higher pitch than formerly, I should
be far from contradicting them. These are indeed the vices
of the times: but for the first of them, I am afraid we must
content ourselves with complaints, instead of offering at a
remedy: for as luxury is always owing to too much wealth,
Providence in its wisdom has so ordered it, that in due course
of time it will destroy itself. The cure therefore of luxury is
poverty; a remedy, which, though we do not care to prescribe
to ourselves, we are preparing at great pains and expense for
those that are to come after us. Of gaming I shall only observe, that, like luxury, it will in time work out its own cure;
and at the rate it goes on at present, one should imagine it
cannot last long.

I know of but one evil more that seems to have gathered
any degree of strength in these times, and that is corruption:
for, as to extravagance and a love of pleasure, I include them
in the article of luxury. And perhaps the evil of corruption,
as it is now practised, may admit of palliation: for though it
has been asserted by certain writers upon ethics, that it is
unlawful to do evil, that good may ensue, yet something may
be said in favour of a candidate for a seat in parliament, who,
if he should be tempted to commit the small evil of bribing a
borough or a few particulars in a county, it is, no doubt, in
order to effect so great a good as the preservation of the liberty,
the property, the happiness, the virtue, and the religion of a
whole nation.

As to all other vices, I believe they will be found to exist
among us pretty much in the same degree as heretofore, forms
only changing. Our grandfathers used to get drunk with
strong beer and port; we get drunk with claret and champaign. They would lie abominably to conceal their wenching;
we lie as abominably in boasting of ours. They stole slily
in at the back-door of a bagnio; we march in boldly at the
fore-door, and immediately steal out slily at the back-door.
Our mothers were prudes; their daughters coquets. The

first dressed like modest women, and perhaps were wantons; the last dress like women of the town, and perhaps are virtuous. Those treated without hanging out a sign; these hang out a sign without intending to treat. To be still more particular; the abuse of power, the views of patriots, the flattery of dependents, and the promises of great men, are, I believe, pretty much the same now as in former ages. Vices that we have no relish for, we part with for those we like; giving up avarice for prodigality, hypocrisy for profligacy, and lewdness for play.

But as I have instanced in this essay the particular vices of the times, it would be doing them injustice if I neglected to observe, that humanity, charity, and the civilities of life, never abounded so much as now. I must also repeat, what has already been taken notice of in these papers, that our virtues receive a lustre, and our vices a softening, by manners and decorum.

There is a folly indeed (for I will not call it a vice) with which the ladies of this age are particularly charged: it is,that not only their airs and their dress, but even their faces are French. I wish with all my heart that I could preserve my integrity, and vindicate my fair countrywomen from this imputation; but I am sorry to say it, what by travelling abroad, and by French milliners, mantua-makers and hair-cutters at home, our politest assemblies seem to be filled with foreigners. But how will it astonish many of my readers to be told, that while they are extolling the days of good Queen Bess, they are complimenting that very reign in which these fashions were originally introduced! But because in a matter of so much consequence no man's bare word should be taken, I shall make good my assertion by publishing an authentic letter, written by that subtle minister Sir William Cecil (afterwards Lord Burleigh) to Sir Henry Norris, Queen Elizabeth's ambassador at the court of France. This letter was originally printed in the year sixteen hundred and sixty-three, among a collection of state letters called *Scrinia Ceciliana,* or Mysteries of Government, and is as follows:

"SIR,

"The queen's majesty would fain have a tailor that had skill to make her apparel both after the French and Italian manner: and she thinketh that you might use some means to obtain some one such there as serveth the queen, without mentioning any manner of request in the queen's majesty's name.   First to cause my lady your wife to use some such means to get one, as thereof knowledge might not come to the queen's mother's ears, of whom the queen's majesty thinketh thus; that if she did understand that it were a matter wherein her majesty might be pleasured, she would offer to send one to the queen's majesty: nevertheless if it cannot be so obtained by this indirect means, then her majesty would have you devise some other good means to obtain one that were skilful.

"Yours in all truth,
"W. CECIL"

I shall only observe upon this letter (which I confess to be a masterpiece for subtilty and contrivance) that if by the introduction and increase of French fashions, our religion and government are also in time to be French (which many worthy patriots and elderly gentlewomen are in dreadful apprehension of) we ought no doubt to throw off all regard to the memory of Queen Elizabeth, and to lament that her minister was not impeached of high-treason, for advising and encouraging so pernicious an attempt against that Magna Charta of dress, the old English Ruff and Fardingale.

JOHN HAWKESWORTH

1715(?) Was born in London, of humble parents.

1744 Succeeded Samuel Johnson as compiler of parliamentary debates for the *Gentlemen's Magazine*.

1746-1749 Contributed poetry to the *Gentlemen's Magazine*.

1752-1754 Founded—with Johnson, Bathurst, and Warton—and edited the *Adventurer*.

1755 Published the *Works of Jonathan Swift*, in twelve volumes.

1756 Altered, at the request of David Garrick, Dryden's *Amphitryon*, which was produced at Drury Lane.

Received the degree of LL.D. at the hands of Archbishop Herring.

Became the superintendent of the school for young ladies conducted by his wife at Bromley, having failed in his intention of practicing in the ecclesiastical courts.

Became estranged from Johnson.

1759 Adapted Southerne's *Oroonoko* for production at Drury Lane.

1760 Wrote an oratorio, *Zimri*, the music for which was composed by John Stanley.

1761 Published *Almoran and Hamet*, an Oriental story.

1765 Was appointed reviewer of new books for the *Gentlemen's Magazine*.

1766 Published *Letters Written by the Late Jonathan Swift, 1703-1740*.

1769 Sat for his portrait to Sir Joshua Reynolds.

1771 Was appointed by Lord Sandwich, at the instigation of David Garrick, to revise and publish an account of certain voyages to the South Seas.

1773 Published *An Account of the Voyages Undertaken by Order of His Present Majesty for Making Discoveries in the Southern Hemisphere, of Joseph Banks, Esq.*, a work for which he is said to have received £6,000.

Died as the result of a fever, aggravated by the attacks of the press on the *Voyages*, and was buried at Bromley.

1774 Thurlow attacked the *Voyages* as being an example of the exploitation of literary work possible under the then existing copyright laws.

FROM GREENHORN TO BLOOD[1]

To the Adventurer,
Sir,

Though the characters of men have, perhaps, been essen‹
tially the same in all ages, yet their external appearance has
changed with other peculiarities of time and place, and they
have been distinguished by different names, as new modes of
expression have prevailed: a periodical writer, therefore,
who catches the picture of evanescent life, and shows the
deformity of follies which in a few years will be so changed as
not to be known, should be careful to express the character
when he describes the appearance, and to connect it with
the name by which it then happens to be called. You have
frequently used the terms *Buck* and *Blood*, and have given
some account of the characters which are thus denominated;
but you have not considered them as the last stages of a
regular progression, nor taken any notice of those which pre-
cede them. Their dependence upon each other is, indeed,
so little known, that many suppose them to be distinct and
collateral classes, formed by persons of opposite interests,
tastes, capacities, and dispositions: the scale, however, consists of eight degrees: *Greenhorn, Jemmy, Jessamy, Smart,
Honest Fellow, Joyous Spirit, Buck*, and *Blood*. As I have
myself passed through the whole series, I shall explain each
station by a short account of my life, remarking the periods
when my character changed its denomination, and the particular incidents by which the change was produced.

My father was a wealthy farmer in Yorkshire; and when I
was near eighteen years of age, he brought me up to London,
and put me apprentice to a considerable shop-keeper in the
city. There was an awkward modest simplicity in my manner, and a reverence of religion and virtue in my conversation. The novelty of the scene that was now placed before
me, in which there were innumerable objects that I never con-

---

[1] *Adventurer*, No. 100. Saturday, October 20, 1753.

ceived to exist, rendered me attentive and credulous; peculiarities, which, without a provincial accent, a slough in my gait,
a long lank head of hair, an unfashionable suit of drab-
coloured cloth, would have denominated me a *Greenhorn*, or,
in other words, a *Country Put* very green.

Green, then, I continued even in externals, near two years;
and in this state I was the object of universal contempt and
derision; but being at length wearied with merriment and
insult, I was very sedulous to assume the manners and appearance of those, who in the same station were better treated.
I had already improved greatly in my speech; and my father
having allowed me thirty pounds a year for apparel and
pocket-money, the greater part of which I had saved, I bespoke a suit of clothes of an eminent city tailor, with several
waistcoats and breeches, and two frocks for a change: I cut
off my hair, and procured a brown bob periwig of Wilding, of
the same colour with a single row of curls just round the bottom, which I wore very nicely combed, and without powder:
my hat, which had been cocked with great exactness in an
equilateral triangle, I discarded, and purchased one of a
more fashionable size, the fore corner of which projected
near two inches further than those on each side, and was
moulded into the shape of a spout: I also furnished myself
with a change of white thread stockings, took care that my
pumps were varnished every morning with a new German
blacking-ball; and when I went out, carried in my hand a
little switch, which, as it has been long appendant to the
character that I had just assumed, has taken the same name,
and is called a *Jemmy*.

I soon perceived the advantage of this transformation.
My manner had not, indeed, kept pace with my dress; I was
still modest and diffident, temperate and sober, and consequently still subject to ridicule: but I was now admitted into
company, from which I had before been excluded by the
rusticity of my appearance; I was rallied and encouraged by
turns; and I was instructed both by precept and example.
Some offers were made of carrying me to a house of private

entertainment, which then I absolutely refused; but I soon found the way into the playhouse, to see the last two acts, and the farce: here I learned that by breaches of chastity no man was thought to incur either guilt or shame; but that, on the contrary, they were essentially necessary to the character of a fine gentleman. I soon copied the original, which I found to be universally admired, in my morals, and made some farther approaches to it in my dress; I suffered my hair to grow long enough to comb back over the fore-top of my wig, which when I sallied forth to my evening amusement, I changed to a queue; I tied the collar of my shirt with half an ell of black riband, which appeared under my neck-cloth; the fore corner of my hat was considerably elevated and shortened so it no longer resembled a spout, but the corner of a minced pie; my waistcoat was edged with a narrow lace, my stockings were silk, and I never appeared without a pair of clean gloves. My address, from its native masculine plainness, was converted to an excess of softness and civility, especially when I spoke to the ladies. I had before made some progress in learning to swear; I had proceeded by *fegs, faith, pox, plague, 'pon my life, 'pon my soul, rat it,* and *zookers,* to *zauns* and *the divill.* I now advanced to *by Jove, 'fore ged, ged's curse it,* and *demme:* but I still uttered these interjections in a tremulous tone, and my pronunciation was feminine and vicious. I was sensible of my defects, and, therefore, applied with great diligence to remove them. I frequently practised alone, but it was a long time before I could swear so much to my own satisfaction in company, as by myself. My labour, however, was not without its reward; it recommended me to the notice of the ladies, and procured me the gentle appellation of *Jessamy.*

I now learned among other grown gentlemen to dance, which greatly enlarged my acquaintance; I entered into a subscription for country dances once a week at a tavern, where each gentleman engaged to bring a partner: at the same time I made considerable advances in swearing; I could pronounce *demme* with a tolerable air and accent, give the vowel its full sound, and look with confidence in the face of the person to whom I spoke. About this time my father's elder brother died, and left me an estate of near five hundred pounds *per annum*. I now bought out the remainder of my time; and this sudden accession of wealth and independence gave me immediately an air of greater confidence and freedom. I laid out near one hundred and fifty pounds in clothes, though I was obliged to go into mourning: I employed a court tailor to make them up; I exchanged my queue for a bag; I put on a sword, which, in appearance, at least, was a Toledo; and in proportion as I knew my dress to be elegant, I was less solicitous to be neat. My acquaintance now increased every hour; I was attended, flattered, and caressed; was often invited to entertainments, supped every night at a tavern, and went home in a chair; was taken notice of in public places, and was universally confessed to be improved into a *Smart*.

There were some intervals in which I found it necessary to abstain from wenching; and in these, at whatever risk, I applied myself to the bottle, a habit of drinking came insensibly upon me, and I was soon able to walk home with a bottle and a pint. I had learned a sufficient number of fashionable toasts, and got by heart several toping and several bawdy songs, some of which I ventured to roar out with a friend hanging on my arm as we scoured the street after our nocturnal revel. I now laboured with indefatigable industry to increase these acquisitions: I enlarged my stock of healths; made great progress in singing, joking, and story-telling; swore well; could make a company of staunch topers drunk; always collected the reckoning, and was the last man that departed. My face began to be covered with red pimples, and my eyes to be weak; I became daily more negligent of my dress, and more blunt in my manner; I professed myself a foe to starters and milk-sops, declared that there was no enjoyment equal to that of a bottle and a friend, and soon gained the appellation of an *Honest Fellow*.

By this distinction I was animated to attempt yet greater

excellence; I learned several feats of mimicry of the under players, could take off known characters, tell a staring story, and humbug with so much skill, as sometimes to take in a knowing one. I was so successful in the practice of these arts, to which, indeed, I applied myself with unwearied diligence and assiduity, that I kept my company roaring with applause, till their voices sunk by degrees, and they were no longer able either to hear or to see. I had now ascended another scale in the climax, and was acknowledged, by all who knew me, to be a *Joyous Spirit*.

After all these topics of merriment were exhausted, and I had repeated my tricks, my stories, my jokes, and my songs, till they grew insipid, I became mischievous; and was continually devising and executing frolics, to the unspeakable delight of my companions, and the injury of others. For many of them I was prosecuted, and frequently obliged to pay large damages: but I bore all these losses with an air of jovial indifference; I pushed on in my career, I was more desperate in proportion as I had less to lose: and being deterred from no mischief by the dread of its consequences, I was said to run at all, and complimented with the name of *Buck*.

My estate was at length mortgaged for more than it was worth; my creditors were importunate; I became negligent of myself and of others: I made a desperate effort at the gaming-table, and lost the last sum that I could raise; my estate was seized by the mortgagee; I learned to pack cards and to cog a die; became a bully to whores; passed my nights in a brothel, the street, or the watch-house; was utterly insensible of shame, and lived upon the town as a beast of prey in a forest. Thus I reached the summit of modern glory, and had just acquired the distinction of a *Blood*, when I was arrested for an old debt of three hundred pounds, and thrown into the King's Bench prison.

These characters, Sir, though they are distinct, yet do not at all differ, otherwise than as shades of the same colour, and though they are stages of a regular progression, yet the whole progress is not made by every individual: some are so soon initiated in the mysteries of the town, that they are never publicly known in their Greenhorn state; others fix long in their Jemmyhood, others are Jessamies at fourscore, and some stagnate in each of the higher stages for life. But I request that they may never hereafter be confounded either by you or your correspondents. Of the Blood, your brother adventurer, Mr. Wildgoose, though he assumes the character, does not seem to have a just and precise idea as distinct from the Buck, in which class he should be placed, and will probably die; for he seems determined to shoot himself, just at the time when his circumstances will enable him to assume the higher distinction.

But the retrospect upon life, which this letter has made necessary, covers me with confusion, and aggravates despair. I cannot but reflect, that among all these characters, I have never assumed that of a Man. Man is a reasonable being, which he ceases to be, who disguises his body with ridiculous fopperies, or degrades his mind by detestable brutality. These thoughts would have been of great use to me, if they had occurred seven years ago. If they are of use to you, I hope you will send me a small gratuity for my labour, to alleviate the misery of hunger and nakedness: but dear Sir, let your bounty be speedy, lest I perish before it arrives.

I am your humble servant

NOMENTANUS

RICHARD OWEN CAMBRIDGE

1717   Was born in London, the son of a merchant.
Studied at Eton.

1734   Entered St. John's College, Oxford,

1736   Published a poem on the marriage of Frederick, Prince of Wales, in *Oxford Congratulatory Verses.*

1737   Left Oxford without taking a degree, and became a member of Lincoln's Inn.

1741   Married the granddaughter of Sir John Trenchard, Secretary of State under William III.
Removed to Whitminster in Gloucester.

1748   Inherited a fortune from his uncle and took up his residence in London.

1751   Removed to Twickenham, where he remained during the rest of his life.
Published *The Scribleriad*, a mock-heroic poem in the manner of Pope.

1752   Published *A Dialogue Between a Member of Parliament and His Servant*, a satiric poem in imitation of Horace.

1753–1756 Contributed twenty-one papers to the *World.*

1754   Published *The Intruder* and *The Fable of Jotham*, imitations of Horace.

1756   Published *The Fakeer* and *An Elegy Written in an Empty Bath Assembly Room.*

1761   Published *History of the War upon the Coast of Coromandel*, a treatise upon Indian history which remained authoritative for many years.

1802   Died at Twickenham.

FROM SUPERFLUITY TO NECESSITY

IT IS an observation of the Duke de Rochefaucault, "that there are many people in the world who would never have been in love if they had never heard talk of it." As strange

---

¹*World*, No. 72. Thursday, May 16, 1754.

as this assertion may appear, there is nothing more certain, than that mankind pursue with much greater ardour, what they are talked into an admiration of, than what they are prompted to by natural passions; nay, so great is the infatuation, that we frequently see them relinquishing real gratifications, for the sake of following ideal notions, or the accidental mode of thinking of the present times.

The story of the princess Parizade in the Arabian tales, is a proper illustration of what I have here advanced. I shall give my readers a short abstract of this story, as it may furnish matters for reflection, and a very useful moral, to such of them as regulate their whole conduct, and even their desires, by fashion.

This princess, the happiest as well as most beautiful of her sex, lived with her two beloved brothers in a splendid palace, situated in the midst of a delightful park, and the most exquisite gardens in the east. It happened one day, while the princes were hunting, that an old woman came to the gate, and desired admittance to the oratory, that she might say her prayers. The princess no sooner knew of her request than she granted it, giving orders to her attendants, that after the good woman's prayers were ended, they should show her all the apartments of the palace, and then bring her into the hall where she herself was sitting. Everything was performed as directed; and the princess, having regaled her guest with some fruits and sweet-meats, among many other questions, asked her what she thought of the palace.

"Madam," answered the old woman, "your palace is beautiful, regular, and magnificently furnished; its situation is delightful, and its gardens are beyond compare. But yet, if you will give me leave to speak freely, there are three things wanting to make it perfect."—"My good mother," interrupted the princess Parizade, "what are those three things? I conjure you in God's name to tell me what they are; and if there be a possibility of obtaining them, neither difficulties nor dangers shall stop me in the attempt." "Madam," replied the old woman, "the first of these three things is the

Talking Bird, the second is the Singing Tree, and the third
is the Yellow or Golden Water." "Ah, my good mother,"
cried the princess, "how much am I obliged to you for the
knowledge of these things! They are no doubt the greatest
curiosities in the world, and unless you can tell me where
they are to be found, I am the most unhappy of women."
The old woman satisfied the princess in that material point,
and then took her leave.

The story goes on to inform us, that when the two princes
returned from hunting, they found the princess Parizade so
wrapt up in thought, that they imagined some great misfortune had befallen her, which when they had conjured her
to acquaint them with, she only lifted up her eyes to look
upon them, and then fixed them again upon the ground,
telling them that nothing disturbed her. The entreaties of
the two princes, however, at last prevailed, and the princess
addressed them in the following manner.

"You have often told me, my dear brothers, and I have
always believed, that this house, which our father built, was
complete in everything, but I have learnt this day that it
wants three things; these are the Talking Bird, the Singing
Tree, and the Yellow Water. An old woman has made this
discovery to me, and told me the place where they are to be
found, and the way thither. Perhaps you may look upon
these rarities as trifles; but think what you please, I am fully
persuaded that they are absolutely necessary; and whether
you value them or not, I cannot be easy without them."

The sequel tells us, that after the princess Parizade had
expressed herself with this proper spirit upon the occasion,
the brothers, in pity to her wants, went in pursuit of these
necessaries, and that failing in the enterprize, they were one
after another turned into stone.

The application of this tale is so universal, that the enu-
merating particulars is almost an unnecessary labour.
The whole fashionable world are so many Parizades; and
things not only useless in their natures, but also ugly in themselves, from having been once termed charming by some

fashionable leaders of modern taste, are now become so necessary that nobody can do without them.

But though this story happens to be told of a lady, the folly it particularizes is chiefly to be found in the other sex: I mean, in respect to the pernicious consequences attending vain and chimerical pursuits.

If we enter into the strictest examination of these idle longings of the women, we shall find that they seldom amount to anything more than a dissipation of their pin money, without any other ill consequence than that of turning their thoughts from some real good, which they actually possess, to an imaginary expectation. The passion for shells, old china, and the like, is confessedly trifling; but it is only blameable in proportion to the anxiety with which it is pursued: but what is this in comparison to the desolation of ambition, the waste of magnificence, and the ruin of play?

Madame Montespan's coach and six mice was not a more idle, though it was a less mischievous folly, than the armies of her lover, Lewis the fourteenth. The ambition of that monarch to emulate the conquerors of antiquity; of Cæsar to rival Alexander; of Alexander to resemble the hero of his darling poem, the *Iliad;* the designs of Pyrrhus, and the project of Xerxes; what were they but counterparts to a passion for the Talking Bird, the Singing Tree, and the Yellow Water?

To descend a little into private life, how many do we see daily talked into a rage for building, gardening, painting, and divers other expenses, to the embarrassing a fortune which would more than sufficiently supply the necessaries of life? Among the numbers who have changed a sober plan of living for one of riot and excess, the greatest part have been converted by the arguments in a drinking song. Thousands have taken the same fruitless and expensive journey, because they have heard that it is very John Trott not to have visited France, and that a person who has not been abroad has seen nothing. I was once told by a gentleman, who had undone himself by keeping running horses, that he owed his ruin to a strong impression made upon him, when a boy, by his father's butler, who happened to declare in his hearing, "that it was a creditable thing to keep good cattle; and that if he was a gentleman, he should take great pleasure in being always well mounted."

But to apply our fable to the most recent instance of this species of infatuation: How often have we seen an honest country gentleman, who has lived a truly happy life, blessed in his family, amused with his farms and gardens, entertained by his own beneficence, usefully employed in the administration of justice, or in reconciling the differences of his litigious neighbours, but who being talked into an opinion of the great service a man might do his country, as well as honour to himself, by getting into parliament, has given up all his real enjoyments and useful occupations for this imaginary phantom, which has only taught him by experience, what he might have learnt from example, that the family interest, as it is called, is too often the destruction of the family estate.

As to all those gentlemen who have gained their elections, I most sincerely wish them joy; and for those who have been disappointed, and who now may have leisure to turn their thoughts from their country to themselves, I beg leave to recommend to them the pleasures, and I may add, the duties of domestic life: in comparison of which all other advantages are nothing more than the Talking Bird, the Singing Tree, and the Yellow Water.

HORACE WALPOLE
EARL OF ORFORD

1717 Was born in London, the fourth son of Sir Robert Walpole, first earl of Orford.

1727 Entered Eton, where began his acquaintance with Thomas Gray.

1735 Entered King's College, Cambridge.

1738 Became "usher of the exchequer," "comptroller of the pipe," and "clerk of the estreats," appointments made through the influence of his father as Prime Minister.

1739 Left Cambridge, and went abroad with Thomas Gray. Quarreled with Gray.

1741 Returned to England.

1741–1767 Served as a member of Parliament.

1746 Wrote the prologue for Rowe's *Tamerlaine* for presentation at the court.
Contributed to the *Museum*.
Wrote *The Beauties*.
Resumed his friendship with Gray.

1747 Removed to Twickenham, buying, subsequently the property known as "Strawberry Hill," which he filled with art treasures.

1753 Contributed to the *World*.

1757 Established a private printing press at Strawberry Hill.
Published *A Letter from Xo Ho, a Chinese Philosopher at London, to His Friend Lien Chi, at Pekin*, a work which probably suggested Goldsmith's *Citizen of the World*.

1762 Published *Anecdotes of Painting in England*, the work which caused Thomas Chatterton to seek his patronage.

1764 Published *The Castle of Otranto*, the forerunner of the "Gothic romance."

1767 Published *Historic Doubts of Richard Third*.

1768 Published *The Mysterious Mother*, a tragedy.

1778 Produced *Nature Will Prevail*, a fairy comedy, at the Haymarket.

1797 Died in London.

POLITENESS[1]

I am never better pleased than when I can vindicate the honour of my native country; at the same time I would not endeavour to defend it preposterously, nor to contradict the eyes, the senses of mankind, out of stark good patriotism. The fluctuating condition of the things of this world necessarily produces a change in manners and morals, as well as in the face of countries and cities. Climates cannot operate so powerfully on constitutions, as to preserve the same character perpetually to the same nations. I do not doubt but in some age of the world the Bœotians will be a very lively whimsical people, and famous for their repartees; and that our neighbour islanders will be remarkable for the truth of their ideas, and for the precision with which they will deliver the conceptions. Some men are so bigoted to antiquated notions, that if they were, even in this age, to write a panegyric on old England, they would cram their composition with encomiums on our good nature, our bravery, and our hospitality. This indeed might be a panegyric on old England, but would have very little resemblance to the modern characteristics of the nation. Our good nature was necessarily soured by the spirit of the party; our courage has been a little cramped by the act of parliament that restrained prize-fighting; and hospitality is totally impracticable, since a much more laudable custom has been introduced, and prevailed universally, of paying the servants of other people much more than their master's dinner cost. Yet we shall always have virtues sufficient to countenance very exalted panegyrics: and if some of our more heroic qualities are grown obsolete, others of a gentler cast, and better calculated for the help of society, have grown up and diffused themselves in their room. While we were rough and bold, we could not be polite; while we feasted half a dozen wapentakes with sirloins of beef, and sheep roasted whole, we could not attend

---

[1] *World*, No. 103. Thursday, December 19, 1754.

to the mechanism of a plate, no bigger than a crown piece, loaded with the legs of canary birds, dressed *à la Pompadour*. Let nobody start at my calling this a polite nation. It shall be the business of this paper to prove that we are the most polite nation in Europe; and that France must yield to us in the extreme delicacy of our refinements. I might urge, as a glaring instance in which that nation has forfeited her title to politeness, the impertinent spirit of her parliaments, which, though couched in very civilly-worded remonstrances, is certainly at bottom very ill-bred. They have contradicted their monarch, and crossed his clergy in a manner not to be defended by a people who pique themselves upon complaisance and attentions.—But I abominate politics: and when I am writing in defence of politeness, shall certainly not blend so coarse a subject with so civil a theme.

It is not virtue that constitutes the politeness of a nation, but the art of reducing vice to a system that does not shock society. Politeness (as I understand the word) is an universal desire of pleasing others (that are not too much below one) in trifles, for a little time; and of making one's intercourse with them agreeable to both parties, by civility without ceremony, by ease without brutality, by complaisance without flattery, by acquiescence without sincerity. A clergyman who puts his patron into a sweat by driving him round the room, till he has found the coolest place for him, is not polite. When Bubbamira changes her handkerchief before you, and wipes her neck, rather than leave you alone while she should perform the refreshing office in the next room, I should think she is not polite. When Boncœur shivers on your dreary hill, where for twenty years you have been vainly endeavouring to raise reluctant plantations, and yet profess that only some of the trees have been a little kept back by the late dry season, he is not polite; he is more; he is kind. When Sophia is really pleased with the stench of a kennel, because her husband likes that she should go and look at a favourite litter, she must not pretend to politeness;

she is only a good wife. If this definition, and these instances
are allowed me, it will be difficult to maintain that the nations
who have had the most extensive renown for politeness, had
any pretensions to it. The Greeks called all the rest of the
world barbarians: the Romans went still farther, and treated
them as such. Alexander, the best-bred hero amongst the
former, I must own, was polite, and showed great attentions
to Darius's family; but I question, if he had not extended his
attentions a little farther to the princess Statira, whether he
could be pronounced quite well-bred. As to the Romans, so
far were they from having any notion of treating foreigners
with regard, that there is not one classic author that mentions
a single ball or masquerade given to any stranger of distinction. Nay, it was a common practice with them to tie kings,
queens, and women of the first fashion of other countries in
couples, like hounds, and drag them along their *via Piccadillia*
in triumph, for the entertainment of their shop-keepers and
'prentices. A practice that we should look upon with horror!
What would the *Examiner* have said, if the duke of Marlborough had hauled Marshall Tallard to St. Paul's or the
Royal Exchange, behind his chariot? How deservedly
would the French have called us savages, if we had made
Marshall Bellisle pace along the kennel in Fleet-street, or up
Holborn, while some of our ministers or generals called it an
ovation?

The French, who attempt to succeed the Romans in
empire, and who affect to have succeeded them in politeness,
have adopted the same way of thinking, though so contrary
to true good-breeding. They have no idea that an Englishman or a German ever sees a suit of clothes till he arrives at
Paris. They wonder, if you talk of a coach at Vienna, or of a
soupe at London: and are so confident of having monopolized
all the arts of civilized life, that with the greatest complaisance in the world, they affirm to you, that they suppose your
dukes and duchesses live in caves, with only the property of
wider forests than ordinary, and that *les milords Anglois*,
with a great deal of money, live upon raw flesh, and ride races

without breeches or saddles. At their houses they receive
you with wonder that shocks you, or with indifference that
mortifies you; and if they put themselves to the torture of
conversing with you, after you have taken infinite pains to
acquire their language, it is merely to inform you, that you
neither know how to dress like a sensible man, nor to eat,
drink, game, or divert yourself like a christian. How different are our attentions to foreigners! how open our houses to
their nobility, our purses to their tradesmen! But without
drawing antitheses between our politeness and their ill-
breeding, I shall produce an instance in which we have
pushed our refinements on the duties of society beyond what
the most civilized nations ever imagined. We are not only
well-bred in common intercourse, but our very crimes are
transacted with such a softness of manners, that though they
may injure, they are sure never to affront our neighbour.
The instance I mean, is, the extreme good-breeding that has
been introduced into the science of robbery; which (considering how very frequent it is become) would really grow a
nuisance to society, if the professors of it had not taken all
imaginable precautions to make it as civil a commerce, as
gaming, conveyancing, toad-eating, pimping, or any of the
money-inveigling arts, which have already got an established
footing in the world. A highwayman would be reckoned a
brute, a monster, if he had not all manner of attention not to
frighten the ladies; and none of the great Mr. Nash's laws
are more sacred than that of restoring any favourite bauble
to which a robbed lady has a particular partiality. Now
turn your eyes to France. No people upon earth has less of
the *scavoir vivre*[1] than their banditti. No Tartar has less
douceur[2] in his manner than a French highwayman. He
takes your money without making you a bow, and your life
without making you an apology. This obliges their government to keep up numerous *guets*,[3] a severe police, racks,

[1]Good breeding.
[2]Gentleness.
[3]Watchmen.

gibbets, and twenty troublesome things, which might all be avoided, if they would only reckon and breed up their thieves to be good company. I know that some of our latest imported young gentlemen affirm that the Sieur Mandriew, the terror of the eastern provinces, learned the dance of Marseille himself, and has frequently supped with the incomparable Jelliot. But till I hear whether he dies like a gentleman, I shall forbear to rank him with the *petits-maîtres*[1] of our own Tyburn. How extreme is the *politesse* of the latter! Mrs. Chenevix has not more insinuation when she sells a snuff-box of *papier mâché*, or a bergamot toothpick-case, than a highwayman when he begs to know if you have no rings or bank-bills.

An acquaintance of mine was robbed a few years ago, and very near shot through the head by the going off of a pistol of the accomplished Mr. M'Lean; yet the whole affair was conducted with the greatest good-breeding on both sides. The robber, who had only taken a purse this way, because he had that morning been disappointed of marrying a great fortune, no sooner returned to his lodgings, than he sent the gentleman two letters of excuses, which, with less wit than the epistles of Voiture, had ten times more natural and easy politeness in the turn of their expression. In the postscript, he appointed a meeting at Tyburn at twelve at night, where the gentleman might purchase again any trifles he had lost; and my friend has been blamed for not accepting the rendez-vous, as it seemed liable to be construed by ill-natured people into a doubt of the honour of a man, who had given him all the satisfaction in his power, for having unluckily been near shooting him through the head.

The Lacedæmonians were the only people, except the English, who seem to have put robbery on a right foot; and I have often wondered how a nation that had delicacy enough to understand robbing on the highway, should at the same time have been so barbarous, as to esteem poverty, black-

---

[1]Beaux.

broth, and virtue! We had no highwaymen, that were men
of fashion, till we had exploded plum-porridge.

But of all the gentlemen of the road who have conformed
to the manner of the great world, none seem to me to have
carried true politeness so far as a late adventurer, whom I
beg leave to introduce to my readers under the title of the
Visiting Highwayman. This refined person made it a rule
to rob none but people he visited; and whenever he designed
an impromptu of that kind, dressed himself in a rich suit,
went to a lady's house, asked for her, and not finding her at
home, left his name with her porter, after inquiring which
way she was gone. He then followed, or met her on her return home, proposed his demands, which were generally for
some favourite ring or snuff-box that he had seen her wear,
and which he had a mind to wear for her sake; and then letting her know that he had been to wait on her, took his leave
with a cool bow, and without scampering away, as other men
of fashion do from a visit with really the appearance of having
stolen something.

As I do not doubt but such of my fair readers, as propose
being at home this winter, will be impatient to send this
charming smuggler (Charles Fleming by name) a card for
their assemblies, I am sorry to tell them that he was hanged
last week.

JOSEPH WARTON

1722 Was born in Surrey, the son of a clergyman, and the elder brother of Thomas Warton.
Attended grammar school at Basingstoke.

1735 Elected a scholar at Winchester School, where he formed a friendship with Gilbert White, later a famous biologist; and with William Collins, later one of the best known poets of his day.

1739 Published a poem in the *Gentlemen's Magazine*, which was favorably noticed by Dr. Johnson.

1740 Entered Oriel College, Oxford.

1744 Received the B. A. degree from Oxford, and took orders, acting as his father's curate until the death of the latter in 1745.
Published *Ode on Reading West's Pindar*.

1746 Published *Odes on Various Subjects*.

1748 Married Mary Daman.

1754 Issued an edition of Virgil in both Latin and English.
Contributed to the *World*.

1753–1756 Contributed twenty-four papers to the *Adventurer*.

1754 Became rector of Tunworth.

1755 Became second-master at the Winchester School.

1756 Issued the first volume of the *Essay on the Genius and Work of Pope*.

1759 Received the M. A. degree from Oxford.

1766 Became head-master of the Winchester School.

1768 Received the B.D. and D.D. degrees from Oxford.

1772 Occurred the death of his wife.

1773 Married Charlotte Nicholas.

1782 Issued the second volume of the *Essay on Pope*.

1793 Resigned as head-master of the Winchester School and retired to Wickham.

1797 Issued an edition of the work of Pope, in nine volumes.

1800 Died, and was buried in Winchester Cathedral.

A VISIT TO BEDLAM WITH DEAN SWIFT: A VISION[1]

To the Adventurer,

Sir,

Montesquieu wittily observes, that by building professed madhouses, men tacitly insinuate, that all who are out of their senses are to be found only in those places. This remark having made some impression on my mind, produced last night the following vision.

I imagined that Bedlam had been ordered to be rebuilt upon a more extensive plan by act of parliament; and that Dean Swift, calling at my lodgings, offered to accompany me to see the new-erected edifice, which, he observed, was not half capacious enough before to contain the various species of madness that are to be found in this kingdom. As we walked through the galleries, he gave me the following account of the several inhabitants.

The lady in the first apartment had prevailed upon her husband, a man of study and economy, to indulge her with a rout twice a week at her own house. This soon multiplied her obligations to the company she kept, and in a fortnight she insisted upon two more. His lordship venturing to oppose her demand with steady resolution, but with equal tenderness, the lady complained, that the rights of quality and fortune were invaded, that her credit was lost with the fashionable world, and that ignorance and brutality had robbed her of the pleasures of a reasonable being, and rendered her the most unhappy wife in Great Britain. The cause of her complaints, however, still subsisted, and by perpetually brooding over it she at length turned her brain.

Next to her is a dramatic writer, whose comedy having been justly damned, he began to vent his spleen against the public, by weekly abuses of the present age; but as neither the play nor his defences of it were read, his indignation continually increased, till at length it terminated in madness.

---

[1]*Adventurer*, No. 109. Tuesday, November 20, 1753.

He on the right hand is a philosopher, who has lost his reason in a fruitless attempt to discover the cause of electricity.

He on the left is a celebrated jockey of noble birth, whose favourite mare, that had enjoyed three triumphs in former seasons, was distanced a few days ago at Newmarket.

Yonder meagre man has bewildered his understanding by closely studying the doctrine of the chances, in order to qualify himself for a professorship which will be shortly established and amply endowed at an eminent chocolate-house, where lectures on this important subject are constantly to be read.

An unforeseen accident turned the head of the next unfortunate prisoner. She had for a long time passed for fifteen years younger than she was, and her lively behaviour and airy dress concurred to help forward the imposition; till one evening, being animated with an extraordinary flow of spirits, she danced out seven of her artificial teeth, which were immediately picked up, and delivered to her with great ceremony by her partner.

The merchant in the neighbouring cell had resolved to gain a plum. He was possessed of seventy thousand pounds, and eagerly expected a ship that was to complete his wishes. But the ship was cast away in the channel, and the merchant is distracted for his loss.

That disconsolate lady had for many years assiduously attended an old gouty uncle, had assented to all his absurdities, and humoured all his foibles, in full expectation of being made his executrix; when happening one day to affirm that his gruel had sack enough in it, contrary to his opinion, he altered his will immediately, and left all to her brother; which affords her no consolation, for avarice is able to subdue the tenderness of nature.

Behold the beautiful and virtuous Theodora! Her fondness for an ungrateful husband was unparalleled. She detected him in the arms of a disagreeable and affected prostitute, and was driven to distraction.

Is my old friend the commentator here likewise? Alas!

he has lost his wits in inquiring whether or no the ancients wore perukes? as did his neighbour Cynthio, by receiving a frown from his patron at the last levee.

The fat lady, upon whom you look so earnestly, is a grocer's wife in the city. Her disorder was occasioned by her seeing at court, last Twelfth night, the daughter of Mr. Alderman Squeeze, oil-man, in a sack far richer and more elegant than her own.

The next chamber contains an adventurer who purchased thirty tickets in the last lottery. As he was a person of a sanguine complexion, and lively imagination, he was sure of gaining the ten thousand pounds by the number of his chances. He spent a month in surveying the counties that lie in the neighbourhood of the metropolis, before he could find out an agreeable site for the fine house he intended to build. He next fixed his eye on a most blooming and beautiful girl, whom he designed to honour as his bride. He bespoke a magnificent coach, and the ornaments of his harness were to be of his own invention. Mr. Degagee, the taylor, was ordered to send to Paris for the lace with which his wedding clothes were to be adorned. But in the midst of these preparations for prosperity, all his tickets were drawn blanks; and instead of his villa on the banks of the Thames, you now see him in these melancholy lodgings.

His neighbour in the next apartment was an honest footman, who was likewise to try his fortune in the same lottery: and who, obtaining a very large and unexpected sum, could not stand the shock of such good fortune, but grew mad with excess of joy.

You wonder to see that cell beautified with Chinese vases and urns. It is inhabited by that famous virtuoso Lady Harriet Brittle, whose opinion was formerly decisive at all auctions, where she was usually appealed to about the genuineness of porcelain. She purchased, at an exorbitant price, a Mandarin, and a Jos, that were the envy of all the female connoisseurs, and were allowed to be inestimable. They were to be placed at the upper end of a little rock-work temple

of Chinese architecture, in which neither propriety, proportion, nor true beauty, were considered, and were carefully
packed up in different boxes; but the brutish waggoner happening to overturn his carriage, they were crushed to pieces.
The poor lady's understanding could not survive so irreparable a loss; and her relations, to soothe her passion, have provided those Chelsea urns with which she has decorated her
chamber, and which she believes to be the true Nanquin.

Yonder miserable youth, being engaged in a hot contention at a fashionable brothel about a celebrated courtezan,
killed a sea officer with whose face he was not acquainted;
but who proved upon inquiry to be his own brother, who had
been ten years absent in the Indies.

Look attentively into the next cell; you will there discover
a lady of great worth and fine accomplishment, whose father
condemned her to the arms of a right honourable debauchee,
when he knew she had fixed her affections irrevocably on
another, who possessed an unincumbered estate, but wanted
the ornament of a title. She submitted to the orders of a
stern father with patience, obedience, and a breaking heart.
Her husband treated her with that contempt which he
thought due to a citizen's daughter; and besides communicated to her an infamous distemper, which her natural
modesty forbade her to discover in time; and the violent
medicines which were afterwards administered to her by an
unskilful surgeon, threw her into a delirious fever, from which
she could never be recovered.

Here the Dean paused; and looking upon me with great
earnestness, and grasping my hand closely, spoke with an
emphasis that awakened me; —"Think me not so insensible
a monster, as to deride the lamentable lot of the wretches
we have now surveyed. If we laugh at the follies, let us at
the same time pity the manifold miseries of man."

I am, Sir,

Your humble servant,

SOPHRON

SIR JOSHUA REYNOLDS

1723 Was born in Devonshire, the son of a Fellow of Balliol College. Was educated by his father.

1731 Manifested a decided talent in drawing.

1741 Became apprenticed to Thomas Hudson, a fashionable London portrait painter.

1743-1746 Lived at Plympton with his father. Began to be known as a painter.

1746 Removed to Plymouth Dock, residing with his sisters. Continued to paint portraits, influenced now by William Gandy of Exeter.

1749-1752 Accompanied Commodore Keppel to Algeria, visiting Lisbon, Gibraltar, Leghorn, and later visiting the chief galleries of Italy and France.

1753 Began to outstrip Thomas Hudson in popularity, by reason of the character and force of his portrait of Keppel. Became acquainted with Dr. Samuel Johnson.

1755-1760 Produced many of his finest paintings.

1759 Produced *Venus*, perhaps his best imaginative work.

1760 Established himself in a house in Leicester Square. Contributed three papers on art to the *Idler*, which set forth the germ of his later *Discourses*.

1761 Came into his full powers through the portrait of Sterne.

1764 Suggested that the Literary Club be formed, the membership of which included Johnson, Burke, Goldsmith, Gibbon, Garrick, and many of the distinguished literary men of the time.

1768 Became first president of the Royal Academy. Was knighted by George III.

1769-1790 Delivered his fifteen *Discourses*.

1770 Exhibited companion portraits of Johnson and Goldsmith. Was accorded the dedication of Goldsmith's *Deserted Village*.

1771 Painted companion portraits of the king and queen.

1772 Was elected Alderman of Plympton, his native town.

1773 Was awarded the degree of D.C.L. by Oxford University.

1780 Painted the portrait of himself for the Academy.

1783 Painted Mrs. Siddons as "The Tragic Muse."

1784 Became "Painter to the King."
     Became an executor of the estate of Dr. Johnson upon the death of the latter.
     Commissioned by Empress Catherine of Russia to paint a picture for her. Painted "The Infant Hercules Strangling the Serpents," for which he received fifteen hundred guineas.
1787 Painted "The Duchess of Devonshire Playing with Her Infant Daughter."
1789 Lost the sight of his left eye and was forced to stop painting in order to save that of the other.
1791 Was accorded the dedication of Boswell's *Life of Johnson.*
1792 Died as the result of a tumor which developed in the region of the left eye.

TRUE IDEA OF BEAUTY[1]

To the Idler,
Sir,

Discoursing in my last letter on the different practice of the Italian and Dutch painters, I observed, that "the Italian painter attends only to the invariable, the great and general ideas which are fixed and inherent in universal nature."

I was led into the subject of this letter by endeavouring to fix the original cause of this conduct of the Italian masters. If it can be proved that by this choice they selected the most beautiful part of the creation, it will show how much their principles are founded on reason, and, at the same time, discover the origin of our ideas of beauty.

I suppose it will be easily granted, that no man can judge whether any animal be beautiful in its kind, or deformed, who has seen only one of that species; that is as conclusive in regard to the human figure, so that if a man, born blind, was to recover his sight, and the most beautiful woman was brought before him, he could not determine whether she was handsome or not; nor, if the most beautiful and most deformed were produced, could he any better determine to which he should

---

[1] *Idler,* No. 82. Saturday, November 10, 1759.

give the preference, having seen only these two. To distinguish beauty, then, implies the having seen many individuals of that species. If it is asked, how is more skill acquired by the observation of greater numbers? I answer that, in consequence of having seen many, the power is acquired, even without seeking after it, of distinguishing between accidental blemishes and excrescences which are continually varying the surface of Nature's works, and the invariable general form which Nature most frequently produces, and always seems to intend in her productions.

Thus amongst the blades of grass or leaves of the same tree, though no two can be found exactly alike, yet the general form is invariable: A naturalist, before he chose one as a sample, would examine many, since, if he took the first that occurred, it might have, by accident or otherwise, such a form as that it would scarcely be known to belong to that species; he selects, as the painter does, the most beautiful, that is, the most general form of nature.

Every species of the animal as well as the vegetable creation may be said to have a fixed or determinate form towards which nature is continually inclining, like various lines terminating in the centre; or it may be compared to pendulums vibrating in different directions over one central point, and as they all cross the centre, though only one passes through any other point, so it will be found that perfect beauty is oftener produced by nature than deformity; I do not mean than deformity in general, but than any one kind of deformity. To instance in a particular part of a feature: the line that .orms the ridge of the nose is beautiful when it is straight; this then is the central form, which is oftener found than either concave, convex, or any other irregular form that shall be proposed. As we are then more accustomed to beauty than deformity, we may conclude that to be the reason why we approve and admire it, as we approve and admire customs and fashions of dress for no other reason than that we are used to them, so that though habit and custom cannot be said to be the cause of beauty, it is certainly the cause of our liking it; and I have no doubt but that, if we were more used to deformity than beauty, deformity would then lose the idea now annexed to it, and take that of beauty; as, if the whole world should agree that *yes* and *no* should change their meaning, *yes* would then deny, and *no* would affirm.

Whoever undertakes to proceed further in this argument, and endeavours to fix a general criterion of beauty respecting different species, or to show why one species is more beautiful than another, it will be required from him first to prove that one species is really more beautiful than another. That we prefer one to the other, and with very good reason, will be readily granted; but it does not follow from thence that we think it more a beautiful form; for we have no criterion of form by which to determine our judgment. He who says a swan is more beautiful than a dove, means little more than that he has more pleasure in seeing a swan than a dove, either from the stateliness of its motions, or its being a more rare bird; and he who gives the preference to the dove, does it from some association of ideas of innocence that he always annexes to the dove; but, if he pretends to defend the preference he gives to one or the other by endeavouring to prove that this more beautiful form proceeds from a particular gradation of magnitude, undulation of a curve, or direction of a line, or whatever other conceit of his imagination he shall fix on as a criterion of form, he will be continually contradicting himself, and find at last that the great Mother of Nature will not be subjected to such narrow rules. Among the various reasons why we prefer one part of her works to another, the most general, I believe, is habit and custom; custom makes, in a certain sense, white black, and black white; it is custom alone determines our preference of the colour of the Europeans to the Ethiopians; and they for the same reason, prefer their own colour to ours. I suppose nobody will doubt, if one of their painters were to paint the goddess of beauty, but that he would represent her black, with thick lips, flat nose, and woolly hair; and, it seems to me, he would act very unnaturally if he did not, for by what criterion will any one dispute the propriety of his idea? We, indeed, say, that the form and colour of the European is preferable to that of the Ethiopian; but I know of no reason we have for it, but that we are more accustomed to it. It is absurd to say, that beauty is possessed of attractive powers, which irresistibly seize the corresponding mind with love and admiration, since that argument is equally conclusive in the favour of the white and the black philosopher.

The black and white nations must, in respect of beauty, be considered as of different kinds, at least a different species of the same kind; from one of which to the other, as I observed, no inference can be drawn.

Novelty is said to be one of the causes of beauty; that novelty is a very sufficient reason why we should admire, is not denied; but because it is uncommon, is it therefore beautiful? The beauty that is produced by colour, as when we prefer one bird to another, though of the same form, on account if its colour, has nothing to do with this argument, which reaches only to form. I have here considered the word *beauty* as being properly applied to form alone. There is a necessity of fixing this confined sense; for there can be no argument, if the sense of the word is extended to everything that is approved. A rose may as well be said to be beautiful because it has a fine smell, as a bird because of its colour. When we apply the word *beauty* we do not mean always by it a more beautiful form, but something valuable on account of its rarity, usefulness, colour, or any other property. A horse is said to be a beautiful animal; but, had a horse as few good qualities as a tortoise, I do not imagine that he would be then esteemed beautiful.

A fitness to the end proposed, is said to be another cause of beauty; but supposing we were proper judges of what form is the most proper in an animal to constitute strength or swiftness, we always determine concerning its beauty, before we exert our understanding to judge of its fitness.

From what has been said, it may be inferred, that the works of nature, if we compare one species with another, are all equally beautiful; and that preference is given from custom, or some association of ideas; and that, in creatures of the same species, beauty is the medium or centre of all various forms.

To conclude, then, by way of corollary; if it has been proved, that the painter, by attending to the invariable and general ideas of nature, produces beauty, he must, by regarding minute particularities and accidental discriminations, deviate from the universal rule, *and pollute his canvas with deformity*.[1]

---

[1] Said to have been added by Johnson.

COLMAN AND THORNTON

GEORGE COLMAN

1732 Born in Florence, the son of Francis Colman, envoy to Tuscany.

1733 Occurred the death of his father, upon which he became the ward of William Pulteney, afterward the Earl of Bath.

1746 Entered Westminster School, where he began to write, his first composition being *Verses to the Right Honorable Lord Viscount Pulteney.*

1751 Entered Christ Church College, Oxford.

1753 Contributed his first published work, "A Vision," to the *Adventurer*, No. 90.

1754–1756 Founded and edited, with Bonnell Thornton, the *Connoisseur.*

1755 Received the B.A. degree at Oxford.

1757 Called to the bar.
Made the acquaintance of David Garrick.

1759 Received the M.A. degree and started upon the Oxford Circuit in the practice of law, a profession which he abandoned for literature only upon the death of the Earl of Bath, in 1764.
Published *Ode to Obscurity* and *Oblivion*, parodies upon the work of Mason and Gray, and began to be known as a writer.

1760 Produced *Polly Honeycomb*, his first play, at Drury Lane.

1761 Produced *The Jealous Wife*, a comedy modelled upon *Tom Jones*, which became the most popular play of the time.

1761–1762 Edited, with Thornton, the *St. James Chronicle*, to which he contributed a series of fifteen papers called *The Genius.*

1764 Occurred the death of the Earl of Bath, who willed him 900 guineas a year.
Became a member of the Literary Club.

1765 Published a translation of the *Comedies* of Terence.

1766 Produced *The Clandestine Marriage*, a play written in collaboration with Garrick.
Occurred the estrangement from Garrick.

1767 Produced *The English Merchant*, a comedy based upon Voltaire's *L'Ecossaise*, which brought him, subsequently, a satiric letter from Voltaire.

Occurred the death of his mother, from whom he inherited a large estate, part of which he used for the purchase of Covent Garden—to the further annoyance of Garrick.

1767–1774 Managed Covent Garden.

1776 Obtained control of the Haymarket Theater.

1781 Produced John Gay's *Beggars' Opera*.

1783 Published a translation of Horace's *Art of Poetry*,

1785 Suffered a stroke of paralysis.

1787 Published *Prose on General Occasions Accompanied with Some Pieces in Verse*, a collected edition of his miscellaneous writings.

1794 Died as the result of paralysis, and was buried in Kensington Church.

BONNELL THORNTON

1724 Was born in London, the son of an apothecary.

1739 Was admitted to Westminster School as a queen's scholar.
Met William Cowper, and, through him, George Colman.

1743 Entered Christ's Church College, Oxford.

1743–1752 Contributed to the *Student*, an Oxford and Cambridge miscellany.
Founded *Have at Ye All, or The Drury Lane Journal*, a venture in imitation of Fielding's *Covent Garden Journal*.
Contributed to the *Adventurer*.

1747 Received the B.A. degree.

1750 Received the M.A. degree.

1754 Received the M.B. degree.
Founded and edited, with George Colman, the *Connoisseur*.

1761–1762 Edited, with Colman, the *St. James Chronicle*.

1762 Contributed to *St. James' Magazine*.

1763 Issued a burlesque *Ode on St. Cecilia's Day*.

1764 Married Sylvia Braithwaite.

1767 Issued *The Battle of the Wigs*, a burlesque upon the disputes between the licentiates and the fellows of the College of Physicians.
Issued a translation of the *Comedies* of Plautus.

1768 Died, and was buried in Westminster Abbey.

ON CHRISTMAS[1]

————*Age, libertate Decembri,*
Quando ita majores voluerunt, utere.[2]
Hor. *Sat.* II, 7, 4.

AT THIS season of the year it has always been customary for the lower part of the world to express their gratitude to their benefactors; while some of a more elevated genius among them clothe their thoughts in a kind of holiday dress, and once in the year rise into poets. Thus the bellman bids good-night to all his masters and mistresses in couplets; the news-carrier hawks his own verses; and the very lamp-lighter addresses his worthy customers in rhyme. As a servant to the public, I should be wanting in the due respect to my readers, if I also did not take this earliest opportunity of paying them the compliments of the season, and (in the phrase of their barbers, tailors, shoemakers, and other tradesmen) wish them a merry Christmas and a happy new year.

Those old-fashioned mortals, who have been accustomed to look upon this season with extraordinary devotion, I leave to con over the explanation of it in Nelson: it shall at present be my business to show the different methods of celebrating it in these kingdoms. With the generality, Christmas is looked upon as a festival in the most literal sense, and held sacred by good eating and drinking. These, indeed, are the most distinguishing marks of Christmas: the revenue from the malt-tax and the duty upon wines, &c., on account of these twelve days, has always been found to increase considerably: and it is impossible to conceive the slaughter that is made among the poultry and the hogs in different parts of the country, to furnish the prodigious number of turkeys and chines, and collars of brawn, that travel up, as presents, to the metropolis on this occasion. The

---

[1]*Connoisseur*, No. 48.   December 26, 1754.

[2]Come, let us, like our jovial sires of old,
With gambols and mince-pies our Christmas hold.

jolly cit looks upon this joyous time of feasting with as much pleasure as on the treat of a new-elected alderman, or a lord-mayor's day. Nor can the country farmer rail more against the Game Act than many worthy citizens who have ever since been debarred of their annual hare; while their ladies can never enough regret their loss of the opportunity of displaying their skill, in making a most excellent pudding in the belly. But these notable housewives have still the consolation of hearing their guests commend the mince-pies without meat, which we are assured were made at home, and not like the ordinary heavy things from the pastry-cooks. These good people would, indeed, look upon the absence of mince-pies as the highest violation of Christmas; and have remarked with concern the disregard that has been shown of late years to that old English repast: for this excellent British olio is as essential to Christmas, as pancake to Shrove Tuesday, tansy to Easter, furmenty to Midlent Sunday, or goose to Michaelmas day. And they think it no wonder that our finical gentry should be so loose in their principles, as well as weak in their bodies, when the solid, substantial, Protestant mince-pie has given place among them to the Roman Catholic aumulets.

As this season used formerly to be welcomed in with more than usual jollity in the country, it is probable that the Christmas remembrances, with which the wagons and stage-coaches are at this time loaded, first took their rise from the laudable custom of distributing provisions at this severe quarter of the year to the poor. But these presents are now seldom sent to those who are really in want of them, but are designed as compliments to the great from their inferiors, and come chiefly from the tenant to his rich landlord, or from the rector of a fat living, as a kind of tithe, to his patron. Nor is the old hospitable English custom of keeping open house for the poor neighbourhood, any longer regarded. We might as soon expect to see plum-porridge fill a tureen at the ordinary at White's, as that the lord of the manor should assemble his poor tenants to make merry at the great house.

The servants now swill the Christmas ale by themselves in the hall, while the squire gets drunk with his brother fox hunters in the smoking-room.

There is no rank of people so heartily rejoiced at the arrival of this joyful season, as the order of servants, journeymen, and apprentices, and the lower sort of people in general. No master or mistress is so rigid as to refuse them a holiday; and by remarkable good luck the same circumstance, which gives them an opportunity of diverting themselves, procures them money to support it, by the tax which custom has imposed upon us in the article of Christmas boxes. The butcher and the baker send their journeymen and apprentices to levy contributions on their customers, which are paid back again in the usual fees to Mr. John and Mrs. Mary. This serves the tradesman as a pretence to lengthen out his bill, and the master and mistress to lower the wages on account of the vails. The Christmas box was formerly the bounty of well-disposed people, who were willing to contribute something towards rewarding the industrious, and supplying them with necessaries. But the gift is now almost demanded as a right; and our journeymen, apprentices, &c., are grown so polite, that instead of reserving their Christmas box for its original use, their ready cash serves them only for present pocket-money; and instead of visiting their friends and relations, they commence the fine gentlemen of the week. The six-penny hop is crowded with ladies and gentlemen from the kitchen; the sirens of Catherine-street charm many a holiday gallant into their snares; and the play-houses are filled with beaux, wits, and critics, from Cheapside and Whitechapel. The barrows are surrounded with raw lads setting their halfpence against oranges; and the greasy cards and dirty cribbage-board employ the genteeler gamesters in every ale-house. A merry Christmas has ruined many a promising young fellow, who has been flush of money at the beginning of the week, but before the end of it has committed a robbery on the till for more.

But in the midst of this general festivity there are some so far from giving into any extraordinary merriment, that they seem more gloomy than usual, and appear with faces as dismal as the month in which Christmas is celebrated. I have heard a plodding citizen most grievously complain of the great expense of housekeeping at this season, when his own and his wife's relations claim the privilege of kindred to eat him out of house and home: then again, considering the present total decay of trade, and the great load of taxes, it is a shame, they think, that poor shop-keepers should be so fleeced and plundered, under the pretence of Christmas boxes. But if tradesmen have any reason to murmur at Christmas, many of their customers, on the other hand, tremble at its approach; as it is made a sanction to every petty mechanic, to break in upon their joy, and disturb a gentleman's repose at this time by bringing in his bill.

Others, who used to be very merry at this season, have within this year or two been quite disconcerted. To put them out of their old way is to put them out of humour; they have therefore quarrelled with the almanac, and refuse to keep their Christmas according to Act of Parliament. My cousin Village informs me that this obstinacy is very common in the country; and that many still persist in waiting eleven days for their mirth, and defer their Christmas till the blowing of the Glastonbury thorn. In some, indeed, this cavilling with the calendar has been only the result of close economy; who, by evading the expense of keeping Christmas with the rest of the world, find means to neglect it when the general time of celebrating it is over. Many have availed themselves of this expedient: and I am acquainted with a couple who are enraged at the New Style on another account; because it puts them to double expenses, by robbing them of the opportunity of keeping Christmas day and their wedding day at the same time.

As to persons of fashion, this annual carnival is worse to them than Lent, or the empty town in the middle of summer. The boisterous merriment, an awkward affectation of politeness among the vulgar, interrupts the course of their refined pleasures, and drives them out of town for the holidays. The few who remain are very much at a loss how to dispose of their time; for the theatres at this season are opened only for the reception of schoolboys and apprentices, and there is no public place where a person of fashion can appear, without being surrounded with the dirty inhabitants of St. Giles's, and the brutes from the Wapping side of Westminster. These unhappy sufferers are really to be pitied; and since Christmas day has to persons of distinction a great deal of insipidity about it, I cannot enough applaud an ingenious lady, who sent cards round to all her acquaintance, inviting them to a rout on that day; which they declared was the happiest thought in the world, because Christmas day is so like Sunday.

ESSAY WRITING[1]

Est brevitate opus, ut currat sententia, neu se
Impediat verbis lassas onerantibus aures:
Et sermone opus est, modo tristi, saepe jocoso.[2]
                                   Hor. *Sat.* I, x, 10.

AMONG the several degrees of authors, there are none, perhaps, who have more obstacles to surmount at their setting out, than the writers of periodical essays.   Talk with a modern critic, and he will tell you, that a new paper is a vain attempt after the inimitable *Spectator* and others; and that all the proper subjects are already pre-occupied, and that it is equally impossible to find out a new field for observation, as to discover a new world.   With these prejudices the public are prepared to receive us: and while they expect to be cloyed with the stale repetition of the same fare, though tossed up in a different manner, they sit down with but little relish for the entertainment.

---

[1]*Connoisseur*, No. 71.   Thursday, June 5, 1755.
[2]"I write as I would talk; am short, and clear;
   Not clog'd with words, that load the wearied ear:
   A grave, dull, essay now and then goes down;
   But folks expect to laugh with Mr. Town."

That the *Spectator* first led the way, must undoubtedly be acknowledged: but that his followers must for that reason be always supposed to tread in his steps, can by no means be allowed. In the high road of life there are several extensive walks, as well as bye-paths, which we may strike into, without the necessity of keeping the same beaten track with those that have gone before us. New objects for ridicule will continually present themselves; and even the same characters will appear different by being differently disposed, as in the same pack of cards, though ever so often shuffled, there will never be two hands exactly alike.

After this introduction, I hope to be pardoned, if I indulge myself in speaking a word or two concerning my own endeavours to entertain the public. And first, whatever objections the reader may have had to the subjects of my papers, I shall make no apology for the manner, in which I have chosen to treat them. The dread of falling into (what they are pleased to call) colloquial barbarisms, has induced some unskilful writers to swell their bloated diction with uncouth phrases and the affected jargon of pedants. For my own part, I never go out of the common way of expression, merely for the sake of introducing a more sounding word with a Latin termination. The English language is sufficiently copious and expressive without any further adoption of new terms; and the native words seem to me to have far more force than any foreign auxiliaries, however pompously ushered in: as British soldiers fight our battles better than the troops taken into our pay.

The subjects of my essays have been chiefly such as I thought might recommend themselves to the public notice by being new and uncommon. For this reason I purposely avoided the worn-out practice of retailing scraps of morality, and affecting to dogmatize on the common duties of life. In this point, indeed, the *Spectator* is inimitable; nor could I hope to say any thing new upon these topics after so many excellent moral and religious essays, which are the principal ornament of that work. I have therefore contented myself with exposing vice and folly by painting mankind in their natural colours, without assuming the rigid air of a preacher, or the moroseness of a philosopher. I have rather chosen to undermine our fashionable excesses by secret sapping, than to storm them by open assault. In a word, upon all occasions I have endeavoured to laugh people into a better behaviour: as I am convinced, that the sting of reproof is not less sharp for being concealed; and advice never comes with a better face, than when it comes with a laughing one.

There are some points in the course of this work, which perhaps might have been treated with a more serious air. I have thought it my duty to take every opportunity of exposing the absurd tenets of our modern Free-thinkers and Enthusiasts. The Enthusiast is, indeed, much more difficult to cure than the Free-thinker; because the latter, with all his bravery, cannot but be conscious that he is wrong; whereas the former may have deceived himself into a belief, that he is certainly in the right; and the more he is opposed, the more he considers himself as "patiently suffering for the truth's sake." Ignorance is too stubborn to yield to conviction; and on the other hand those, whom "a little learning has made mad," are too proud and self-sufficient to hearken to the sober voice of reason. The only way left us, therefore, is to root out superstition, by making its followers ashamed of themselves: and as for our Free-thinkers, it is but right to turn their boasted weapons of ridicule against them; and as they themselves endeavour to banter others out of every serious and virtuous notion, we too (in the language of the psalmist) should "laugh them to scorn, and have them in derision."

It is with infinite pleasure, that I find myself so much encouraged to continue my labours, by the kind reception which they have hitherto met with from the public: and Mr. Baldwin with no less pleasure informs me, that as there are but few numbers left of the folio edition, he intends to collect them into two pocket volumes. The reader cannot conceive, how much I already pride myself on the charming figure, which my works will make in this new form: and I shall endeavour to render these volumes as complete as I possibly can, by several considerable additions and amendments. Though contracted into the small space of a twelves volume, I still hope to maintain my former dignity; like the devils in Milton's *Pandæmonium.*

> . . . To smallest forms
> Reduc'd their shapes immense, and were at large.

The *Spectator* has very elegantly compared his single papers, as they came out, to "cherries on a stick," of the dearness of which the purchasers cannot complain, who are willing to gratify their taste with choice fruit at its earliest production. I have considered my own papers as so many flowers, which joined together would make up a pretty nosegay; and though each of them, singly taken, may not be equally admired for their odours, they may receive an additional fragrance by a happy union of their sweets.

The learned decoration in the front of my papers, though perhaps it has sometimes put my scholarship to a stand, I could by no means dispense with: for such is the prevalence of custom, that the most finished essay without a motto would appear to many people as maimed and imperfect, as a beautiful face without a nose. But custom has imposed upon us a new task of giving translations to these mottos; and it has been the usual method to copy them promiscuously from Dryden or Francis: though (as Denham has remarked of translation in general) "the spirit of the original is evaporated in the transfusion, and nothing is left behind but a mere *caput mortuum.*"[1] A motto, as it stands in the original, may be very apposite to the subject of the essay, though nothing to the purpose in the common translation; and it frequently derives all its elegance from an humorous application, in a different sense to what it bears in the author, but of which not the least trace can appear in the version. For this reason I have determined to give entire new translations, or rather

---

[1]Death's head.

imitations of all the mottos and quotations, adapted to the present times. And these, I flatter myself, will reflect an additional beauty on my work; as some of them admit of epigrammatic turns, while others afford room for lively and picturesque allusions to modern manners. In this dress they will at least appear more of a piece with the essays themselves; and not like the patch-work of random translations.

In the meantime I shall only add, that if any nobleman, gentleman, or rich citizen, is ambitious to have his name prefixed to either of these volumes, he is desired to send in proposals, together with a list of his virtues and good qualities, to the publisher; and the dedications shall be disposed of to the best bidder.

None but principals will be treated with.

BRIDE-CAKES[1]

Melle soporatam et medicatis frugibus offam
Objicit.——[2]

Virg. Æn. VI, 420.

As EVERY marriage is a kind of family festival, the wedding day is honoured with various celebrities, and distinguished like the fifth of November, the birthdays of the royal family or any other public day, with many demonstrations of joy: the happy couple are drest in their richest suits, the bells ring all day, and the evening is concluded with the merry ceremony of throwing the stocking. But these festivities are not always so religiously observed in town; where many a pair of quality are tacked together with the utmost privacy, and immediately after sneak out of town, as if they were ashamed to show their faces after what they had done. In the country, when the squire or any other person of dis-

---

[1] *Connoisseur*, No. 95. Thursday, November 20, 1755.

[2] The honey'd cake will lose its sweetness soon,
And prove a bitter in the honey-moon.

tinction is married, the honey-moon is almost a continued
carnival; and every marriage is accounted more or less likely
to be prosperous, in proportion to the number of deer, oxen,
and sheep, that are killed on the occasion, and the hogsheads
of wine and tuns of ale, with which they are washed down.
By the last post I received an account from my cousin
Village, of the wedding of a near relation, with a particular
detail of the magnificence of the entertainment, the splendour
of the ball, and the universal joy of the whole manor. At
the same time I received compliments from the new married
couple, with a large slice of the bride-cake; the virtues of which
are well known to every girl of thirteen. I was never in
possession of this nuptial charm before: but I was so much
delighted with this matrimonial token, and it excited in my
mind so many reflections on conjugal happiness, that (though
I did not lay it under my pillow) it gave occasion to the following dream.

I found myself in the middle of a spacious building, which
was crowded with a variety of persons of both sexes; and upon
inquiry was told, that it was the temple of the god of marriage;
and that every one, who had an inclination to sacrifice to that
deity, was invited to approach a large altar, which was covered with a great number of cakes of different shapes and appearance. Some of these were moulded into the form of
hearts; and others were woven into true lovers' knots: some
were strewed with sugar, and stuck about with sweet-meats;
some were covered with gold; some were stamped with
coronets; and others had their tops embellished with glittering
toys, that represented a fine house, a set of jewels, or a coach
and six. Plutus and Cupid were busily employed in distributing these cakes (which were all of them marked with
the word Matrimony, and called bride-cakes) to different
persons, who were allowed to choose for themselves, according to their different views and inclinations.

I observed several hasten to the altar, who all appeared
to be variously affected by their choice. To some the cakes
seemed of so delicious a flavour, that they imagined they

should never be surfeited; while others, who found the taste very agreeable at first, in a short time declared it to be flat and insipid. However, I could not help remarking, that many more (particularly among the quality) addressed themselves to Plutus than to Cupid.

Being desirous to take a nearer view of the company, I pushed through the crowd, and placed myself close by the altar. A young couple now advanced, and applying to Cupid, desired him to reach them one of the cakes, in the shape of a double heart pierced through with darts: but just as they were going to share it betwixt them, a crabbed old fellow, whom I found to be the girl's father, stepp'd up, broke the cake in two, and obliged the young lady to fix upon another, which Plutus picked out for her, and which represented the figure of a fine gentleman in gilt gingerbread.

An old fellow of sixty-two, who had stolen one day from the business of the alley, next came towards the altar, and seemed to express a strong desire for a cake. Plutus, who recollected him at first sight, immediately offered him one, which, though very mouldy and coarse, was gilt all over; but he was astonished at the old gentleman's refusing it, and petitioning Cupid for a cake of the most elegant form and sweetest ingredients. The little god at first repulsed him with indignation, but afterwards sold it to him for a large sum of money: a circumstance, which amazed me beyond expression, but which I soon found was very commonly practised in this temple. The old fellow retired with his purchased prize; and though I imagined he might still have a colt's tooth remaining, after having for some time mumbled it between his old gums in vain, it lay by him untouched and unenjoyed.

I was afterwards very much disgusted with the many instances that occurred, of these delicate morsels being set up to sale: and I found, that their price rose and fell, like that of beef or mutton, according to the glut or scarcity of the market. I was particularly affected with the disposal of the two following. A young gentleman and lady were approaching the altar, and had agreed to take between them a cake of a plain form but delicious flavour, marked Love and Competence; but a person of quality stepping forward persuaded the false female to join with him, and receive from Plutus one much more glittering, marked Indifference and Large Settlement. Another lady was coming up with a Knight of the Bath, being tempted by a cake with a red ribband streaming from it, like the flags on a Twelfth-cake; but was prevailed on by a person of greater rank and distinction to accept a more showy cake, adorned with a blue ribband and a coronet.

A buxom dame of an amorous complexion came next and begged very hard for a cake. She had before received several, which suited her tooth, and pleased her palate so excessively, that as soon as she had dispatched one, she constantly came to Cupid for another. She now seized her cake with great transport, and retiring to a corner with it, I could discern her greedily mumbling the delicious morsel, though she had fairly worn out six and twenty of her teeth in the service. After this an ancient lady came tottering up to the altar, supported by a young fellow in a red coat with a shoulder-knot. Plutus gave him a stale cake marked with the word *Jointure* in large golden capitals, which he received with some reluctance, while the old lady eagerly snatched another from Cupid, (who turned his head aside from her) on which I could plainly discover the word *Dotage*.

A rich rusty bachelor of the last century then came bustling through the crowd. He brought with him a red-cheeked country girl of nineteen. As he approached the altar, he met several coming from it with cakes which he had refused; some of which were marked Riches, some Family, some Beauty, and one or two Affection. The girl he brought with him proved to be his dairy maid, whom he had for some time past been in vain attempting to bring over to his wishes; but at last finding his design impracticable, he came with her to the altar. He seemed, indeed, a little ashamed of his undertaking, and betrayed a good deal of awkwardness in his manner, and deportment. However, as soon as he had taken his cake, he retired; and determined to spend the rest of his days with his milch-cow in the country.

To satisfy a modest longing, there now advanced a maiden lady in the bloom of three-score. She had, it seems, heretofore, refused several offers from Cupid and Plutus; but being enraged to find that they had now given over all thoughts of her, she seized by the hand a young ensign of the guards, and carried him to the altar, whence she herself snatched up a cake, and divided it with her gallant. She was highly delighted with the taste of it at first; but her partner being very soon cloyed, she too late discovered, that the half which she held in her hand was signed Folly, and that which she had forced upon her paramour was marked Aversion.

A little, pert, forward miss in a frock and hanging sleeves ran briskly up to Cupid, and begged for a cake:—what it was she did not care; but a cake she must and would have, of one kind or another. She had just stretched out her hand to receive one from Cupid, when her mamma interposed, sent the child back again blubbering to the boarding school, and carried off the cake herself.

An old woman, fantastically drest, then burst into the temple, and ran raving up to the altar, crying out, that she would have a husband. But the poor lady seemed likely to be disappointed; for, as she could prevail on no one to join hands with her, both Cupid and Plutus refused to favour her with a cake. Furious with rage and despair, she snatched one off the altar; and seizing on the first man that came in her way, which unfortunately happened to be myself, she would have forcibly crammed it down my throat. As the least crumb of it was as disagreeable as a drench to a horse, I began to spawl, and sputter, and kick; and though the flurry of spirits, which it occasioned, awaked me, I thought I had the nauseous taste of it still in my mouth.

CHARACTER OF A SPORTING PARSON[1]

Gaudit equis, canibusque, et aprici gramine campi.[2]
Hor. *Ars. Poet.*, 162.

MY COUSIN VILLAGE, from whom I had not heard for some time, has lately sent me an account of a Country Parson; which I dare say will prove entertaining to my town readers, who can have no other idea of our clergy, than what they have collected from the spruce and genteel figures, which they have been used to contemplate here in doctors' scarfs, pudding-sleeves, starched bands, and feather-top grizzles. It will be found from my cousin's description, that these reverend ensigns of orthodoxy are not so necessary to be displayed among rustics; and that, when they are out of the pulpit or surplice, the good pastors may, without censure, put on the manners as well as dress of a groom or whipper-in.

DONCASTER, Jan. 14, 1756

DEAR COUSIN,

I am just arrived here, after having paid a visit to our old acquaintance Jack Quickset, who is now become the Reverend Mr. Quickset, Rector of —— parish in the North-Riding of the county, a living worth upwards of three hundred pounds *per ann.* As the ceremonies of ordination have occasioned no alteration in Jack's morals or behaviour, the figure he makes in the church is somewhat remarkable: but as there are many other incumbents of country livings whose clerical characters will be found to tally with his, perhaps a slight sketch, or, as I may say, rough draught of him, with some account of my visit, will not be unentertaining to your readers.

Jack, hearing that I was in this part of the world, sent

---

[1]*Connoisseur*, No. 105. Thursday, January 29, 1756.

[2]To spring a covey, or unearth a fox,
In rev'rend sportsmen is right orthodox.

me a very hearty letter, informing me, that he had been double-japanned (as he called it) about a year ago, and was the present incumbent of ——; where if I would favour him with my company, he would give me a cup of the best Yorkshire stingo, and would engage to show me a noble day's sport, as he was in a fine open country with plenty of foxes. I rejoiced to hear he was so comfortably settled, and set out immediately for his living. When I arrived within the gate, my ears were alarmed with such a loud chorus of "no mortals on earth are so happy as we," that I began to think I had made a mistake: till observing its close neighbourhood to the church convinced me, that this could be no other than the parsonage-house. On my entrance, my friend (whom I found in the midst of a room-full of fox hunters in boots and bob-wigs) got up to welcome me to ——, and embracing me, gave me the full flavour of his stingo by belching in my face, as he did me the honour of saluting me. He then introduced me to his friends; and placing me at the right hand of his own elbow-chair, assured them, that I was a very honest cock, and loved a chase of five and twenty miles on end as well as any of them; to preserve the credit of which character, I was obliged to comply with an injunction to toss off a pint bumper of port, with the foot of the fox dipped and squeezed into it to give a zest to the liquour.

The whole economy of Jack's life is very different from that of his brethren. Instead of having a wife and a house full of children, (the most common family of country clergymen,) he is single; unless we credit some idle whispers in the parish, that he is married to his housekeeper. The calm amusements of piquet, chess, and back-gammon, have no charms for Jack, who sees "his dearest action in the field," and boasts, that he has a brace of as good hunters in his stable, as ever leg was laid over. Hunting and shooting are the only business of his life; fox-hounds and pointers lie about in every parlour; and he is himself, like Pistol, always in boots. The estimation in which he holds his friends, is rated according to their excellence as sportsmen; and to be able to make a good shot, or hunt a pack of hounds well, are most recommending qualities.

His parishioners often earn a shilling and a cup of ale at his house, by coming to acquaint him, that they have found an hare sitting, or a fox in cover. One day, while I was alone with my friend, the servant came in to tell him, that the clerk wanted to speak with him. He was ordered in; but I could not help smiling, when (instead of giving notice of a burying, christening, or some other church business, as I expected) I found the honest clerk only came in to acquaint his reverend superior, that there was a covey of patridges, of a dozen brace at least, not above three fields from the house.

Jack's elder brother, Sir Thomas Quickset, who gave him the benefice, is lord of the manor: so that Jack has full power to beat up the game unmolested. He goes out three times a week with his brother's hounds, whether Sir Thomas hunts or not; and has besides a deputation from him as lord of the manor, consigning the game to his care, and empowering him to take away all guns, nets, and dogs from persons not duly qualified. Jack is more proud of this office, than many other country clergymen are of being in the commission for the peace. Poaching is in his eye the most heinous crime in the two tables; nor does the care of souls appear to him half so important a duty as the preservation of the game.

Sunday, you may suppose, is as dull and tedious to this ordained sportsman, as to any fine lady in town; not that he makes the duties of his function any fatigue to him, but as this day is necessarily a day of rest from the usual toils of shooting and the chase. It happened, that the first Sunday after I was with him he engaged to take care of a church, in the absence of a neighbouring clergyman, which was about twenty miles off. He asked me to accompany him; and the more to encourage me, he assured me, that we would ride over as fine a champaign open country as any in the north. Accordingly I was roused by him in the morning before daybreak by a loud hollowing of "hark to Merriman," and the repeated smacks of his half-hunter; and after we had fortified our stomachs with several slices of hung beef and a horn or two of stingo, we sallied forth. Jack was mounted upon a hunter, which he assured me was never yet thrown out: and as we rode along, he could not help lamenting, that so fine a soft morning should be thrown away upon a Sunday; at the same time remarking, that the dogs might run breast high.

Though we made the best of our way over hedge and ditch, and took everything, we were often delayed by trying if we could prick a hare, or by leaving the road to examine a piece of cover and he frequently made me stop, while he pointed out the particular course that Reynard took, or the spot where he had earth'd. At length we arrived on full gallop at the church, where we found the congregation waiting for us: but as Jack had nothing to do but to alight, pull his band out of the sermon-case, give his brown scratch bob a shake, and clap on the surplice, he was presently equipped for the service. In short, he behaved himself both in the desk and pulpit to the entire satisfaction of all the parish as well as the squire of it; who, after thanking Jack for his excellent dis-course, very cordially took us home to dinner with him.

I shall not trouble you with an account of our entertain-ment at the squire's; who, being himself as keen a sportsman as ever followed a pack of dogs, was hugely delighted with Jack's conversation. Church and king, and another particu-lar toast, (in compliment, I suppose, to my friend's clerical character) were the first drank after dinner; but these were directly followed by a pint bumper to horses sound, dogs hearty, earths stopt, and foxes plenty. When we had run over again with great joy and vociferation, as many chases as the time would permit, the bell called us to evening prayers: after which, though the squire would fain have had us stay and take a hunt with him, we mounted our horses at the church-door, and rode home in the dark; because Jack had engaged to meet several of his brother-sportsmen, who were to lie all night at his own house, to be in readiness to make up for the loss of Sunday, by going out a cock-shooting very early next morning.

I must leave it to you, cousin, to make what reflections you please on this character; only observing, that the country can furnish many instances of these ordained sportsmen, whose thoughts are more taken up with the stable or the dog-kennel than the church: and, indeed it will be found, that our friend Jack and all of his stamp are regarded by their parishioners, not as parsons of the parish, but rather as squires in orders.

I am, dear cousin, yours, &c.

OLIVER GOLDSMITH

1728 Was born in Ireland, the son of a clergyman.
1734–1745 Went to school in Lissoy, Athlone, and Edgeworthstown.
1745 Entered Trinity College, Dublin.
1749 Began a futile effort to become a clergyman; attempted to teach school; began to study law.
1752 Began the study of medicine at Edinburgh.
1754 Went abroad.
1756 Took up residence in London, where he served as assistant to an apothecary, as an actor, as a school teacher, and as a doctor.
1757 Became a contributor to the *Monthly Review*.
1758 Was rejected by the College of Surgeons.
1759 Contributed to *The Bee*, a short-lived periodical.
1761 Was introduced to Dr. Samuel Johnson.
1762 Contributed a series of essays called *The Citizen of the World* to the *Ledger*.
1764 Became a member of the Literary Club, and published *The Traveller*, a poem which marked the beginning of his fame.
1765 Published a collected edition of his essays.
1766 Published *The Vicar of Wakefield*.
1767 Produced *The Good-Natured Man*.
1769 Published *The Roman History*.
1770 Published *The Deserted Village*, and went abroad.
1771 Produced *She Stoops to Conquer*.
1774 Published *Retaliation* and *An History of the Earth and Animated Nature*.
        Died, and was buried in Temple Church.

ON THE USE OF LANGUAGE[1]

THE manner in which most writers begin their treatises on the use of language is generally thus: "Language has been granted to man in order to discover his wants and necessities, so as to have them relieved by society. Whatever we desire,

---

[1] *Bee*, No. III. Saturday, October 20, 1759.

whatever we wish, it is but to clothe those desires or wishes in words, in order to fruition. The principal use of language, therefore," say they, "is to express our wants, so as to receive a speedy redress."

Such an account as this may serve to satisfy grammarians and rhetoricians well enough; but men who know the world maintain very contrary maxims: they hold, and I think with some show of reason, that he who best knows how to conceal his necessities and desires is the most likely person to find redress, and that the true use of speech is not so much to express our wants as to conceal them.

When we reflect on the manner in which mankind generally confer their favors, we shall find that they who seem to want them least are the very persons who most liberally share them. There is something so attractive in riches that the large heap generally collects from the smaller; and the poor find as much pleasure in increasing the enormous mass as the miser who owns it sees happiness in its increase. Nor is there in this anything repugnant to the laws of true morality. Seneca himself allows that, in conferring benefits, the present should always be suited to the dignity of the receiver. Thus, the rich receive large presents, and are thanked for accepting them. Men of middling stations are obliged to be content with presents something less; while the beggar, who may be truly said to want indeed, is well paid if a farthing rewards his warmest solicitations.

Every man who has seen the world, and has had his ups and downs in life, as the expression is, must have frequently experienced the truth of this doctrine, and must know that to have much, or to seem to have it, is the only way to have more. Ovid finely compares a man of broken fortune to a falling column; the lower it sinks, the greater weight it is obliged to sustain. Thus, when a man has no occasion to borrow, he finds numbers willing to lend him. Should he ask his friend to lend him an hundred pounds, it is possible, from the largeness of his demand, he may find credit for twenty; but should he humbly only sue for a trifle, it is two to one whether he might be trusted for twopence.   A certain young fellow at George's, whenever he had occasion to ask his friend for a guinea, used to prelude his request as if he wanted two hundred, and talked so familiarly of large sums that none could ever think he wanted a small one.   The same gentleman, whenever he wanted credit for a new suit from his tailor, always made the proposal in laced clothes; for he found by experience that if he appeared shabby on these occasions, Mr. Lynch had taken an oath against trusting; or, what was every bit as bad, his foreman was out of the way, and would not be at home these two days.

There can be no inducement to reveal our wants except to find pity, and by this means relief; but before a poor man opens his mind in such circumstances, he should first consider whether he is contented to lose the esteem of the person he solicits, and whether he is willing to give up friendship only to excite compassion.   Pity and friendship are passions incompatible with each other, and it is impossible that both can reside in any breast for the smallest space without impairing each other.   Friendship is made up of esteem and pleasure; pity is composed of sorrow and contempt: the mind may for some time fluctuate between them, but it never can entertain both together.

Yet, let it not be thought that I would exclude pity from the human mind.   There is scarcely any who are not in some degree possessed of this pleasing softness; but it is at best but a short-lived passion and seldom affords distress more than transitory assistance.   With some it scarcely lasts from the first impulse till the hand can be put into the pocket; with others it may continue for twice that space; and on some of extraordinary sensibility I have seen it operate for half an hour.   But, last as it may, it generally produces but beggarly effects; and where, from this motive, we give farthings, from others we give always pounds.   In great distress, we sometimes, it is true, feel the influence of tenderness strongly; when the same distress solicits a second time, we then feel with diminished sensibility, but, like the repetition of an echo, every new impulse becomes weaker, till at last our sensations lose every mixture of sorrow, and degenerate into downright contempt.

Jack Spindle and I were old acquaintances; but he's gone. Jack was bred in a compting-house, and his father, dying just as he was out of his time, left him an handsome fortune and many friends to advise with. The restraint in which he had been brought up had thrown a gloom upon his temper, which some regarded as an habitual prudence, and, from such considerations, he had every day repeated offers of friendship. Those who had money were ready to offer him their assistance that way; and they who had daughters, frequently, in the warmth of affection, advised him to marry. Jack, however, was in good circumstances; he wanted neither money, friends, nor a wife, and therefore modestly declined their proposals.

Some errors in the management of his affairs, and several losses in trade, soon brought Jack to a different way of thinking; and he at last thought it his best way to let his friends know that their offers were at length acceptable. His first address was therefore to a scrivener who had formerly made him frequent offers of money and friendship at a time when, perhaps, he knew those offers would have been refused.

Jack, therefore, thought he might use his old friend without any ceremony, and, as a man confident of not being refused, requested the use of an hundred guineas for a few days, as he had just then had an occasion for money. "And pray, Mr. Spindle," replied the scrivener, "do you want all this money?"—"Want it, sir!" says the other; "if I did not want it, I should not have asked for it."—"I am sorry for that," says the friend; "for those who want money when they come to borrow will want money when they should come to pay. To say the truth, Mr. Spindle, money is money nowadays. I believe it is all sunk in the bottom of the sea, for my part; and he that has got a little is a fool if he does not keep what he has got "

Not quite disconcerted by this refusal, our adventurer was resolved to apply to another, whom he knew to be the very best friend he had in the world. The gentleman whom he now addressed received his proposal with all the affability that could be expected from generous friendship. "Let me see; you want an hundred guineas; and pray, dear Jack, would not fifty answer?"—"If you have but fifty to spare, sir, I must be contented."—"Fifty to spare! I do not say that, for I believe I have but twenty about me."—"Then I must borrow the other thirty from some other friend."—"And, pray," replied the friend, "would it not be the best way to borrow the whole money from that other friend? and then one note will serve for all, you know. Lord, Mr. Spindle, make no ceremony with me at any time; you know I'm your friend, and when you choose a bit of dinner or so——You, Tom, see the gentleman down.—You won't forget to dine with us now and then. Your very humble servant."

Distressed, but not discouraged, at this treatment, he was at last resolved to find that assistance from love which he could not have from friendship. Miss Jenny Dismal had a fortune in her own hands, and she had already made all the advances that her sex's modesty would permit. He made his proposal, therefore, with confidence, but soon perceived "No bankrupt ever found the fair one kind." Miss Jenny and Master Billy Galloon were lately fallen deeply in love with each other, and the whole neighbourhood thought it would soon be a match.

Every day now began to strip Jack of his former finery; his clothes flew piece by piece to the pawnbrokers, and he seemed at length equipped in the genuine mourning of antiquity. But still he thought himself secure from starving. The numberless invitations he had received to dine, even after his losses, were yet unanswered; he was therefore now resolved to accept of a dinner because he wanted one; and in this manner he actually lived among his friends a whole week without being openly affronted. The last place I saw poor Jack was at the Rev. Dr. Gosling's. He had, as he fancied, just nicked the time, for he came in as the cloth was laying. He took a chair without being desired, and talked for some time without being attended to. He assured the company that nothing procured so good an appetite as a walk to White Conduit House, where he had been that morning. He looked at the table-cloth, and praised the figure of the damask; talked of a feast where he had been the day before, but that the venison was overdone. All this, however, procured the poor creature no invitation, and he was not yet sufficiently hardened to stay without being asked; wherefore, finding the gentleman of the house insensible to all his fetches, he thought proper at last to retire, and mend his appetite by a walk in the Park.

You then, O ye beggars of my acquaintance, whether in rags or lace, whether in Kent Street or the Mall, whether at the Smyrna or St. Giles's; might I advise you as a friend, never seem in want of the favor which you solicit. Apply to every passion but pity for redress. You may find relief from vanity from self-interest, or from avarice, but seldom from compassion. The very eloquence of a poor man is disgusting; and that mouth which is opened ever for flattery is seldom expected to close without a petition.

If, then, you would ward off the grip of poverty, pretend to be a stranger to her, and she will at least use you with ceremony. Hear not my advice, but that of Ofellus. If you be caught dining upon a halfpenny porringer of pease-soup and potatoes, praise the wholesomeness of your frugal repast. You may observe that Dr. Cheyne has prescribed pease-broth for the gravel; hint that you are not one of those who are always making a god of your belly. If you are obliged to wear a flimsy stuff in the midst of winter, be the first to remark that stuffs are very much worn at Paris. If there be found some irreparable defects in any part of your equipage which cannot be concealed by all the arts of sitting cross-legged, coaxing, or darning, say that neither you nor Sampson Giddeon were ever very fond of dress. Or, if you be a philosopher, hint that Plato and Seneca are the tailors you choose to employ; assure the company that men ought to be content with a bare covering, since what is now the pride of some was formerly our shame.

In short, however caught, do not give up, but ascribe to the frugality of your disposition what others might be apt to attribute to the narrowness of your circumstances, and appear rather to be a miser than a beggar. To be poor and to seem poor is a certain method never to rise. Pride in the great is hateful, in the wise it is ridiculous; beggarly pride is the only sort of vanity I can excuse.

A CITY NIGHT PIECE[1]

THE clock has struck two, the expiring taper rises and sinks in the socket, the watchman forgets the hour in slumber, the laborious and the happy are at rest, and nothing now wakes but guilt, revelry, and despair. The drunkard once more fills the destroying bowl, the robber walks his midnight round, and the suicide lifts his guilty arm against his own sacred person.

Let me no longer waste the night over the page of antiquity or the sallies of contemporary genius, but pursue the solitary walk, where vanity, ever changing, but a few hours past walked before me, where she kept up the pageant, and now, like a froward child, seems hushed with her own importunities.

What a gloom hangs all around! The dying lamp feebly emits a yellow gleam; no sound is heard but of the chiming clock or the distant watch-dog. All the bustle of human pride is forgotten, and this hour may well display the emptiness of human vanity.

There may come a time when this temporary solitude may be made continual, and the city itself, like its inhabitants, fade away, and leave a desert in its room.

What cities, as great as this, have once triumphed in existence; had their victories as great as ours; joy as just, and as unbounded as we; and, with short-sighted presumption, promised themselves immortality—posterity can hardly

[1]*Bee*, No. IV. Saturday, October 27, 1759.

trace the situation of some. The sorrowful traveller wanders over the awful ruins of others, and, as he beholds, he learns wisdom and feels the transience of every sublunary possession.

Here stood their citadel, but now grown over with weeds; there their senate-house, but now the haunt of every noxious reptile; temples and theatres stood here, now only an undistinguished heap of ruins. They are fallen, for luxury and avarice first made them feeble. The rewards of state were conferred on amusing, and not on useful, members of society. Thus true virtue languished, their riches and opulence invited the plunderer, who, though once repulsed, returned again, and at last swept the defendants into undistinguished destruction.

Here few appear in those streets which but some few hours ago were crowded! and those who appear no longer now wear their daily mask, nor attempt to hide their lewdness or their misery.

But who are those who make the streets their couch, and find a short repose from wretchedness at the doors of the opulent? These are strangers, wanderers, and orphans, whose circumstances are too humble to expect redress, and their distresses too great even for pity. Some are without the covering even of rags, and others emaciated with disease; the world seems to have disclaimed them; society turns its back upon their distress, and has given them up to nakedness and hunger. These poor shivering females have once seen happier days, and been flattered into beauty. They have been prostituted to the gay luxurious villain, and are now turned out to meet the severity of winter in the streets: perhaps now !ying at the door of their betrayers, they sue to wretches whose hearts are insensib!e to calamity, or debauchees who may curse, but will not relieve, them.

Why, why, was I born a man, and yet see the suffering of wretches I cannot relieve! Poor houseless creatures! the world will give you reproaches, but will not give you relief. The slightest misfortunes, the most imaginary uneasinesses of the rich, are aggravated with all the power of eloquence, and

engage our attention; while you weep unheeded, persecuted
by every subordinate species of tyranny, and finding enmity
in every law.

Why was this heart of mine formed with so much sensibility! or why was not my fortune adapted to its impulse!
Tenderness, without a capacity of relieving, only makes the
heart that feels it more wretched than the object which sues
for assistance.

But let me turn from a scene of such distress to the sancti-
fied hypocrite, who has been talking of virtue till the time of
bed, and now steals out to give a loose rein to his vices under
the protection of midnight—vices more atrocious because he
attempts to conceal them. See how he pants down the dark
alley, and, with hastening steps, fears an acquaintance in
every face. He has passed the whole day in company he
hates, and now goes to prolong the night among company
that as heartily hate him. May his vices be detected! may
the morning rise upon his shame! Yet I wish to no purpose:
villainy, when detected, never gives up, but boldly adds impudence to imposture.

A VISIT TO WESTMINSTER ABBEY[1]

I AM just returned from Westminster Abbey, the place of
sepulture for the philosophers, heroes, and kings of England.
What a gloom do monumental inscriptions and all the venerable remains of deceased merit inspire! Imagine a temple
marked with the hand of antiquity, solemn as religious awe,
adorned with all the magnificence of barbarous profusion,
dim windows, fretted pillars, long colonnades, and dark
ceilings. Think, then, what were my sensations at being introduced to such a scene. I stood in the midst of the temple
and threw my eyes round on the walls, filled with the statues,
the inscriptions, and the monuments of the dead.

Alas! I said to myself, how does pride attend the puny

[1]*Citizen of the World.* Letter XIII.

child of dust even to the grave! Even humble as I am, I possess more consequence in the present scene than the greatest hero of them all; they have toiled for an hour to gain a transient immortality, and are at length retired to the grave where they have no attendant but the worm, none to flatter but the epitaph.

As I was indulging such reflections, a gentleman, dressed in black, perceiving me to be a stranger, came up, entered into conversation, and politely offered to be my instructor and guide through the temple. "If any monument," said he, "should particularly excite your curiosity, I shall endeavour to satisfy your demands." I accepted with thanks the gentleman's offer, adding that "I was come to observe the policy, the wisdom, and the justice of the English, in conferring rewards upon deceased merit. If adulation like this," continued I, "be properly conducted, as it can no ways injure those who are flattered, so it may be a glorious incentive to those who are now capable of enjoying it. It is the duty of every good government to turn this monumental pride to its own advantage; to become strong in the aggregate from the weakness of the individual. If none but the truly great have a place in this awful repository, a temple like this will give the finest lessons of morality, and be a strong incentive to true ambition. I am told that none have a place here but characters of the most distinguished merit." The man in black seemed impatient at my observations; so I discontinued my remarks, and we walked on together to take a view of every particular monument in order as it lay.

As the eye is naturally caught by the finest objects, I could not avoid being particularly curious about one monument, which appeared more beautiful than the rest. "That," said I to my guide, "I take to be the tomb of some very great man. By the peculiar excellence of the workmanship, and the magnificence of the design, this must be a trophy raised to the memory of some king who has saved his country from ruin, or law-giver who has reduced his fellow-citizens from anarchy into just subjection." "It is not requisite," replied my companion, smiling, "to have such qualifications in order to have a very fine monument here. More humble abilities will suffice." "What! I suppose, then, the gaining two or three battles, or the taking half a score towns, is thought a sufficient qualification?" "Gaining battles, or taking towns," replied the man in black, "may be of service; but a gentleman may have a very fine monument here without ever seeing a battle or a siege." "This, then, is the monument of some poet, I presume, of one whose wit has gained him immortality?" "No, sir," replied my guide, "the gentleman who lies here never made verses; and as for wit, he despised it in others because he had none himself." "Pray, tell me then, in a word," said I, peevishly, "what is the great man who lies here particularly remarkable for?" "Remarkable, sir!" said my companion; "why, sir, the gentleman that lies here is remarkable, very remarkable—for a tomb in Westminster Abbey." "But, head of my ancestors! how has he got here! I fancy he could never bribe the guardians of the temple to give him a place. Should he not be ashamed to be seen among company where even moderate merit would look like infamy?" "I suppose," replied the man in black, "the gentleman was rich, and his friends, as is usual in such a case, told him he was great. He readily believed them; the guardians of the temple, as they got by the self-delusion, were ready to believe him too; so he paid his money for a fine monument; and the workman, as you see, has made him one of the most beautiful. Think not, however, that this gentleman is singular in his desire of being buried among the great; there are several others in the temple, who, hated and shunned by the great while alive, have come here, fully resolved to keep them company now they are dead."

As we walked along to a particular part of the temple, "There," says the gentleman, pointing with his finger, "that is the Poets' Corner; there you see the monuments of Shakespeare, and Milton, and Prior, and Drayton." "Drayton!" I replied. "I never heard of him before; but I have been told of one Pope; is he there?" "It is time enough," replied my guide, "these hundred years; he is not long dead; people have not done hating him yet." "Strange," cried I; "can any be found to hate a man whose life was wholly spent in entertaining and instructing his fellow-creatures?" "Yes," says my guide, "they hate him for that very reason. There is a set of men called answerers of books, who take upon them to watch the republic of letters, and distribute reputation by the sheet; they somewhat resemble the eunuchs in a seraglio, who are incapable of giving pleasure themselves, and hinder those who would. These answerers have no other employment but to cry out Dunce, and Scribbler; to praise the dead, and revile the living; to grant a man of confessed abilities some small share of merit; to applaud twenty blockheads, in order to gain the reputation of candour; and to revile the moral character of the man whose writings they cannot injure. Such wretches are kept in pay by some mercenary bookseller, or more frequently the bookseller himself takes this dirty work off their hands, as all that is required is to be very abusive and very dull. Every poet of any genius is sure to find such enemies; he feels, though he seems to despise, their malice; they make him miserable here, and, in the pursuit of empty fame, at last he gains solid anxiety.

"Has this been the case with every poet I see here?" cried I. "Yes, with every mother's son of them," replied he, "except he happened to be born a mandarin. If he has much money, he may buy reputation from your book-answerers, as well as a monument from the guardians of the temple."

"But are there not some men of distinguished taste, as in China, who are willing to patronize men of merit, and soften the rancour of malevolent dulness?" "I own there are many," replied the man in black; "but, alas, sir, the book-answerers crowd about them, and call themselves the writers of books; and the patron is too indolent to distinguish; thus poets are kept at a distance, while their enemies eat up all their rewards at the mandarin's table."

Leaving this part of the temple, we made up to an iron

gate, through which my companion told me we were to pass, in order to see the monuments of the kings. Accordingly I marched up without further ceremony, and was going to enter, when a person, who held the gate in his hand, told me I must pay first. I was surprised at such a demand, and asked the man whether the people of England kept a show? whether the paltry sum he demanded was not a national reproach? whether it was not more to the honour of the country to let their magnificence or their antiquities be openly seen, than thus meanly to tax a curiosity which tended to their own honour? "As for your questions," replied the gate-keeper, "to be sure they may be very right, because I don't understand them; but, as for that there threepence, I farm it from one—who rents it from another—who hires it from a third—who leases it from the guardians of the temple, and we all must live." I expected, upon paying here, to see something extraordinary, since what I had seen for nothing filled me with so much surprise: but in this I was disappointed; there was little more within than black coffins, rusty armour, tattered standards, and some few slovenly figures in wax. I was sorry I had paid, but I comforted myself by considering it would be my last payment. A person attended us, who, without once blushing, told a hundred lies; he talked of a lady who died by pricking her finger; of a king with a golden head, and twenty such pieces of absurdity. "Look ye there, gentlemen," says he, pointing to an old oak chair, "there's a curiosity for ye! in that chair the kings of England were crowned; you see also a stone underneath, and that stone is Jacob's pillow." I could see no curiosity either in the oak chair or the stone; could I, indeed, behold one of the old kings of England seated in this, or Jacob's head laid upon the other, there might be something curious in the sight; but in the present case there was no more reason for my surprise than if I should pick a stone from their streets, and call it a curiosity merely because one of the kings happened to tread upon it as he passed in a procession.

From hence our conductor led us through several dark

walks and winding ways, uttering lies, talking to himself, and flourishing a wand which he held in his hand. He reminded me of the black magicians of Kobi. After we had been almost fatigued with a variety of objects, he at last desired me to consider attentively a certain suit of armour, which seemed to show nothing remarkable. "This armour," said he, "belonged to General Monk." "Very surprising that a general should wear armour!" "And pray," added he, "observe this cap: this is General Monk's cap." "Very strange indeed, very strange, that a general should have a cap also! Pray, friend, what might this cap have cost originally?" "That, sir," says he, "I don't know; but this cap is all the wages I have for my trouble." "A very small recompense truly," said I. "Not so very small," replied he, "for every gentleman puts some money into it, and I spend the money." "What, more money! still more money!" "Every gentleman gives something, sir." "I'll give thee nothing," returned I; "the guardians of the temple should pay you your wages, friend, and not permit you to squeeze thus from every spectator. When we pay our money at the door to see a show, we never give more as we are going out. Sure, the guardians of the temple can never think they get enough. Show me the gate; if I stay longer, I may probably meet with more of those ecclesiastical beggars."

Thus leaving the temple precipitately, I returned to my lodgings, in order to ruminate over what was great, and to despise what was mean, in the occurrences of the day.

THE CHARACTER OF THE MAN IN BLACK[1]

THOUGH fond of many acquaintances, I desire an intimacy only with a few. The man in black whom I have often mentioned is one whose friendship I could wish to acquire, because he possesses my esteem. His manners, it is true, are tinctured with some strange inconsistencies; and he may be

---

[1]*Citizen of the World.* Letter XXVI.

justly termed a humourist in a nation of humourists. Though he is generous even to profusion, he affects to be thought a prodigy of parsimony and prudence; though his conversation be replete with the most sordid and selfish maxims, his heart is dilated with the most unbounded love. I have known him profess himself a manhater, while his cheek was glowing with compassion; and while his looks were softened into pity I have heard him use the language of the most unbounded ill-nature. Some affect humanity and tenderness, others boast of having such dispositions from nature; but he is the only man I ever knew who seemed ashamed of his natural benevolence. He takes as much pains to hide his feelings as any hypocrite would to conceal his indifference; but on every unguarded moment the mask drops off, and reveals him to the most superficial observer.

In one of our late excursions into the country, happening to discourse upon the provision that was made for the poor in England, he seemed amazed how any of his countrymen could be so foolishly weak as to relieve occasional objects of charity, when the laws had made such ample provision for their support. "In every parish-house," says he, "the poor are supplied with food, clothes, fire, and a bed to lie on; they want no more; I desire no more myself; yet still they seem discontented. I am surprised at the inactivity of our magistrates in not taking up such vagrants, who are only a weight upon the industrious; I am surprised that the people are found to relieve them, when they must be at the same time sensible that it in some measure encourages idleness, extravagance, and imposture. Were I to advise any man for whom I had the least regard, I would caution him by all means not to be imposed upon by their false pretences; let me assure you, sir, they are impostors, every one of them, and rather merit a prison than relief."

He was proceeding in this strain earnestly to dissuade me from an imprudence of which I am seldom guilty, when an old man, who still had about him the remnants of tattered finery, implored our compassion. He assured us that he was no common beggar, but forced into the shameful profession to support a dying wife and five hungry children. Being prepossessed against such falsehoods, his story had not the least influence upon me; but it was quite otherwise with the man in black: I could see it visibly operate upon his countenance, and effectually interrupt his harangue. I could easily perceive that his heart burnt to relieve the five starving children, but he seemed ashamed to discover his weakness to me. While he thus hesitated between compassion and pride, I pretended to look another way, and he seized this opportunity of giving the poor petitioner a piece of silver, bidding him at the same time, in order that I should hear, go work for his bread, and not tease passengers with such impertinent falsehoods for the future.

As he fancied himself quite unperceived, he continued as we proceeded to rail against beggars with as much animosity as before; he threw in some episodes on his own amazing prudence and economy, with his profound skill in discovering impostors; he explained the manner in which he would deal with beggars were he a magistrate; hinted at enlarging some of the prisons for their reception, and told two stories of ladies that were robbed by beggarmen. He was beginning a third to the same purpose when a sailor with a wooden leg once more crossed our walks, desiring our pity and blessing our limbs. I was for going on without taking any notice, but my friend, looking wishfully upon the poor petitioner, bid me stop, and he would show me with how much ease he could at any time detect an impostor.

He now, therefore, assumed a look of importance, and in an angry tone began to examine the sailor, demanding in what engagement he was thus disabled and rendered unfit for service. The sailor replied, in a tone as angrily as he, that he had been an officer on board a private ship-of-war, and that he had lost his leg abroad, in defence of those who did nothing at home. At this reply all my friend's importance vanished in a moment; he had not a single question more to ask; he now only studied what method he should take to relieve him unobserved. He had, however, no easy part to act, as he was obliged to preserve the appearance of ill-nature before me, and yet relieve himself by relieving the sailor. Casting, therefore, a furious look upon some bundles of chips which the fellow carried in a string at his back, my friend demanded how he sold his matches; but, not waiting for a reply, desired in a surly tone to have a shilling's worth. The sailor seemed at first surprised at this demand, but soon recollecting himself, and presenting his whole bundle, "Here, master," says he, "take all my cargo, and a blessing into the bargain."

It is impossible to describe with what air of triumph my friend marched off with his new purchase; he assured me that he was firmly of opinion that those fellows must have stolen their goods, who could thus afford to sell them for half value. He informed me of several different uses to which those chips might be applied; he expatiated largely upon the savings that would result from lighting candles with a match, instead of thrusting them into the fire. He averred, that he would as soon have parted with a tooth as his money to those vagabonds, unless for some valuable consideration. I cannot tell how long this panegyric upon frugality and matches might have continued, had not his attention been called off by another object more distressful than either of the former. A woman in rags, with one child in her arms, and another on her back, was attempting to sing ballads, but with such a mournful voice that it was difficult to determine whether she was singing or crying. A wretch who, in the deepest distress, still aimed at good-humour was an object my friend was by no means capable of withstanding; his vivacity and his discourse were instantly interrupted; upon this occasion his very dissimulation had forsaken him. Even in my presence he immediately applied his hands to his pockets, in order to relieve her; but guess his confusion when he found he had already given away all the money he carried about him to former objects. The misery painted in the woman's visage was not half so strongly expressed as the agony in his. He continued to search for some time, but to no purpose, till, at length recollecting himself, with a face of ineffable good-nature, as he had no money, he put into her hands his shilling's worth of matches.

BEAU TIBBS[1]

I

THOUGH naturally pensive, yet am I fond of gay company, and take every opportunity of thus dismissing the mind from duty. From this motive I am often found in the centre of a crowd; and wherever pleasure is to be sold, am always a purchaser. In those places, without being remarked by any, I join in whatever goes forward; work my passions into a similitude of frivolous earnestness, shout as they shout, and condemn as they happen to disapprove. A mind thus sunk for a while below its natural standard is qualified for stronger flights, as those first retire who would spring forward with greater vigour.

Attracted by the serenity of the evening, my friend and I lately went to gaze upon the company in one of the public walks near the city. Here we sauntered together for some time, either praising the beauty of such as were handsome, or the dresses of such as had nothing else to recommend them. We had gone thus deliberately forward for some time, when, stopping on a sudden, my friend caught me by the elbow, and led me out of the public walk. I could perceive by the quickness of his pace, and by his frequently looking behind, that he was attempting to avoid somebody who followed: we now turned to the right, then to the left; as we went forward, he still went faster; but in vain: the person whom he attempted to escape hunted us through every doubling, and gained upon us each moment, so that at last we fairly stood still, resolving to face what we could not avoid.

Our pursuer soon came up, and joined us with all the familiarity of an old acquaintance. "My dear Drybone,"

[1]*Citizen of the World.* Letter LIV.

cries he, shaking my friend's hand, "where have you been hiding yourself this half a century? Positively I had fancied you were gone to cultivate matrimony and your estate in the country." During the reply I had an opportunity of surveying the appearance of our new companion: his hat was pinched up with peculiar smartness; his looks were pale, thin, and sharp; round his neck he wore a broad black riband, and in his bosom a buckle studded with glass; his coat was trimmed with tarnished twist; he wore by his side a sword with a black hilt; and his stockings of silk, though newly washed, were grown yellow by long service. I was so much engaged with the peculiarity of his dress that I attended only to the latter part of my friend's reply, in which he complimented Mr. Tibbs on the taste of his clothes, and the bloom in his countenance.

"Pshaw, pshaw, Will," cried the figure, "no more of that, if you love me: you know I hate flattery,—on my soul I do; and yet, to be sure, an intimacy with the great will improve one's appearance, and a course of venison will fatten; and yet, faith, I despise the great as much as you do; but there are a great many damned honest fellows among them, and we must not quarrel with one half, because the other wants breeding. If they were all such as my Lord Mudler, one of the most good-natured creatures that ever squeezed a lemon, I should myself be among the number of their admirers. I was yesterday to dine at the Duchess of Piccadilly's. My lord was there. 'Ned,' says he to me, 'Ned,' says he, 'I'll hold gold to silver I can tell where you were poaching last night.' 'Poaching, my lord?' says I: 'faith, you have missed already; for I stayed at home, and let the girls poach for me. That's my way; I take a fine woman as some animals do their prey—stand still, and, swoop, they fall into my mouth.'"

"Ah, Tibbs, thou art a happy fellow," cried my companion, with looks of infinite pity; "I hope your fortune is as much improved as your understanding in such company?"

"Improved!" replied the other: "you shall know,—but let it go no farther—a great secret—five hundred a year to begin with—my lord's word of honour for it. His lordship took me

down in his own chariot yesterday, and we had a *tête-à-tête*
dinner in the country, where we talked of nothing else."

"I fancy you forget, sir," cried I; "you told us but this
moment of your dining yesterday in town."

"Did I say so?" replied he coolly. "To be sure, if I said
so, it was so. Dined in town! Egad, now I do remember, I
did dine in town; but I dined in the country too; for you must
know, my boys, I eat two dinners. By the by, I am grown as
nice as the devil in my eating. I'll tell you a pleasant affair
about that: we were a select party of us to dine at Lady Gro-
gram's,—an affected piece, but let it go no farther—a secret.—
Well, there happened to be no asafœtida in the sauce to a turkey, upon which, says I, 'I'll hold a thousand guineas, and say
done first, that'—But, dear Drybone, you are an honest
creature; lend me half-a-crown for a minute or two, or so, just
till—but harkee, ask me for it the next time we meet, or it
may be twenty to one but I forget to pay you."

When he left us, our conversation naturally turned upon so
extraordinary a character. "His very dress," cries my friend,
"is not less extraordinary than his conduct. If you meet him
this day, you find him in rags; if the next, in embroidery.
With those persons of distinction of whom he talks so familiarly he has scarce a coffee-house acquaintance. However,
both for the interests of society, and perhaps for his own,
Heaven has made him poor; and while all the world perceive
his wants, he fancies them concealed from every eye. An
agreeable companion, because he understands flattery; and
all must be pleased with the first part of his conversation,
though all are sure of its ending with a demand on their purse.
While his youth countenances the levity of his conduct, he
may thus earn a precarious subsistence; but when age comes
on, the gravity of which is incompatible with buffoonery,
then will he find himself forsaken by all; condemned in the
decline of life to hang upon some rich family whom he once
despised, there to undergo all the ingenuity of studied contempt, to be employed only as a spy upon the servants, or a
bugbear to fright the children into obedience."—*Adieu.*

II[1]

I AM apt to fancy I have contracted a new acquaintance whom it will be no easy matter to shake off. My little beau yesterday overtook me again in one of the public walks, and, slapping me on the shoulder, saluted me with an air of the most perfect familiarity. His dress was the same as usual, except that he had more powder in his hair, wore a dirtier shirt, a pair of temple spectacles, and his hat under his arm.

As I knew him to be a harmless, amusing little thing, I could not return his smiles with any degree of severity: so we walked forward on terms of the utmost intimacy, and in a few minutes discussed all the usual topics preliminary to particular conversation. The oddities that marked his character, however, soon began to appear; he bowed to several well-dressed persons, who, by their manner of returning the compliment, appeared perfect strangers. At intervals he drew out a pocket-book, seeming to take memorandums, before all the company, with much importance and assiduity. In this manner he led me through the length of the whole walk, fretting at his absurdities, and fancying myself laughed at not less than him by every spectator.

When we were got to the end of our procession, "Blast me," cries he, with an air of vivacity, "I never saw the Park so thin in my life before! There's no company at all today; not a single face to be seen."

"No company!" interrupted I peevishly; "no company, where there is such a crowd? Why, man, there's too much. What are the thousands that have been laughing at us but company?"

"Lord, my dear," returned he, with the utmost good humour, "you seem immensely chagrined; but, blast me, when the world laughs at me, I laugh at the world, and so we are even. My Lord Tripp, Bill Squash the Creolian, and I, sometimes make a party at being ridiculous; and so we say and do a thousand things for the joke's sake. But I see you are grave,

---

[1]*Citizen of the World.* Letter LV.

and if you are for a fine grave sentimental companion, you shall dine with me and my wife today; I must insist on't. I'll introduce you to Mrs. Tibbs, a lady of as elegant qualifications as any in nature; she was bred, but that's between ourselves, under the inspection of the Countess of All-Night. A charming body of voice; but no more of that,—she shall give us a song. You shall see my little girl too, Carolina Wilhelmina Amelia Tibbs, a sweet pretty creature! I design her for my Lord Drumstick's eldest son; but that's in friendship, let it go no farther; she's but six years old, and yet she walks a minuet, and plays on the guitar immensely already. I intend she shall be as perfect as possible in every accomplishment. In the first place, I'll make her a scholar: I'll teach her Greek myself, and learn that language purposely to instruct her; but let that be a secret."

Thus saying, without waiting for a reply, he took me by the arm, and hauled me along. We passed through many dark alleys and winding ways; for, from some motives to me unknown, he seemed to have a particular aversion to every frequented street; at last, however, we got to the door of a dismal looking house in the outlets of the town, where he informed me he chose to reside for the benefit of the air.

We entered the lower door, which ever seemed to lie most hospitably open; and I began to ascend an old and creaking staircase, when, as he mounted to show me the way, he demanded whether I delighted in prospects; to which answering in the affirmative, "Then," says he, "I shall show you one of the most charming in the world out of my windows; we shall see the ships sailing, and the whole country for twenty miles round, tip-top, quite high. My lord Swamp would give ten thousand guineas for such a one; but, as I sometimes pleasantly tell him, I always love to keep my prospects at home, that my friends may visit me the oftener."

By this time we were arrived as high as the stairs would permit us to ascend, till we came to what he was facetiously pleased to call the first floor down the chimney; and knocking at the door, a voice from within demanded, "Who's there?"

My conductor answered that it was him.   But this not satis-
fying the querist, the voice again repeated the demand; to
which he answered louder than before; and now the door was
opened by an old woman with cautious reluctance.

When we were got in, he welcomed me to his house with
great ceremony, and turning to the old woman, asked where
was her lady?   "Good troth," replied she, in a peculiar dialect, "she's washing your twa shirts at the next door, because
they have taken an oath against lending out the tub any
longer."—

"My two shirts!" cried he in a tone that faltered with confusion; "what does the idiot mean?"

"I ken what I mean weel enough," replied the other; "she's
washing your twa shirts at the next door, because——"

"Fire and fury, no more of thy stupid explanations!" cried
he; "go and inform her we have got company.   Were that
Scotch hag," continued he, turning to me, "to be forever in
my family, she would never learn politeness, nor forget that
absurd poisonous accent of hers, or testify the smallest specimen of breeding or high life; and yet it is very surprising too,
as I had her from a parliament man, a friend of mine from
the Highlands, one of the politest men in the world; but that's
a secret."

We waited some time for Mrs. Tibbs' arrival, during which
interval I had a full opportunity of surveying the chamber
and all its furniture, which consisted of four chairs with old
wrought bottoms, that he assured me were his wife's embroidery; a square table that had been once japanned; a cradle
in one corner, a lumbering cabinet in the other; a broken
shepherdess, and a mandarin without a head, were stuck over
the chimney; and round the walls several paltry unframed
pictures which, he observed, were all his own drawing.

"What do you think, sir, of that head in the corner, done
in the manner of Grisoni?   There's the true keeping in it;
it's my own face, and though there happens to be no likeness,
a Countess offered me an hundred for its fellow.   I refused
her, for hang it! that would be mechanical, you know."

The wife at last made her appearance, at once a slattern and a coquette; much emaciated, but still carrying the remains of beauty. She made twenty apologies for being seen in such odious dishabille, but hoped to be excused, as she had stayed out all night at the gardens with the Countess, who was excessively fond of the horns. "And, indeed, my dear," added she, turning to her husband, "his lordship drank your health in a bumper."

"Poor Jack!" cries he; "a dear good-natured creature, I know he loves me. But I hope, my dear, you have given orders for dinner; you need make no great preparations neither, there are but three of us; something elegant and little will do,—a turbot, an ortolan, a——"

"Or what do you think, my dear," interrupts the wife, "of a nice pretty bit of ox-cheek, piping hot, and dressed with a little of my own sauce?"

"The very thing!" replies he; "it will eat best with some smart bottled beer: but be sure to let us have the sauce his Grace was so fond of. I hate your immense loads of meat; that is country all over; extremely disgusting to those who are in the least acquainted with high life."

By this time my curiosity began to abate, and my appetite to increase: the company of fools may at first make us smile, but at last never fails of rendering us melancholy; I therefore pretended to recollect a prior engagement, and, after having shown my respect to the house, according to the fashion of the English, by giving the servant a piece of money at the door, I took my leave; Mr. Tibbs assuring me that dinner, if I stayed, would be ready at least in less than two hours.

AT VAUXHALL[1]

THE people of London are as fond of walking as our friends at Pekin of riding: one of the principal entertainments of the citizens here in summer is to repair about nightfall to a garden

---

[1] *Citizen of the World.* Letter LXXI.

not far from town, where they walk about, show their best clothes and best faces, and listen to a concert provided for the occasion.

I accepted an invitation a few evenings ago from my old friend, the man in black, to be one of a party that was to sup there, and at the appointed hour waited upon him at his lodgings. There I found the company assembled and expecting my arrival. Our party consisted of my friend in superlative finery, his stockings rolled, a black velvet waistcoat which was formerly new, and his gray wig combed down in imitation of hair; a pawnbroker's widow, of whom, by-the-bye, my friend was a professed admirer, dressed out in green damask, with three gold rings on every finger; Mr. Tibbs, the second-rate beau I have formerly described, together with his lady, in flimsy silk, dirty gauze instead of linen, and a hat as big as an umbrella.

Our first difficulty was in settling how we should set out. Mrs. Tibbs had a natural aversion to the water, and the widow, being a little in flesh, as warmly protested against walking; a coach was therefore agreed upon; which being too small to carry five, Mr. Tibbs consented to sit in his wife's lap. In this manner, therefore, we set forward, being entertained by the way with the bodings of Mr. Tibbs, who assured us he did not expect to see a single creature for the evening above the degree of a cheese-monger; that this was the last night of the Gardens, and that consequently we should be pestered with the nobility and gentry from Thames Street and Crooked Lane, with several other pathetic ejaculations, probably inspired by the uneasiness of his situation.

The illuminations began before we arrived, and I must confess that upon entering the Gardens I found every sense overpaid with more than expected pleasure; the lights everywhere glimmering through the scarcely-moving trees—the full-bodied concert bursting on the stillness of the night—the natural concert of the birds in the more retired part of the grove, vying with that which was formed by art—the company gayly dressed, looking satisfaction, and the tables spread with various delicacies—all conspired to fill my imagination with the visionary happiness of the Arabian lawgiver, and lifted me into an ecstasy of admiration. "Head of Confucius," cried I to my friend, "this is fine! this unites rural beauty with courtly magnificence. If we except the virgins of immortality that hang on every tree, and may be plucked at every desire, I do not see how this falls short of Mohammed's paradise!" "As for virgins," cries my friend, "it is true they are a fruit that do not much abound in our gardens here; but if ladies, as plenty as apples in autumn, and as complying as any houri of them all, can content you, I fancy we have no need to go to heaven for paradise."

I was going to second his remarks, when we were called to a consultation by Mr. Tibbs and the rest of the company, to know in what manner we were to lay out the evening to the greatest advantage. Mrs. Tibbs was for keeping the genteel walk of the garden, where, she observed, was always the very best company; the widow, on the contrary, who came but once a season, was for securing a good standing-place to see the water-works, which she assured us would begin in less than an hour at farthest; a dispute, therefore, began, and as it was managed between two of very opposite characters, it threatened to grow more bitter at every reply. Mrs. Tibbs wondered how people could pretend to know the polite world who had received all their rudiments of breeding behind a counter; to which the other replied that, though some people sat behind counters, yet they could sit at the head of their own tables too, and carve three good dishes of hot meat whenever they thought proper; which was more than some people could say for themselves, that hardly knew a rabbit and onions from a green goose and gooseberries.

It is hard to say where this might have ended, had not the husband, who probably knew the impetuosity of his wife's disposition, proposed to end the dispute by adjourning to a box, and try if there was anything to be had for supper that was supportable. To this we all consented; but here a new distress arose: Mr. and Mrs. Tibbs would sit in none but a genteel box, a box where they might see and be seen—one, as they expressed it, in the very focus of public view; but such a box was not easy to be obtained; for though we were perfectly convinced of our own gentility and the gentility of our appearance, yet we found it a difficult matter to persuade the keepers of the boxes to be of our opinion: they chose to reserve genteel boxes for what they judged more genteel company.

At last, however, we were fixed, though somewhat obscurely, and supplied with the usual entertainment of the place. The widow found the supper excellent, but Mrs. Tibbs thought everything detestable. "Come, come, my dear," cries the husband, by way of consolation, "to be sure we can't find such dressing here as we have at Lord Crump's, or Lady Crimp's; but for Vauxhall dressing it is pretty good; it is not their victuals, indeed, I find fault with, but their wine; their wine," cries he, drinking off a glass, "indeed, is most abominable."

By this last contradiction the widow was fairly conquered in point of politeness. She perceived now that she had no pretensions in the world to taste; her very senses were vulgar, since she had praised detestable custard and smacked at wretched wine; she was therefore content to yield the victory, and for the rest of the night to listen and improve. It is true, she would now and then forget herself, and confess she was pleased, but they soon brought her back again to miserable refinement. She once praised the painting of the box in which we were sitting, but was soon convinced that such paltry pieces ought rather to excite horror than satisfaction; she ventured again to commend one of the singers, but Mrs. Tibbs soon let her know, in the style of a connoisseur, that the singer in question had neither ear, voice, nor judgment.

Mr. Tibbs, now willing to prove that his wife's pretensions to music were just, entreated her to favour the company with a song; but to this she gave a positive denial: "For you know very well, my dear," says she, "that I am not in voice to-day, and when one's voice is not equal to one's judgment what signifies singing? Besides, as there is no accompaniment, it would be but spoiling music." All these excuses, however, were overruled by the rest of the company, who, though one would think they already had music enough, joined in the entreaty. But particularly the widow, now willing to convince the company of her breeding, pressed so warmly that she seemed determined to take no refusal. At last, then, the lady complied, and after humming for some minutes, began with such a voice and such affectation as I could perceive gave but little satisfaction to any except her husband. He sat with rapture in his eye, and beat time with his hand on the table.

You must observe, my friend, that it is the custom of this country, when a lady or gentleman happens to sing, for the company to sit as mute and motionless as statues. Every feature, every limb must seem to correspond in fixed attention; and while the song continues they are to remain in a a state of universal petrifaction. In this mortifying situation we had continued for some time, listening to the song and looking with tranquillity, when the master of the box came to inform us that the water-works were going to begin. At this information I could instantly perceive the widow bounce from her seat; but, correcting herself, she sat down again, repressed by motives of good-breeding. Mrs. Tibbs, who had seen the water-works a hundred times, resolving not to be interrupted, continued her song without any share of mercy, nor had the smallest pity on our impatience. The widow's face, I own, gave me high entertainment; in it I could plainly read the struggle she felt between good-breeding and curiosity; she talked of the water-works the whole evening before, and seemed to have come merely in order to see them; but then she could not bounce out in the very middle of a song, for that would be forfeiting all pretensions to high life or high-lived company ever after. Mrs. Tibbs, therefore, kept on singing, and we continued to listen, till at last, when the song was just concluded, the waiter came to inform us that the water-works were over.

"The water-works over!" cried the widow; "the water-works over already! that's impossible; they can't be over so soon!" "It is not my business," replied the fellow, "to contradict your ladyship; I'll run again and see." He went, and soon returned with a confirmation of the dismal tidings. No ceremony could now bind my friend's disappointed mistress; she testified her displeasure in the openest manner; in short, she now began to find fault in turn, and at last insisted upon going home just at the time that Mr. and Mrs. Tibbs assured the company that the polite hours were going to begin, and that the ladies would instantaneously be entertained with the horns. *Adieu.*

THOMAS WARTON

1728 Was born at Basingstoke, the son of a clergyman, and the brother of Joseph Warton.
Studied with his father until he reached the age of sixteen.

1744 Entered Trinity College, Oxford.

1745 Published *Five Pastoral Eclogues.*

1747 Received the B.A. degree, took orders, and engaged in tutorial work in the university.
Published *The Pleasures of Melancholy.*

1749 Published *The Triumph of Isis,* which began his academic reputation.

1750 Received the M.A. degree.

1751 Issued *Newmarket,* a satire.

1754 Published *Observations on the Faerie Queen of Spenser,* which established his reputation as a critic.
Began his acquaintance with Dr. Johnson.

1755 Obtained for Dr. Johnson the M.A. degree from Oxford.

1757 Was elected professor of poetry at Oxford.

1758–1759 Contributed to the *Idler.*

1758 Published a selection of Latin metrical inscriptions.

1766 Published a collection of Greek inscriptions.

1767 Obtained the B.D. degree.

1770 Published an edition of Theocritus.

1771 Was elected a fellow of the London Society of Antiquaries.
Was appointed to a parish in Oxfordshire.

1774 Published the first volume of the *History of English Poetry from the Close of the Eleventh to the Commencement of the Eighteenth Century,* the second volume appearing in 1778, and the third in 1781.

1782 Issued a pamphlet in the Chatterton controversy, showing the Rowley poems to have been forgeries.
Became a member of the Literary Club.

1785 Was elected Camden professor of history at Oxford.
Was created poet-laureate.
Published an edition of Milton's minor poems.

1790 Died as the result of a paralytic stroke, and was buried in the chapel at Oxford.

CHARACTER OF SAM SOFTLY[1]

SAM SOFTLY was bred a sugar-baker; but succeeding to a considerable estate on the death of his elder brother, he retired early from business, married a fortune, and settled in a country house near Kentish-town. Sam, who formerly was a sportsman, and in his apprenticeship used to frequent Barnet races, keeps a high chaise, with a brace of seasoned geldings. During the summer months the principal passion and employment of Sam's life is to visit, in this vehicle, the most eminent seats of the nobility and gentry in different parts of the kingdom, with his wife and some select friends. By these periodical excursions Sam gratifies many important purposes. He shows his chaise to the best advantage; he indulges his insatiable curiosity for finery, which, since he has turned gentleman, has grown upon him to an extraordinary degree; he discovers taste and spirit; and, what is above all, he finds frequent opportunities of displaying to the party, at every house he sees, his knowledge of family connections. At first Sam was contented with driving a friend between London and his villa. Here he prided himself in pointing out the boxes of the citizens on each side of the road, with an accurate detail of their respective failure or successes in trade; and harangued on the several equipages that were accidentally passing. Here, too, the seats interspersed on the surrounding hills, afforded ample matter for Sam's curious discoveries. For one, he told his companions, a rich Jew had offered money; and that a retired widow was courted at another, by an eminent dry-salter. At the same time he discussed the utility, and enumerated the expenses, of the Islington turnpike. But Sam's ambition is at present raised to nobler undertakings.

When the happy hour of the annual expedition arrives, the seat of the chaise is furnished with Ogilvy's *Book of Roads*, and a choice quantity of cold tongues. The most alarming

[1] *Idler*, No. 93. Saturday, January 26, 1760.

disaster which can happen to our hero, who thinks he throws a whip admirably well, is to be overtaken on a road which affords no quarter for wheels. Indeed, few men possess more skill or discernment for concerting and conducting a party of pleasure. When a seat is to be surveyed, he has a peculiar talent in selecting some shady bench in the park, where the company may most commodiously refresh themselves with cold tongue, chicken, and French rolls; and is very sagacious in discovering what cool temple in the garden will be best adapted for drinking tea, brought for this purpose, in the afternoon, and from which the chaise may be resumed with the greatest convenience. In viewing the house itself, he is principally attracted by the chairs and beds, concerning the cost of which his minute inquiries generally gain the clearest information. An agate table easily diverts his eyes from the most capital strokes of Rubens, and a Turkey carpet has more charms than a Titian. Sam, however, dwells with some attention on the family portraits, particularly the most modern ones; and as this is a topic on which the house-keeper usually harangues in a more copious manner, he takes this opportunity of improving his knowledge of intermarriages. Yet, notwithstanding this appearance of satisfaction, Sam has some objection to all he sees. One house has too much gilding; at another, the chimney-pieces are all monuments: at a third, he conjectures that the beautiful canal must certainly be dried up in a hot summer. He despises the statues at Wilton, because he thinks he can see much better carving at Westminster Abbey. But there is one general objection which he is sure to make at almost every house, particularly at those which are most distinguished. He allows that all the apartments are extremely fine, but adds, with a sneer, that they are too fine to be inhabited.

Misapplied genius most commonly proves ridiculous. Had Sam, as Nature intended, contentedly continued in the calmer and less conspicuous pursuits of sugar-baking, he might have been a respectable and useful character. At present he dissipates his life in a specious idleness, which neither improves himself nor his friends. Those talents which might have benefited society, he exposes to contempt by false pretensions. He affects pleasures which he cannot enjoy, and is acquainted only with those subjects on which he has no right to talk, and which it is no merit to understand.

WILLIAM COWPER

1731 Was born at Great Berkhampstead, the son of a clergyman.

1737 Entered Dr. Pitman's school in Herfordshire.
Occurred the death of his mother.

1739 Was removed from the school because of persecution by a fellow student.

1739–1741 Was treated for serious eye trouble.

1741 Entered Westminster School, where he met George Colman.

1745 Suffered a severe attack of smallpox, which is said to have removed the cause of his eye trouble.

1748 Entered the Middle Temple.

1749–1752 Served as an articled clerk to a solicitor named Chapman.

1754 Was called to the bar.

1755–1756 Had a love affair with his cousin, Theodora, which was broken off by the girl's father because of the relationship; neither ever married.

1756 Occurred the death of his father.
Joined the Nonesense Club, composed of literary men—among others, George Colman and Bonnell Thornton.
Contributed to *The Connoisseur*.

1759 Bought chambers in the Inner Temple.

1761 Contributed to the *St. James's Chronicle*.

1763 Attempted suicide at the thought of undergoing examination, for the appointment as "reading clerk and clerk of the committees," and rapidly developed symptoms of insanity.
Was confined in a private sanitarium at St. Albans.

1765 Was removed, upon his recovery, to Huntingdon, where he became a resident in the home of the Unwins.
Became deeply interested in religion.

1773 Suffered a second attack of insanity, brought on by the deepening of his religious fervor, and again showed suicidal tendencies.
Was taken care of by John Newton, a clergyman, who subsequently came to exert a powerful influence over him.

1774 Returned to live with the Unwins, much improved in health.

1779 Published *Olney Hymns*, written under the encouragement of John Newton.

1780–1781 Wrote *Progress of Error, Truth, Table Talk,* and *Expostu-lation.*

1782 Published *Poems by William Cowper, of the Inner Temple, Esq.*

1784 Addressed the famous letter, *On Hares,* to the *Gentlemen's Magazine.*

1785 Published *The Task,* the volume containing also *John Gilpin* and *Trocinium.*

1786 Published a second edition of *The Task,* and found himself among the first poets of the day.
       Received an anonymous annuity, probably bestowed by his cousin Theodora.

1787 Suffered a third attack of insanity.

1791 Published a translation of Homer.

1800 Died, and was buried in Dereham Church.

COUNTRY CHURCHES[1]

Delicta majorum immeritus lues,
Romane, donec templa refeceris
Aedesque labentes Deorum, et
Faeda nigro simulacra fumo.[2]
                              Hor. *Car.* III, 6, 1–4.

Mr. Village to Mr. Town,
Dear Cousin,

The country at present, no less than the metropolis, abounding with politicians of every kind, I began to despair of picking up any intelligence, that might possibly be enter-taining to your readers. However, I have lately visited some of the most distant parts of the kingdom with a clergy-man of my acquaintance: I shall not trouble you with an account of the improvements that have been made in the seats we saw according to the modern taste, but proceed to give you some reflections, which occurred to us on observing

---

[1]*Connoisseur,* No. 134. Thursday, August 19, 1756.
[2]"The tott'ring tow'r, and mould'ring walls repair.
And fill with decency the house of pray'r:
Quick to the needy curate bring relief.
And deck the parish-church without a brief."

several country churches, and the behaviour of their congregations.

The ruinous condition of some of these edifices gave me
great offence; and I could not help wishing, that the honest
vicar, instead of indulging his genius for improvements, by
inclosing his gooseberry-bushes within a Chinese rail, and
converting half an acre of his glebe land into a bowling green,
would have applied part of his income to the more laudable
purpose of sheltering his parishioners from the weather, during their attendance on divine service. It is no uncommon
thing to see the parsonage-house well thatched, and in exceeding good repair, while the church perhaps has scarce any
other roof than the ivy that grows over it. The noise of
owls, bats, and magpies, makes a principal part of the church-
music in many of these ancient edifices; and the walls, like a
large map, seem to be portioned out into capes, seas, and pro-
montories, by the various colours with which the damps have
stained them. Sometimes, the foundation being too weak to
support the steeple any longer, it has been found expedient
to pull down that part of the building, and to hang the bells
under a wooden shed on the ground beside it. This is the
case in a parish in Norfolk, through which I lately passed,
and where the clerk and the sexton, like the two figures at St.
Dunstan's, serve the bells in capacity of clappers, by striking
them alternately with a hammer.

In other churches I have observed, that nothing unseemly
or ruinous is to be found, except in the clergyman, and the
appendages of his person. The squire of the parish, or his
ancestors perhaps, to testify their devotion, and to leave a
lasting monument to their magnificence, have adorned the
altar-piece with the richest of crimson velvet, embroidered
with vine-leaves and ears of wheat; and have dressed up the
pulpit with the same splendour and expense; while the gentleman, who fills it, is exalted, in the midst of all this finery,
with a surplice as dirty as a farmer's frock, and a periwig
that seems to have transferred its faculty of curling to the
band, which appears in full buckle beneath it.

But if I was concerned to see several distressed pastors, as well as many of our country churches in a tottering condition, I was more offended with the indecency of worship in others. I could wish that the clergy would inform their congregations, that there is no occasion to scream themselves hoarse in making the responses; that the town-crier is not the only person qualified to pray with due devotion; and that he who bawls the loudest may, nevertheless, be the wickedest fellow in the parish. The old women too in the aisle might be told, that their time would be better employed in attending to the sermon, than in fumbling over their tattered testaments till they have found the text; by which time the discourse is near drawing to a conclusion; while a word or two of instruction might not be thrown away upon the younger part of the congregation, to teach them, that making posies in summer time, and cracking nuts in autumn, is no part of the religious ceremony.

The good old practice of psalm-singing is, indeed, wonderfully improved in many country churches since the days of Sternhold and Hopkins; and there is scarce a parish-clerk, who has so little taste as not to pick his staves out of the New Version. This has occasioned great complaints in some places, where the clerk has been forced to bawl by himself, because the rest of the congregation cannot find the psalm at the end of their prayer-books; while others are highly disgusted at the innovation, and stick as obstinately to the Old Version as to the old style. The tunes themselves have also been new-set to jiggish measures; and the sober drawl, which used to accompany the first two staves of the hundredth psalm with the *Gloria Patri*, is now split into as many quavers as an Italian air. For this purpose there is in every county an itinerant band of vocal musicians, who make it their business to go round to all the churches in their turns, and after a prelude with the pitch-pipe, astonish the audience with hymns set to the new Winchester measure, and anthems of their own composing. As these new-fashioned psalmodists are necessarily made up of young men and maids, we may

naturally suppose, that there is a perfect concord and sym-
phony between them: and, indeed, I have known it happen,
that these sweet singers have more than once been brought
into disgrace, by too close an unison between the thorough-
bass and the treble.

It is a difficult matter to decide, which is looked upon as
the greatest man in a country church, the parson or his clerk.
The latter is most certainly held in higher veneration, where
the former happens to be only a poor curate, who rides post
every sabbath from village to village, and mounts and dis-
mounts at the church-door. The clerk's office is not only to
tag the prayers with an amen, or usher in the sermon with a
stave; but he is also the universal father to give away the
brides, and the standing god-father to all the new-born
bantlings. But in many places there is a still greater man
belonging to the church, than either the parson or the clerk
himself. The person I mean is the squire; who, like the king,
may be styled head of the church in his own parish. If the
benefice be in his own gift, the vicar is his creature, and of
consequence entirely at his devotion: or, if the care of the
church be left to a curate, the Sunday fees of roast beef and
plum pudding, and a liberty to shoot in the manor, will bring
him as much under the squire's command as his dogs and
horses. For this reason the bell is often kept tolling, and the
people waiting in the churchyard, an hour longer than the
usual time; nor must the service begin till the squire has
strutted up the aisle, and seated himself in the great pew in
the chancel. The length of the sermon is also measured by
the will of the squire, as formerly by the hour-glass: and I
know one parish, where the preacher has always the complaisance to conclude his discourse, however abruptly, the
minute that the squire gives the signal, by rising up after
his nap.

In a village church, the squire's lady or the vicar's wife
are perhaps the only females, that are stared at for their
finery: but in the larger cities and towns, where the newest
fashions are brought down weekly by the stage-coach or wag-

gon, all the wives and daughters of the most topping trades-men vie with each other every Sunday in the elegance of their apparel. I could even trace the gradations in their dress, according to the opulence, the extent, and the distance of the place from London. I was at church in a populous city in the North, where the mace-bearer cleared the way for Mrs. Mayoress, who came sidling after him in an enormous fan-hoop, of a pattern which had never been seen before in those parts. At another church, in a corporation town, I saw several negligees, with furbelowed aprons, which had long dis-puted the prize of superiority: but these were most woefully eclipsed by a burgess's daughter, just come from London, who appeared in a trolloppee or slammerkin, with treble ruffles to the cuffs, pinked and gimped, and the sides of the petticoat drawn up in festoons. In some lesser borough towns, the contest, I found, lay between three or four black and green bibs and aprons: at one a grocer's wife attracted our eyes, by a new-fashion'd cap call'd a Joan; and, at an-other, they were wholly taken up by a mercer's daughter, in a nun's hood.

I need not say anything of the behaviour of the congrega-tions in these more polite places of religious resort; as the same genteel ceremonies are practised there, as at the most fashion-able churches in town. The ladies immediately on their entrance, breathe a pious ejaculation through their fan-sticks, and the beaux very gravely address themselves to the haberdashers bills, glued upon the linings of their hats. This pious duty is no sooner performed, than the exercise of bowing and curtsying succeeds: the locking and unlocking of the pews drowns the reader's voice at the beginning of the service; and the rustling of silks, added to the whispering and tittering of so much good company, renders him totally unintelligible to the very end of it.

I am, dear Cousin, yours &c.

CONVERSATIONAL PESTS[1]

IN THE comedy of *The Frenchman in London*, which we are told was acted at Paris with universal applause for several nights together, there is a character of a rough Englishman, who is represented as quite unskilled in the graces of conversation; and his dialogue consists almost entirely of a repetition of the common salutation of How do you do? Our nation has, indeed, been generally supposed to be of a sullen and uncommunicative disposition; while, on the other hand, the loquacious French have been allowed to possess the art of conversing beyond all other people. The Englishman requires to be wound up frequently, and stops as soon as he is down; but the Frenchman runs on in a continual alarm. Yet it must be acknowledged, that, as the English consist of very different humours, their manner of discourse admits of great variety: but the whole French nation converse alike; and there is no difference in their address between a marquis and a *valet-de-chambre*. We may frequently see a couple of French barbers accosting each other in the street, and paying their compliments with the same volubility of speech, the same grimace and action, as two courtiers on the Thuilleries.

I shall not attempt to lay down any particular rules for conversation, but rather point out such faults in discourse and behaviour, as render the company of half mankind rather tedious than amusing. It is in vain, indeed, to look for conversation, where we might expect to find it in the greatest perfection, among persons of fashion: there it is almost annihilated by universal card-playing: insomuch that I have heard it given as a reason why it is impossible for our present writers to succeed in the dialogue of genteel comedy, that our people of quality scarce ever meet but to game. All their discourse turns upon the odd trick and the four honours: and it is no less a maxim with the votaries of whist than with those of Bacchus, that talking spoils company.

---

[1]*Connoisseur*, No. 138. Thursday, September 16, 1756.

Every one endeavours to make himself as agreeable to society as he can: but it often happens that those who most aim at shining in conversation overshoot their mark. Though a man succeeds, he should not, as is frequently the case, engross the whole talk to himself; for that destroys the very essence of conversation, which is talking together. We should try to keep up conversation like a ball bandied to and fro from one to the other, rather than seize it all to ourselves, and drive it before us like a football. We should likewise be cautious to adapt the matter of our discourse to our company; and not talk Greek before ladies, or of the last new furbelows to a meeting of country justices.

But nothing throws a more ridiculous air over our whole conversation, than certain peculiarities easily acquired, but very difficultly conquered and discarded. In order to display these absurdities in a truer light, it is my present purpose to enumerate such of them as are most commonly to be met with; and first to take notice of those buffoons in society, the Attitudinarians and Face-makers. These accompany every word with a peculiar grimace or gesture: they assent with a shrug, and contradict with a twisting of the neck; are angry by a wry mouth, and pleased in a caper or a minuet step. They may be considered as speaking Harlequins; and their rules of eloquence are taken from the posture-master. These should be condemned to converse only in dumb show with their own persons in the looking-glass: as well as the smirkers and smilers, who so prettily set off their faces, together with their words, by a *je-ne-sçai-quoi*[1] between a grin and a dimple. With these we may likewise rank the affected tribe of mimics, who are constantly taking off the peculiar tone of voice or gesture of their acquaintance: though they are such wretched imitators, that, like bad painters, they are frequently forced to write the name under the picture, before we can discover any likeness.

Next to these, whose elocution is absorbed in action,

---

[1] I know not what.

and who converse chiefly with their arms and legs, we may consider the Professed Speakers. And first, the emphatical; who squeeze, and press, and ram down every syllable with excessive vehemence and energy. These orators are remarkable for their distinct elocution and force of expression: they dwell on the important particles *of* and *the*, and the significant conjunctive *and;* which they seem to hawk up, with much difficulty, out of their own throats, and to cram them, with no less pain, into the ears of their auditors. These should be suffered only to syringe, as it were, the ears of a deaf man, through a hearing-trumpet: though I must confess, that I am equally offended with the whisperers or low-speakers, who seem to fancy all their acquaintance deaf, and come up so close to you, that they may be said to measure noses with you, and frequently overcome you with the full exhalations of a stinking breath. I would have these oracular gentry obliged to talk at a distance through a speaking-trumpet, or apply their lips to the walls of a whispering gallery. The wits, who will not condescend to utter any thing but a *bon mot*, and the whistler or tune-hummers, who never articulate at all, may be joined very agreeably together in concert: and to these tinkling cymbals I would also add the sounding-brass, the bawler, who inquires after your health with the bellowing of a town-crier.

The Tatlers, whose pliable pipes are admirably adapted to the "soft parts of conversation," and sweetly "prattling out of fashion," make very pretty music from a beautiful face and a female tongue; but from a rough manly voice and coarse features, mere nonsense is as harsh and dissonant as a jig from a hurdy-gurdy. The Swearers I have spoken of in a former paper; but the Half-swearers, who split, and mince, and fritter their oaths into *gad's bud*, *ad's fish*, and *demmee*, the Gothic Humbuggers, and those who "nick-name God's creatures," and call a man *a cabbage, a crab, a queer cub, an odd fish,* and *an unaccountable muskin*, should never come into company without an interpreter. But I will not tire my readers' patience by pointing out all the pests of conversation; nor dwell particularly on the Sensibles, who pronounce dogmatically on the most trivial points, and speak in sentences; the Wonderers, who are always wondering what o'clock it is, or wondering whether it will rain or no, or wondering when the moon changes; the Phraseologists, who explain a thing by all that, or enter into particulars with this and that and t'other; and lastly, the Silent Men, who seem afraid of opening their mouths, lest they should catch cold, and literally observe the precept of the Gospel, by letting their conversation be only *yea, yea,* and *nay, nay.*

The rational intercourse kept up by conversation is one of our principal distinctions from brutes. We should therefore endeavour to turn this peculiar talent to our advantage, and consider the organs of speech as the instruments of understanding: we should be very careful not to use them as the weapons of vice or tools of folly, and do our utmost to unlearn any trivial or ridiculous habits, which tend to lessen the value of such an inestimable prerogative. It is, indeed, imagined by some philosophers, that even birds and beasts, though without the power of articulation, perfectly understand one another by the sounds they utter; and that dogs, cats, &c., have each a particular language to themselves, like different nations. Thus it may be supposed that the nightingales of Italy have as fine an ear for their own native woodnotes as any signor or signora for an Italian air; that the boars of Westphalia gruntle as expressively through the nose as the inhabitants in High-German; and that the frogs in the dykes of Holland croak as intelligibly as the natives jabber their Low-Dutch. However this may be, we may consider those whose tongues hardly seem to be under the influence of reason, and do not keep up the proper conversation of human creatures, as imitating the language of different animals. Thus, for instance, the affinity between Chatterers and Monkeys, and Praters and Parrots, is too obvious not to occur at once: Grunters and Growlers may be justly compared to Hogs: Snarlers are Curs, that continually show their teeth, but never bite; and the Spitfire passionate are a sort of wild

Cats, that will not bear stroking, but will purr when they are pleased. Complainers are Screech-Owls; and Story-tellers, always repeating the same dull note, are Cuckoos. Poets, that prick up their ears at their own hideous braying, are no better than Asses: Critics in general are venomous Serpents, that delight in hissing; and some of them, who have got by heart a few technical terms without knowing their meaning, are no other than Magpies. I myself, who have crowed to the whole town for near three years past, may perhaps put my readers in mind of a Dunghill-cock; but as I must acquaint them that they will hear the last of me on this day fortnight, I hope they will then consider me as a Swan, who is supposed to sing sweetly at his dying moments.

HENRY MACKENZIE

1745 Was born in Edinburgh, the son of a physician.
Studied at the University of Edinburgh.
Became articled to George Inglis, a solicitor of Edinburgh.

1765 Went to London to observe the methods of the English
exchequer. Became, upon his return, the partner of his
former employer, later succeeding him as Attorney for the
Crown in Scotland.

1771 Published anonymously *The Man of Feeling*, a sentimental
novel after the manner of Sterne, which made a highly favora-
ble impression.

1773 Published anonymously *The Man of the World*, in contrast to
the earlier work.
Produced *The Prince of Tunis*, a tragedy, at the Edinburgh
Theater.

1776 Married Penuel Grant.

1777 Published anonymously *Julia de Roubigne*, a novel in letters.

1779–1780 Edited the *Mirror*, for which he wrote forty-two papers.

1785–1787 Edited the *Lounger*, for which he wrote fifty-seven papers.

1788 Read a paper, *Account of the German Theatre*, before the Royal
Society of Edinburgh, of which he was one of the earliest
members.

1791 Published *Translations of the Set of Horses by Lessing*.

1807 His three novels and the essays from the *Mirror* and the
Lounger published without his consent as *The Works of Henry
Mackenzie*.

1808 Issued *Miscellaneous Works*, in eight volumes, to offset the
spurious edition.

1831 Died in Edinburgh.

LITERATURE AND THE MAN OF BUSINESS[1]

AMONG the cautions which prudence and worldly wisdom
inculcate in the young, or at least among those sober truths
which experience often pretends to have acquired, is that

---

[1] *Lounger*, No. 100. Saturday, December 30, 1786.

danger which is said to result from the pursuits of letters and of science, in men destined for the labours of business, for the active exertions of professional life. The abstraction of learning, the speculations of science, and the visionary excursions of fancy, are fatal, it is said, to the steady pursuit of common objects, to the habits of plodding industry which ordinary business demands. The fineness of mind, which is created or increased by the study of letters, or the admiration of the arts, is supposed to incapacitate a man for the drudgery by which professional eminence is gained: as a nicely tempered edge applied to a coarse and rugged material is unable to perform what a more common instrument would have successfully achieved. A young man destined for law or commerce, is advised to look only into his folio of precedents, or his method of bookkeeping; and Dulness is pointed to his homage, as that benevolent goddess, under whose protection the honours of station and the blessings of opulence are to be attained; while Learning and Genius are proscribed, as leading their votaries to barren indigence and merited neglect. In doubting the truth of these assertions, I think I shall not entertain any hurtful degree of scepticism, because the general current of opinion seems of late years to have set too strongly in the contrary direction; and one may endeavour to prop the failing cause of literature, without being accused of blamable or dangerous partiality.

In the examples which memory and experience produce of idleness or dissipation, and of poverty, brought on by an indulgence of literary or poetical enthusiasm, the evidence must necessarily be on one side of the question only. Of the few whom learning or genius have led astray, the ill-success or the ruin is marked by the celebrity of the sufferer. Of the many who have been as dull as they were profligate, and as ignorant as they were poor, the fate is unknown, from the insignificance of those by whom it was endured. If we may reason *a priori* on the matter, the chances, I think, should be on the side of literature.

In young minds of any vivacity, there is a natural aversion

to the drudgery of business, which is seldom overcome, till the effervescence of youth is allayed by the progress of time and habit, or till that very warmth is enlisted on the side of their profession, by the opening prospects of ambition or emolument. From this tyranny, as youth conceived it, of attention and of labour, relief is commonly sought from some favourite avocation or amusement, for which a young man either finds or steals a portion of his time, either patiently plods through his task, in expectation of its approach, or anticipates its arrival by deserting his work before the legal period for amusement is arrived. It may fairly be questioned whether the most innocent of those amusements is either so honourable or so safe, as the avocation of learning or of science. Of minds uninformed and gross, whom youthful spirits agitate, but fancy and feeling have no power to impel, the amusements will generally be either boisterous or effeminate, will either dissipate their attention or weaken their force. The employment of a young man's vacant hours is often too little attended to by those rigid masters who exact the most scrupulous observation of the periods destined for business. The waste of time is undoubtedly a very calculable loss; but the waste or the depravation of mind is a loss of a much higher denomination. The votary of study, or the enthusiast of fancy, may incur the first; but the latter will be suffered chiefly by him whom ignorance, or want of imagination has left to the grossness of mere sensual enjoyments.

In this, as in other respects, the love of letters is friendly to sober manners and virtuous conduct, which in every profession is the road to success and to respect. Without adopting the commonplace reflections against some particular departments, it must be allowed, that in mere men of business, there is a certain professional rule of right, which is not always honourable, and though meant to be selfish, very seldom profits. A superior education generally corrects this, by opening the mind to different motives of action, to the feelings of delicacy, the sense of honour, and contempt of wealth, when earned by a desertion of those principles.

The moral beauty of those dispositions may perhaps rather provoke the smile, than excite the imitation, of mere men of business and the world.   But I will venture to tell them, that, even on their own principles, they are mistaken.   The qualities which they sometimes prefer as more calculated for pushing a young man's way in life, seldom attain the end, in contemplation of which they are not so nice about the means. This is strongly exemplified by the ill success of many, who, from their earliest youth, had acquired the highest reputation for sharpness and cunning.   Those trickish qualities look to small advantages unfairly won, rather than to great ones honourably attained.   The direct, the open, and the candid, are the surest road to success in every department of life. It needs a certain superior degree of ability to perceive and to adopt this; mean and uninformed minds seize on corners which they cultivate with narrow views to very little advantage: enlarged and well-informed minds embrace great and honourable objects; and if they fail of obtaining them, are liable to none of those pangs which rankle in the bosom of artifice defeated or of cunning over-matched.

To the improvement of our faculties as well as of our principles, the love of letters appears to be favourable.   Letters require a certain sort of application, though of a kind perhaps very different from that which business would recommend. Granting that they are unprofitable in themselves, as that word is used in the language of the world, yet, as developing the powers of thought and reflection, they may be an amusement of some use, as those sports of children in which numbers are used, familiarise them to the elements of arithmetic. They give room for the exercise of that discernment, that comparison of objects, that distinction of causes, which is to increase the skill of the physician, to guide the speculations of the merchant, and to prompt the arguments of the lawyer; and though some professions employ but very few faculties of the mind, yet there is scarce any branch of business in which a man who can think will not excel him who can only labour.   We shall accordingly find, in many departments

where learned information seemed of all qualities the least
necessary, that those who possessed it in a degree above their
fellows, have found, from the very circumstance, the road to
eminence and wealth.

But I must often repeat, that wealth does not necessarily
create happiness, nor confer dignity; a truth which it may be
thought declamation to insist on, but which the present time
seems particularly to require being told. The influx of
foreign riches and of foreign luxury, which this country has
of late experienced, has almost levelled every distinction but
that of money among us. The crest of noble or illustrious
ancestry has sunk before the sudden accumulation of wealth
in vulgar hands; but that were very little had not the elegance
of manner, had not the dignity of deportment, had not the
pride of virtue, which used to characterise some of our high-
born names, given way to that tide of fortune, which has
lifted the low, the illiterate, and the unfeeling, into stations of
which they were unworthy. Learning and genius have not
always resisted the torrent; but I know no bulwarks better
calculated to resist it; the love of letters is connected with an
independence and delicacy of mind, which is a great preserv-
ative against that servile homage which abject men pay to
fortune; and there is a certain classical pride, which from the
society of Socrates and Plato, Cicero and Atticus, looks down
with an honest disdain on the wealth blown insects of modern
times, neither enlightened by knowledge nor ennobled by
virtue. The *non omnis moriar*[1] of the poet draws on futurity
for the deficiencies of the present; and even in the present,
those avenues of more refined pleasures, which the cultivation
of knowledge, of fancy, and of feeling opens to the mind,
gives to the votary of science a real superiority of enjoyment
in what he possesses, and frees him from much of that envy
and regret which less cultivated spirits feel from their wants.

In the possession, indeed, of what he has attained, in that
rest and retirement from his labours, with the hopes of which

---

[1] I shall not wholly die.

his fatigues were lightened and his cares were soothed, the mere man of business frequently undergoes suffering, instead of finding enjoyment. To be busy as one ought, is an easy art; but to know how to be idle, is a very superior accomplishment. This difficulty is much increased with persons to whom the habit of employment has made some active exertions necessary; who cannot sleep contented in the torpor of indolence, or amuse themselves with those lighter trifles in which he, who inherited idleness as he did fortune, from his ancestors, has been accustomed to find amusement. The miseries and mortifications of the "retired pleasures" of men of business have been frequently matter of speculation to the moralist and of ridicule to the wit. But he who has mixed general knowledge with professional skill and literary amusement with professional labour will have some stock wherewith to support him in idleness, some spring for his mind when unbent from business, some employment for those hours which retirement or solitude has left vacant and unoccupied. Independence in the use of one's time is not the least valuable species of freedom. This liberty the man of letters enjoys: while the ignorant and illiterate often retire from the thraldom of business only to become the slaves of languor, intemperance, or vice.

But the situation in which the advantages of that endowment of mind which letters bestow are chiefly conspicuous is old age, when a man's society is necessarily circumscribed, and his powers of active enjoyments are unavoidably diminished. Unfit for the bustle of affairs and the amusements of his youth an old man, if he has no source of mental exertion or employment, often settles into the gloom of melancholy and peevishness, or petrifies his feelings by habitual intoxication. From an old man whose gratifications were solely derived from those sensual appetites which time has blunted, or from those trivial amusements of which youth only can share, age has cut off almost every source of enjoyment. But to him who has stored his mind with the information, and can still employ it in the amusement of letters, this blank of life is

admirably filled up. He acts, he thinks, and he feels with
that literary world whose society he can at all times enjoy.
There is perhaps no state more capable of comfort to ourselves
or more attractive of veneration from others, than that which
such an old age affords; it is then the twilight of the passions,
when they are mitigated but not extinguished, and spread
their gentle influence over the evening of our days, in alliance
with reason and in amity with virtue.

Nor perhaps, if fairly estimated, are the little polish and
complacencies of social life less increased by the cultivation of
letters, than the enjoyment of solitary or retired leisure. To
the politeness of form and the ease of manner, business is
naturally unfavourable, because business looks to the use,
not the decoration of things. But the man of business who
has cultivated letters, will commonly have softened his feelings, if he has not smoothed his manner or polished his address. He may be awkward, but will seldom be rude; may
trespass in the ignorance of ceremonial, but will not offend
against the substantial rules of civility. In conversation,
the pedantry of profession unavoidably insinuates itself
among men of every calling. The lawyer, the merchant, and
the soldier, (this last perhaps, from obvious enough causes,
the most of the three,) naturally slide into the accustomed
train of thinking and the accustomed style of conversation.
The pedantry of the man of learning is generally the most
tolerable and the least tiresome of any; and he who has mixed
a certain portion of learning with his ordinary profession has
generally corrected, in a considerable degree, the abstraction
of the one, and the coarseness of the other.

In the more important relations of society, in the closer
intercourse of friend, of husband, and of father, that superior
delicacy and refinement of feeling which the cultivation of the
mind bestows, heighten affection into sentiment, and mingle
with such connections a dignity and tenderness which gives
its dearest value to our existence. In fortunate circumstances those feelings enhance prosperity; but in the decline
of fortune, as in the decline of life, their influence and impor-

tance are chiefly felt, they smooth the harshness of adversity, and on the brow of misfortune print that languid smile, which their votaries would often not exchange for the broadest mirth of those unfeelingly prosperous men, who possess good fortune, but have not a heart for happiness.

INDEX